OXFORD practice tests
for the TOEIC® test

with key

TOEIC®IS A REGISTERED TRADEMARK OF EDUCATIONAL TESTING SERVICE (ETS). THIS PUBLICATION (OR PRODUCT) IS NOT ENDORSED OR APPROVED BY ETS OR THE CHAUNCEY GROUP INTERNATIONAL LTD. THE TOEIC® PROGRAM IS ADMINISTERED BY THE CHAUNCEY GROUP INTERNATIONAL LTD., A SUBSIDIARY OF EDUCATIONAL TESTING SERVICE.

1

OXFORD

Oxford University Press, Great Clarendon Street, Oxford OX2 6DP

Oxford New York
Auckland Bangkok Buenos Aires Cape Town Chennai
Dar es Salaam Delhi Hong Kong Istanbul Karachi Kolkata
Kuala Lumpur Madrid Melbourne Mexico City Mumbai
Nairobi São Paulo Shanghai Taipei Tokyo Toronto

OXFORD and OXFORD ENGLISH
are trade marks of Oxford University Press

ISBN 0 19 453526 6

Oxford University Press 2000

First published 2000
Fifth impression 2003

Any websites referred to in this publication are in the public domain
and their addresses are provided by Oxford University Press for
information only.
Oxford University Press disclaims any responsibility for the content.

Printed in China

The author and publisher would like to thank Corels for use of
royalty-free images.

Contents

INTRODUCTION

The Test of English for International Communication (TOEIC) was originally designed to test the English proficiency levels of people engaged in international business. However, the TOEIC® test has proven to be such a reliable measure of a test-taker's English language skills that it is now used for academic admissions, for placement purposes, and for measuring achievement. Over 1,500,000 people take the TOEIC test each year.

TOEIC test format

The TOEIC test is divided into two sections. These are Listening Comprehension and Reading. Each section contains 100 questions. You will need approximately 2½ hours to take the test.

Listening Comprehension		45 minutes
Part I	Photographs	20 questions
Part II	Question-response	30 questions
Part III	Short conversations	30 questions
Part IV	Short talks	20 questions

Reading		75 minutes
Part V	Incomplete sentences	40 questions
Part VI	Error recognition	20 questions
Part VII	Reading comprehension	40 questions

Listening Comprehension

Part I Photographs

In this part, you will see a photograph and you will hear four sentences about it. You must choose the sentence that most closely matches what you see. You will hear the sentences once.

You will identify what you see in the photo. This may include people, objects, actions and locations both general and specific. You will also make assumptions; you may not be able to determine if something is actually taking place, but from the clues in the photo, you can assume that it is.

Traps

The three incorrect sentences will contain words that may make them appear correct. A word may have a similar sound to something in the photo (e.g., a *sheep* rather than the *ship* pictured). The sentence may contain a word which has more

than one meaning (e.g., a *bottle of port wine* rather than a *ship in port*). There may be a suitable word included which is used inappropriately (e.g., *He is opening the window*. There is a *window* in the photo, but nobody is *opening* it).

Strategies

Scan the picture quickly and try to identify as much as you can. Ask yourself questions: Who (gender, description, occupation) is in the photo? What is happening? Where was the photo taken? When listening, focus on the words that are easier to hear, the stressed words, as they carry the overall meaning.

Part II Question-response

In this part, you will hear a question and three possible responses. You must choose the response that best answers the question. You will hear the question and each response once.

The question may ask about people, location, time, an activity, an event, emotions, reasons, or opinions. In short, the question could be on almost any subject.

Traps

As in Part I, words may sound similar or be used out of context. Words from the question may be repeated in the response, but be used inaccurately. In addition, there is a potential trap with grammar. You will hear different types of questions: *wh*-questions (*who, what, when, where, why,* and *how*), *yes/no* questions and tag questions. When you hear a *yes/no* or a tag question, you may assume that the response will begin with *Yes* or *No*. In the TOEIC test, as in real life, the response may answer the question indirectly instead. For example:

> *Is there any cake left?*
>
> *(A) I ate the last piece.*
> *(B) Yes, the lake is on the left.*
> *(C) No, I left early.*

(A) is the correct option. The respondent doesn't answer with *yes/no* as would be expected. However, we know the answer *is* no, because the respondent ate *the last piece*.

Strategies

You will have to exercise your short-term memory. You must remember the question until you have picked the appropriate response. If you really don't know the answer, then guess. Choose the response that sounds most natural to you, don't leave any questions unanswered.

Part III Short conversations

In this part, you will hear a short dialog. You will read a question and four answer choices in your test booklet. You must choose the option that best answers the question. You will only hear the dialog once.

The question will ask about the general idea of the conversation; usually it will not focus on specific details. You will be asked to identify an activity, an emotion, a relationship, or the location of the speakers. In some instances you may have to do some minor calculations based on measurements in the dialog.

Traps
As in Parts I and II, words may sound similar or be used out of context. Words may be repeated in the options, but be used inaccurately. In addition, listen out for words that can add to or change meaning. Listen carefully for words that indicate time (e.g., *before, until, while, afterwards,* etc.) and words that indicate negation (e.g., *not, hardly, seldom, by no means,* etc.).

The dialog may compare two or more things so listen for words that show degrees of comparisons.

Modals (e.g., *can, could, ought to,* etc.) indicate possibility and advisability. Listen carefully for modals to determine the intent of the speakers.

Word order is also a potential trap. A sentence such as *Never has the weather been so unpredictable* means *The weather is usually predictable*.

Strategies
Try to read the question before you hear the dialog. If you have time, read the answer choices as well. Look at *all* the options, before choosing your answer. As you listen, imagine the speakers and their location.

Part IV Short talks

In this part, you will hear a short monologue about which you will read two or three questions in your test booklet. For each question, you must choose the correct answer from four options. You will only hear the monologue once.

The talks can be in the form of recorded announcements, weather forecasts, special bulletins, etc. The questions will ask you to determine the location, the speaker, the time, the event, or a reason.

Traps
The traps that were set for you in Parts I, II and III are set once again.

Strategies
This is a very difficult section because you have to listen carefully and remember specific details. It is important that you try to read the questions before you hear the talk. If you have time, try to read the answer choices as well. However, you should listen to the whole talk before attempting to answer any of the questions. Timing is crucial in this part. If you cannot read and answer the question in the 8 second pause then don't worry, but move on to the next one. Don't get left behind on the tape.

Reading

Part V Incomplete sentences

In this part, you will read a sentence with one word or phrase missing and four possible choices to fill the blank. You will choose the best word or phrase.

Both your knowledge of vocabulary and your knowledge of grammar are tested. You will have to understand the meaning of the sentence to choose a vocabulary item. You may have to apply your knowledge of phrasal verbs and set expressions. You will, in some instances, have to understand the grammatical function of the *blank* to choose the correct grammatical form of a word. The grammar forms tested most frequently are verb tense, pronouns, prepositions, conjunctions and comparisons with adjectives and adverbs.

Traps
In the items that test grammar, many of the choices are attractive because they seem to complete the meaning of the sentence. However, they may not be grammatically correct. You have to pay close attention to the word endings and make sure you choose the correct grammatical form required.

Strategies
You must develop a quick pace for the Reading section. You have 75 minutes for 100 items. There are 60 items in Parts V and VI. You should save most of your time for the reading passages in Part VII. Try to answer a question in 30 seconds. If the

answer is not apparent to you, quickly move on. Return to the unanswered questions after you reach the end of Part VII. Always go back and check your answers at the end if there is time.

Part VI   Error recognition

In this part, you will read a sentence with four words or phrases underlined. You must choose the underlined word or phrase which is incorrectly written.

Only grammar is tested. The focus is mainly on errors with subject/verb agreement, pronoun agreement, and word family distinctions. Errors with prepositions are common and occasionally there will be mistakes with verb tense and verb form.

The words that are *not* underlined are always correct.

Traps
A common trap is to insert a word that does not belong. This is usually a pronoun in the subject position e.g., *The workers they are on strike*, or a pronoun which is incorrectly used e.g., *She is going to interview Mr. Robinson itself*.

Strategies
Check each underlined section for an error. If no error is apparent, take each option and see if that word or phrase fits the sentence grammatically. Do not take time to correct an error (even in your head).

Part VII   Reading

You will read a passage followed by 2–5 questions. You will have to answer the questions based on the information in the passage. Each question has four options.

You will have to interpret the information in advertisements, forms, reports, correspondence, tables, graphs, announcements, articles, and schedules.

Traps
Many of the answer options repeat information that is found in the passage, but in a different context. Make sure the option you choose directly answers the question.

Strategies
Read over the questions before you read the passage. Don't look at the answer options. Read the passage quickly to get a general idea. Don't worry about words you don't understand. Then read it again more carefully and try to find the answers to the questions as you read. After that, choose from the options. The questions usually match the order information is presented in the passage.

Be familiar with the type of passages that will be presented.

Studying for the TOEIC test

As you take a practice test, pay attention to the way you work through the test. Keep track of your time. Note how long you spend on a part; estimate how long you spend on an item. Ask yourself how you can improve your speed. Try to develop your own test-taking rhythm.

Use the cassette tape to develop your memory. After you take a test, go back to the Listening section and play the tape again. Try to repeat each sentence you hear in your head and hold it in your memory. You can also try this in your own language when you listen to the radio or television. Try to repeat exactly what the announcer says. It is possible to improve your ability to remember. For the TOEIC test, a good memory is a necessity.

Use the explanatory answers in the back of this book. Use them to learn why you made an error and how the test tried to trap you. There will be a lot of new words, phrases and ideas in this book. Taking these practice TOEIC tests will not only help you become comfortable with the test, but will definitely help you improve your English.

Answer sheets and Conversion table

In the exam you will have to put your answers on an Answer sheet, and you can practise doing this by using the Answer sheets provided at the back of the book.

A score conversion table is included on the inside back cover. This converts the scores of the Oxford practice tests and does not correlate with the actual TOEIC tests. The table provides you with an approximation of your total actual score for the practice tests, and can be used to assess your performance as you work through them.

Practice Test One

LISTENING COMPREHENSION

In this section of the test, you will have the chance to show how well you understand spoken English. There are four parts to this section, with special directions for each part.

PART I

Directions: For each question, you will see a picture in your test book and you will hear four short statements. The statements will be spoken just one time. They will not be printed in your test book, so you must listen carefully to understand what the speaker says.

When you hear the four statements, look at the picture in your test book and choose the statement that best describes what you see in the picture. Then, on your answer sheet, find the number of the question and mark your answer. Look at the sample below.

Sample Answer
Ⓐ ● Ⓒ Ⓓ

Now listen to the four statements.

Statement (B), "They're having a meeting," best describes what you see in the picture. Therefore, you should choose answer (B).

GO ON TO THE NEXT PAGE ▶

1.

2.

3.

4.

GO ON TO THE NEXT PAGE ▶

5.

6.

7.

8.

GO ON TO THE NEXT PAGE ▶

9.

10.

11.

12.

GO ON TO THE NEXT PAGE ▶

13.

14.

15.

16.

GO ON TO THE NEXT PAGE ▶

17.

18.

19.

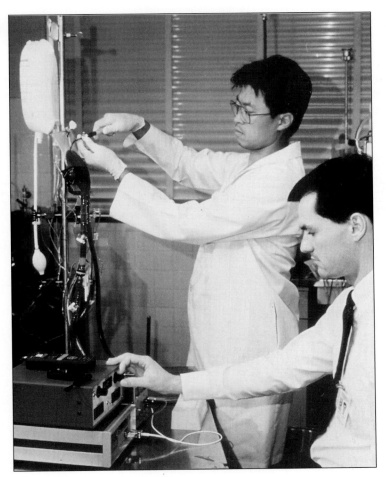

20.

GO ON TO THE NEXT PAGE

PART II

Directions: In this part of the test, you will hear a question spoken in English, followed by three responses, also spoken in English. The question and the responses will be spoken just one time. They will not be printed in your test book, so you must listen carefully to understand what the speakers say. You are to choose the best response to each question.

Now listen to a sample question.

You will hear:

Sample Answer
● Ⓑ Ⓒ

You will also hear:

The best response to the question "How are you?" is choice (A), "I am fine, thank you." Therefore, you should choose answer (A).

21.　Mark your answer on your answer sheet.

22.　Mark your answer on your answer sheet.

23.　Mark your answer on your answer sheet.

24.　Mark your answer on your answer sheet.

25.　Mark your answer on your answer sheet.

26.　Mark your answer on your answer sheet.

27.　Mark your answer on your answer sheet.

28.　Mark your answer on your answer sheet.

29.　Mark your answer on your answer sheet.

30.　Mark your answer on your answer sheet.

31.　Mark your answer on your answer sheet.

32.　Mark your answer on your answer sheet.

33.　Mark your answer on your answer sheet.

34.　Mark your answer on your answer sheet.

35. Mark your answer on your answer sheet.

36. Mark your answer on your answer sheet.

37. Mark your answer on your answer sheet.

38. Mark your answer on your answer sheet.

39. Mark your answer on your answer sheet.

40. Mark your answer on your answer sheet.

41. Mark your answer on your answer sheet.

42. Mark your answer on your answer sheet.

43. Mark your answer on your answer sheet.

44. Mark your answer on your answer sheet.

45. Mark your answer on your answer sheet.

46. Mark your answer on your answer sheet.

47. Mark your answer on your answer sheet.

48. Mark your answer on your answer sheet.

49. Mark your answer on your answer sheet.

50. Mark your answer on your answer sheet.

GO ON TO THE NEXT PAGE ▶

Directions: In this part of the test, you will hear thirty short conversations between two people. The conversations will not be printed in your test book. You will hear the conversations only once, so you must listen carefully to understand what the speakers say.

In your test book, you will read a question about each conversation. The question will be followed by four answers. You are to choose the best answer to each question and mark it on your answer sheet.

51. Where are they?

(A) At a bus stop.
(B) On a train.
(C) In a car.
(D) At a game.

52. What does the man want?

(A) Imported magazines.
(B) Two paperback books.
(C) Greeting cards.
(D) A foreign car.

53. Where are they?

(A) In an engine room.
(B) In an airplane.
(C) In a car.
(D) In a factory.

54. What is known about Paul?

(A) He can build houses.
(B) He is an architect.
(C) He teaches.
(D) He understands blueprints.

55. What is known about the new employee?

(A) He is often sick.
(B) He is an asset to the company.
(C) He knows the manager.
(D) He rarely returns phone calls.

56. Where are they?

(A) In an airport.
(B) In a hotel.
(C) In an office.
(D) In a restaurant.

57. What do these women do for a living?

(A) They are office clerks.
(B) They are architects.
(C) They are caterers.
(D) They are printers.

58. How did Sam get hurt?

(A) He was in the sun too long.
(B) He was playing sports with friends.
(C) He tripped while walking on the beach.
(D) He ran into another car.

59. Where is the key?

(A) In the closet door.
(B) In the key rack.
(C) Beside the water fountain.
(D) On the filing cabinet.

60. How will the correct price be determined?

(A) By calling the company.
(B) By asking the sales rep.
(C) By looking at the price list.
(D) By checking Anthony's invoice.

61. What are they doing now?

(A) Swimming.
(B) Hiking.
(C) Bicycling.
(D) Running.

62. Why is Sue upset?

(A) Someone broke into her car.
(B) She had to pay too much for parking.
(C) She had an accident downtown.
(D) Someone stole her concert tickets.

63. What is Emily going to do?

    (A) Join a fishing club.
    (B) Go and eat in a restaurant.
    (C) Cook the swordfish.
    (D) Prepare a report.

64. Why are there no labels?

    (A) The labels were mailed to the wrong address.
    (B) They were emptied out of the cabinet.
    (C) The marketing clerk forgot to order them.
    (D) They were all used for a large promotion.

65. What is the man considering?

    (A) Hiring a new director.
    (B) Investing in Shundoor.
    (C) Setting a new track record.
    (D) Becoming a broker.

66. What are they talking about?

    (A) What to eat for lunch.
    (B) Whether or not to eat out.
    (C) The time the delivery came.
    (D) The cost of the conference.

67. Where is the house located?

    (A) In the city center.
    (B) In the downtown area.
    (C) In the suburbs.
    (D) In a distant province.

68. What happened to Raul?

    (A) He cut himself with a kitchen knife.
    (B) He wasn't given any help.
    (C) He hurt himself cutting paper.
    (D) He tripped while hurrying.

69. What is the problem?

    (A) The walls need maintenance.
    (B) The carpeting needs to be replaced.
    (C) The volume is too low.
    (D) The office is too noisy.

70. What is the purpose of the ads?

    (A) To increase interest in engineering.
    (B) To expose the condition of the sewer system.
    (C) To promote municipal bonds.
    (D) To support new bridge and tunnel construction.

71. What is broken?

    (A) The computer.
    (B) The air-conditioner.
    (C) The telephone.
    (D) The fax machine.

72. Where are they?

    (A) In a restaurant.
    (B) In an automobile.
    (C) In a hotel.
    (D) In a train car.

73. What does the man want to do?

    (A) Be shown about the islands.
    (B) Buy a guide book.
    (C) Ride in a boat.
    (D) Put up six signs.

74. What is the man interested in?

    (A) The size of the warehouse.
    (B) The location of the conveyor belt.
    (C) How many service elevators there are.
    (D) How big the inventory is.

75. What does the woman want?

    (A) A timetable.
    (B) An earlier training session.
    (C) The express mail service.
    (D) The fast train.

76. What is Jerry's job?

    (A) He is a copier technician.
    (B) He is a sales representative.
    (C) He is a mover.
    (D) He is a lecturer.

GO ON TO THE NEXT PAGE

77. What is Bart concerned about?

   (A) Preparing the report on time.
   (B) An inspection by the chairman of the board.
   (C) Whether or not he can help Judith.
   (D) Convincing all five people to go to the meeting.

78. What is the woman suggesting?

   (A) That the man reads more.
   (B) That he should take his time.
   (C) That flying is better.
   (D) That Paris is very expensive.

79. How many changes were made to win the bid?

   (A) One.
   (B) Two.
   (C) Three.
   (D) Four.

80. Who is the man talking to?

   (A) A baker's delivery service.
   (B) An office supply store salesperson.
   (C) A floral designer.
   (D) A bookstore salesperson.

PART IV

Directions: In this part of the test, you will hear several short talks. Each will be spoken just one time. They will not be printed in your test book, so you must listen carefully to understand and remember what is said.

In your test book, you will read two or more questions about each short talk. The questions will be followed by four answers. You are to choose the best answer to each question and mark it on your answer sheet.

81. Who is the announcement specifically addressed to?

    (A) College students.
    (B) Factory workers.
    (C) The unemployed.
    (D) Potential investors.

82. What is being offered?

    (A) Advice on colleges.
    (B) A course.
    (C) Venture capital.
    (D) Real estate.

83. What claim is made?

    (A) That one will be able to retire early.
    (B) That one can become an independent contractor.
    (C) That one will become financially independent.
    (D) That one can earn money by investing it.

84. What is this report about?

    (A) A complaint by Sharp Penny.
    (B) A stationery supply house order.
    (C) A decision to automate the mailings.
    (D) A reserve account.

85. Who has probably written this report?

    (A) An office manager.
    (B) A mail clerk.
    (C) A Sharp Penny sales rep.
    (D) An office clerk.

86. What is being offered at no charge?

    (A) Training for workers.
    (B) Machine maintenance.
    (C) A half month's rental.
    (D) One month's stationery supply.

87. What is known about Stanley Lake?

    (A) He is a shareholder at the Follenworth Company.
    (B) He prefers to keep to himself.
    (C) He is a door-to-door salesman.
    (D) He is an author.

88. Who is the speaker most likely addressing?

    (A) Book buyers.
    (B) Vice presidents.
    (C) Airport security personnel.
    (D) The marketing staff.

89. Who is most likely to read this notice?

    (A) Bike manufacturers.
    (B) Transportation authorities.
    (C) Bicyclists.
    (D) Bus drivers.

90. What is the purpose of this notice?

    (A) To promote healthier lifestyles.
    (B) To announce the new bike program.
    (C) To sell exercise bikes.
    (D) To announce a new bus schedule.

91. How might the bus operator offer assistance?

    (A) By opening the rack.
    (B) By storing any air pumps in the bus.
    (C) By lifting the bike onto the supports.
    (D) By answering questions.

92. With whom has Myanmar united?

    (A) The European Union.
    (B) The U.S.
    (C) The opponents of the SLORC party.
    (D) The ASEAN.

GO ON TO THE NEXT PAGE

93. What is the response of the U.S. and the European Union?

    (A) Enthusiasm.
    (B) Approval.
    (C) Resignation.
    (D) Opposition.

94. What has Myanmar Shipyards been hired to do?

    (A) To serve as an administrator for the Singapore office.
    (B) To build cargo ships.
    (C) To inspect Jaya Marine Lines International.
    (D) To negotiate contracts with foreign shipping companies.

95. Who is most likely speaking?

    (A) A car manufacturer.
    (B) A construction foreman.
    (C) A tour guide.
    (D) A safety inspector.

96. What is the main point of his message?

    (A) That the market in Venezuela needs more attention.
    (B) That four-doors are more popular than mini-vans.
    (C) That business in Brazil is doing well.
    (D) That South America has excellent markets.

97. Why was Mr. Carreras mentioned?

    (A) To tell the listeners who was handling personnel changes.
    (B) To indicate who had called for stricter safety measures.
    (C) To acknowledge the contribution he has made.
    (D) To let the employees know who the new boss is.

98. What is being advertised?

    (A) Real estate.
    (B) Construction materials and plans.
    (C) Home owner's insurance.
    (D) Free energy conservation audits.

99. Which selling point is emphasized?

    (A) Its aesthetic value.
    (B) Its affordability.
    (C) The ease of assembly.
    (D) The array of color options.

100. How can the reader find out more?

    (A) By visiting Home Dome Builders.
    (B) By ordering a color video.
    (C) By viewing other homes in the neighborhood.
    (D) By ordering a free brochure.

This is the end of the Listening Comprehension portion of Practice Test One. Turn to Part V in your test book.

READING

In this section of the test, you will have a chance to show how well you understand w
There are three parts to this section, with special directions for each part.

PART V

Directions: Questions 101–140 are incomplete sentences. Four words or phrases, marked
(A), (B), (C), (D) are given beneath each sentence. You are to choose the **one** word or phrase that
best completes the sentence. Then, on your answer sheet, find the number of the question and mark
your answer.

You will read:

Because the equipment is very delicate,
it must be handled with ....

(A) caring
(B) careful
(C) care
(D) carefully

Sample Answer

Ⓐ Ⓑ ● Ⓓ

The sentence should read, "Because the equipment is very delicate, it must be handled with care."
Therefore, you should choose answer (C).

Now begin work on the questions.

---

101. If we had seen the demand in advance, we surely .... on the cookbook.

    (A) would stock up
    (B) have stocked up
    (C) had stocked up
    (D) would have stocked up

102. Most of the time in Indonesia was spent .... relatives.

    (A) to visit
    (B) visiting
    (C) going visiting
    (D) go to visit

103. My broker advised me to invest in secured bonds before .... in the stock market.

    (A) invested
    (B) investing
    (C) investment
    (D) I will invest

104. It goes without .... that you'll be paid for all this extra time you're spending on the project.

    (A) telling
    (B) saying
    (C) repeating
    (D) regarding

105. The businessmen discussed the contract at length but never actually signed ....

    (A) anything
    (B) anyone
    (C) another
    (D) anyway

106. The worldwide low inflation rate is expected to continue ....

    (A) at a fast pace
    (B) for a long time
    (C) in a decline
    (D) throughout

GO ON TO THE NEXT PAGE

patient .... examined by the doctor.

(A)   were
(B)   is being
(C)   has
(D)   have been

108.   The Argentineans are protecting their forests because the lumber is very valuable to ....

(A)   they
(B)   ourselves
(C)   them
(D)   we

109.   Travel agents advise .... early, in order to avoid disappointment.

(A)   buying
(B)   postponing
(C)   booking
(D)   canceling

110.   The use of pesticides is having a .... effect on the groundwater.

(A)   devastate
(B)   devastating
(C)   devastated
(D)   devastation

111.   Because of Lucille's managerial skills, the family now has an .... business.

(A)   expanding
(B)   expend
(C)   expanse
(D)   expended

112.   Just as the business was about to go under, he .... the bid for the shopping mall construction.

(A)   was winning
(B)   will win
(C)   had won
(D)   won

113.   We have decided to .... your income with a monthly bonus.

(A)   implement
(B)   compliment
(C)   supplement
(D)   compartment

114.   A study was done to determine the effect .... the change in government policy has had on the small business sector.

(A)   of
(B)   what
(C)   for
(D)   that

115.   The air conditioner will have to be worked on .... the office is in use.

(A)   during
(B)   while
(C)   only
(D)   meanwhile

116.   Your credit history shows that either several loan payments were late .... the bank made a huge error in reporting them.

(A)   and
(B)   but
(C)   nor
(D)   or

117.   Another building will be .... in the downtown area before you know it.

(A)   demolished
(B)   demolishing
(C)   demolish
(D)   demolishes

118.   The meeting is .... over.

(A)   much or little
(B)   here or there
(C)   more or less
(D)   to or from

119. We .... the money to your money market account within three working days.

(A) have been transferred
(B) will transfer
(C) transferring
(D) will be transferred

120. We are sending you what we have now and .... the remainder as soon as it arrives.

(A) will have shipped
(B) will ship
(C) shipped
(D) shipping

121. At election time, every speech is calculated to win ....

(A) preferences
(B) wishes
(C) votes
(D) choices

122. Although most people are .... than I am, they are not as healthy or wise.

(A) wealth
(B) wealthy
(C) wealthily
(D) wealthier

123. Constance breathed a sigh .... relief when she heard that her loan was approved.

(A) to
(B) for
(C) by
(D) of

124. Good management .... to the employees.

(A) will be listened
(B) are listening
(C) listens
(D) listen

125. The newly discovered ore is being extracted by .... of a huge robotic arm.

(A) mean
(B) means
(C) meant
(D) meanings

126. When the computer analyst realized what a .... task it was, he immediately added two more staff to the project.

(A) precise
(B) superfluous
(C) short
(D) formidable

127. I spoke with the real estate agent who told me that the office space would cost $225 .... square foot.

(A) for
(B) in
(C) per
(D) at

128. The human resources department is .... for the hiring and care of our personnel.

(A) respondent
(B) responsive
(C) responding
(D) responsible

129. The air conditioning unit .... for hours by the time you arrive.

(A) will have been running
(B) shall run
(C) will be running
(D) will run

130. We were having so much fun on the ship we were .... to disembark at our destination.

(A) reluctant
(B) doubtful
(C) refusing
(D) hesitant

GO ON TO THE NEXT PAGE

131. The appeal of this training approach is that the students find .... which management style work best for them.

(A) out
(B) up
(C) about
(D) on

132. While you set up the display at the .... of the store, I'll unpack the rest of the goods.

(A) prominence
(B) forward
(C) ahead
(D) front

133. Mrs. Choor has managed the department so well that she'll be up for a .... promotion than she expected.

(A) big
(B) bigger
(C) more
(D) most

134. We would like to .... a teleconference with your public relations office regarding the upcoming merger.

(A) transact
(B) install
(C) perform
(D) arrange

135. We knew the economy was .... a turning point when the interest rates started to fall.

(A) at
(B) about
(C) throughout
(D) inside

136. We have been doing business with them since their ....

(A) incentive
(B) inception
(C) incision
(D) incitement

137. The new clerk wasn't sure under which .... he should file the purchasing documents.

(A) covering
(B) level
(C) rank
(D) category

138. When Mrs. Graf sat down, she asked that the shades be pulled .... because of the bright sunlight.

(A) below
(B) off
(C) down
(D) up

139. By .... what the public liked and didn't like, we were able to fine-tune our ads.

(A) sighting
(B) focusing
(C) predicting
(D) pinpointing

140. We .... with the prime minister for dinner at the Simsbury Hotel tonight.

(A) are meeting
(B) have been met
(C) were met
(D) will be met

PART VI

Directions: In **Questions 141–160**, each sentence has four words or phrases underlined. The four underlined parts of the sentence are marked (A), (B), (C), (D). You are to identify the **one** underlined word or phrase that should be corrected or rewritten. Then, on your answer sheet, find the number of the question and mark your answer.

Example:

Sample Answer
● Ⓑ Ⓒ Ⓓ

All employee are required to wear their
    A   B

identification badges while at work.
    C   D

The underlined word "employee" is not correct in this sentence. This sentence should read, "All employees are required to wear their identification badges while at work." Therefore, you should choose answer (A).

Now begin work on the questions.

141. As your old one, this new copier can collate and
    A   B

 staple the copies in half the time.
   C   D

142. The museum is taking measures to protect its
             A

 paintings from the damaging effects of
          B

 pollutions and utra-violet rays, which are getting
      C

 worse and worse with each passing year.
                D

143. After reviewing our finances, we decided
        A   B

 reduce spending in all departments
   C

 except marketing.
   D

144. Mrs. Barrett, acting as her attorney, defended
           A   B

 Mr. Stevenson in a very determined fashion.
        C   D

145. To make out the lost time, we booked a
       A   B

 direct flight from California to New York.
     C   D

146. One evening, in a restaurant in Madrid, we
    A

 were entertained by several dramatics
       B   C   D

 flamenco dancers.

147. The plane had to fly over above the city
           A   B

 for an hour before getting permission to land.
    C   D

148. The Commission surprised investors by
                   A

 reversing its ruling and freezes all monies in
     B   C   D

 the disputed accounts.

GO ON TO THE NEXT PAGE ▶

149. Since the appliance sales <u>have shot up any</u>,
<u>A</u>
we're <u>going to continue</u> with the marketing plan
<u>B</u>
<u>we've been using</u> since the <u>very start</u>.
<u>C</u> <u>D</u>

150. <u>After</u> downsizing the company, the executives
<u>A</u>
<u>realized that had</u> much more furniture <u>than they</u>
<u>B</u> <u>C</u>
<u>needed</u>.
<u>D</u>

151. When we go <u>on vacation</u>, we prefer <u>swim</u> and
<u>A</u> <u>B</u>
active sports to sightseeing <u>and lying</u>
<u>C</u>
<u>on the beach</u>.
<u>D</u>

152. The <u>shareholders</u> were upset <u>that there weren't</u>
<u>A</u> <u>B</u>
<u>some dividends</u> <u>paid out</u> in the last two
<u>C</u> <u>D</u>
quarters.

153. Before <u>to go</u> elsewhere for new staff, we <u>always</u>
<u>A</u> <u>B</u>
try <u>to hire</u> <u>in house</u>.
<u>C</u> <u>D</u>

154. Because it was <u>structurally unsafe</u> and <u>too</u>
<u>A</u> <u>B</u>
expensive to repair, the <u>75 years old</u> building
<u>C</u>
had to be <u>demolished</u>.
<u>D</u>

155. This summer, the consumer protection agency
<u>are advising</u> consumers to read instructions
<u>A</u>
<u>carefully</u> <u>before using</u> any
<u>B</u> <u>C</u>
<u>outdoor cooking equipment</u>.
<u>D</u>

156. I've <u>looked at</u> several records in your <u>file</u> and
<u>A</u> <u>B</u>
<u>many documents still</u> don't have your
<u>C</u>
<u>new marriage name</u>.
<u>D</u>

157. Ecologists <u>feared</u> the American eagle
<u>A</u>
<u>might be near extinction</u> as there were
<u>B</u>
<u>so few sights</u> of them <u>in the last decade</u>.
<u>C</u> <u>D</u>

158. Standard Tires <u>have</u> agreed to <u>fund</u> any further
<u>A</u> <u>B</u>
<u>research into</u> the <u>manufacture of</u> latex.
<u>C</u> <u>D</u>

159. If the <u>zoning</u> changed, we <u>will be able to</u>
<u>A</u> <u>B</u>
purchase the building <u>down the street</u> and
<u>C</u>
<u>redesign it</u>.
<u>D</u>

160. The <u>factory</u> let go of <u>many its</u> employees
<u>A</u> <u>B</u>
because <u>it had automated</u> so <u>many</u> operations.
<u>C</u> <u>D</u>

PART VII

Directions: Questions 161–200 are based on a selection of reading materials, such as notices, letters, forms, newspaper and magazine articles, and advertisements. You are to choose the **one** best answer (A), (B), (C), or (D) to each question. Then, on your answer sheet, find the number of the question and mark your answer. Answer all questions following each reading selection on the basis of what is **stated** or **implied** in that selection.

Read the following example.

> The Museum of Technology is a "hands-on" museum, designed for people to experience science at work. Visitors are encouraged to use, test, and handle the objects on display. Special demonstrations are scheduled for the first and second Wednesdays of each month at 13:30. Open Tuesday–Friday 12:00–16:30, Saturday 10:00–17:30, and Sunday 11:00–16:30.
>
> When during the month can visitors see special demonstrations?
>
> (A)   Every weekend
> (B)   The first two Wednesdays
> (C)   One afternoon a week
> (D)   Every other Wednesday

Sample Answer
Ⓐ ● Ⓒ Ⓓ

The reading selection says that the demonstrations are scheduled for the first and second Wednesdays of the month. Therefore, you should choose answer (B).

Now begin work on the questions.

Questions 161–162 refer to the following announcement.

ATTENTION HOME OWNERS!

The federal government wants to help you repair and remodel your home. Regardless of how long you have owned your home, its location or condition, or your ethnic background, age, income or marital status, you may be eligible. The purpose of this program is to encourage energy conservation and neighborhood preservation. Title 1 government insurance now allows home owners to make improvements up to $25,000. Improvements may include windows, room conversions, baths, kitchens, roofing, and doors. The work must be done by lender approved contractors.

161. Why is the government offering to loan money?

(A) To help conserve energy sources
(B) To support local contractors
(C) To help businesses with cash flow problems
(D) To specifically repair low income homes

162. What request for improvement would probably be disapproved?

(A) New kitchen counters
(B) Window replacements
(C) Garage construction
(D) Ceiling repairs

GO ON TO THE NEXT PAGE ➤

Questions 163–164 refer to the following document.

RETAIL INSTALLMENT AGREEMENT:

For my records, the Jefferson Company will send an invoice (and payment coupons) along with my order that will indicate the cash price, shipping and handling, amount financed, total sale price (total payments), finance and charge, and annual percentage rate for each item. It will also indicate the number and amount of monthly installments and the amount of sales tax, where applicable. The four-dollar shipping and handling charge and any express shipping charges or sales tax are to be paid with the first installment.

163. What will the person receive from Jefferson Company?

(A) An itemized account of goods
(B) A discount on the cash price
(C) Monthly advertisements
(D) A four-dollar rebate

164. When will the buyer pay?

(A) Before getting the merchandise
(B) Upon delivery
(C) Within one month
(D) In periodic payments

Questions 165–167 refer to the following report.

In the spring of 1994, Holiday Arboreal Farm transplanted 10,000 two-year-old seedlings for Christmas tree production. Of these, 50% were Balsam Fir, 35% Douglas Fir, and 15% were White Pine and Blue Spruce. The Balsam and Douglas Fir would be in the five to six foot range by the sixth growing season after transplanting, with the Balsam having a tendency to reach as high as eight feet, thus making them available to market that year. The White Pine and Spruce would be in the same five to six foot range in the eighth growing year after transplanting. The Balsam and Douglas Fir would be wholesaled for $15.00 and the White Pine and Spruce for $8.00. Any trees not sold in these years could be sold the following years with an increase in size of ten to twelve inches, allowing a price increase of $3.50 per foot.

165. What is the topic of the report?

(A) Furs
(B) Inflation
(C) Holiday gift prices
(D) Trees

166. What affects the price ?

(A) Thickness
(B) Color
(C) Proximity to market
(D) Height

167. What is the purpose of the report?

(A) To encourage nature conservation
(B) To increase sales
(C) To inform about transplanted tree sales
(D) To challenge the price increase

32   Practice Test One

Airtime Technologies, Inc., of Southampton, England, has supplied more than four hundred paging systems to fourteen Chinese provinces since 1989. For instance, it won a 4.5 million dollar contract from the Broadcasting Administrative Committee of the Biendong Province in May. The company's foreign sales are not confined to Asia. It is making healthy inroads in Latin America. In Trinidad and Guyana, an 8 million dollar deal was struck with Allpage, the largest private paging provider in the area. Airtime services its South American customers through its branch offices in Brazil, Mexico and Texas. While the company is blossoming in developing countries, it is also still doing a lot of work in developed countries such as Canada, where there is a joint venture underway. Distributors and marketing personnel are being sought to develop the above-mentioned areas as well as the entire Indonesian region.

168. Where is Airtime Technologies based?

(A) Trinidad
(B) Southampton
(C) Guyana
(D) Texas

169. What does Airtime do in its Mexican office?

(A) Establishes joint ventures with Latin America
(B) Produces pagers in its factories
(C) Provides service to customers in South America
(D) Trains marketing personnel

170. Who is Airtime Technologies looking for?

(A) Technicians who can repair pagers
(B) Chinese broadcasters
(C) Canadian clerical personnel
(D) Sales representatives

GO ON TO THE NEXT PAGE

Questions 171–174 refer to the following advertisement.

To succeed in Saudi Arabia, you need space and a convenient location. Access to transportation, electric power and manpower are also needed. A dynamic and cooperative landlord wouldn't hurt.

The Dammam Industrial Zone has all of this and more, and it's available now. Our location is hard to beat: just ten minutes from King Fahd International Airport. The existing airport highway takes you to the center of the Eastern Province. Plans are underway for improved access to the port of Gizan. Adequate water and power are assured and both you and your management and staff will appreciate the peace and quiet of a rural setting. The Saudi Basic Development Corporation will also provide expert assistance with approvals, licenses and permits. Our situation is perfect for light or heavy manufacturing, as well as for research and development.

171. Which type of business is the advertiser hoping to attract?

(A) Manufacturing companies
(B) Airline companies
(C) Water purification facilities
(D) Management consultants

172. What help is being offered?

(A) Transportation to and from the airport
(B) Securing building permits
(C) Obtaining drivers licenses
(D) Helping the staff to relocate to the area

173. What could the new tenants be assured of?

(A) A skilled work force
(B) Extensive market research
(C) Docking permits at the port of Gizan
(D) Adequate electricity

174. What is particularly favorable about the location?

(A) Warehousing is available in the Eastern Province.
(B) Shipping and docking facilities are available.
(C) It is near an airport.
(D) It is easy to beat the traffic.

Questions 175–177 refer to the following news item.

The bus service between the City Center Subway Station and the Fairfield County Government Center is being expanded to give residents from Huntsville and Lawton easier access to public hearings and other evening events at the government complex. By June 10th, Fairfield connector buses will make six additional round trips between the two stops – four in the middle of the day and two at night. The buses now run only during morning and evening rush hours.

175. Where are the people being bused to?

(A) The government center
(B) Huntsville
(C) The City Center Station
(D) Lawton

176. How many extra trips will Fairfield connector buses make during the day?

(A) Two
(B) Four
(C) Six
(D) Eight

177. When do the connector buses normally run?

(A) In the late morning
(B) In the afternoon
(C) Late at night
(D) During peak hours

Questions 178–180 refer to the following chart.

HOME PRICE	DOWN PAYMENT	MORTGAGE LOAN	MONTHLY PAYMENTS		
			6%	8%	10%
$85,000	$8,500	$73,000	$434	$525	$633
$145,000	$19,000	$129,000	$755	$924	$1,099
$245,000	$44,000	$210,000	$1,210	$1,471	$1,780
$400,000	$85,000	$440,000	$2,110	$2,821	$2,995

178. What is the most expensive home a person could get for an up-front payment of $20,000?

(A) $85,000
(B) $145,000
(C) $245,000
(D) $400,000

179. What is the purpose of the chart?

(A) To sell homes
(B) To compare mortgage rate variables
(C) To advertise low rates
(D) To encourage customers to switch banks

180. Who would be most interested in this chart?

(A) Apartment hunters
(B) Home sellers
(C) Home buyers
(D) The International Revenue Service

GO ON TO THE NEXT PAGE

MANILA RENTALS

The Philippines' equipment rental leader has an immediate opening for a branch administrative assistant at its newest location in Tarlac. Job duties include accounts payable, accounts receivable, bank deposits, office management and general office. Manila Rentals offers a competitive wage, comprehensive benefits package, and 401K, as well as the most lucrative and unique profit sharing plan in the industry.

Manila Rentals uses only the highest quality equipment and glass and dining ware. We have also been rated Number One three years in a row by Consumer Watch Magazine. Qualified candidates should have a minimum of two years of experience in a similar office environment. Good interpersonal and organizational skills a must.

181. How is Manila Rentals different from others in the industry?

(A) It uses only crystal.
(B) It offers above-average wages.
(C) It uses custom-made equipment.
(D) It gives employees a share in company profits.

182. What skills are not listed in the ad?

(A) Office management skills
(B) Computer skills
(C) Interpersonal skills
(D) Bookkeeping skills

183. Who would be most interested in this ad?

(A) A hotel chain that rents dining ware
(B) A senior advertising specialist
(C) Critical consumers
(D) An unemployed office worker

Electromagnetic Fields

Electromagnetic fields (EMFs) are produced any time an electric current runs through a wire or an appliance. Wherever you find electricity, you will find EMFs. In today's electrical environment, EMFs are everywhere. Atlantic Gas & Electric has detected them near power generators, around radio and transmission stations, under power lines, and near electrical outlets, lights, office equipment and computer terminals.

The idea that electromagnetic fields could be dangerous to your health is not entirely new. Soviet scientists began reporting on them as early as 1972 when they noticed that switchyard workers who were regularly exposed to high levels of electromagnetic fields near the Omsk Power Station experienced strange health effects. There were increased levels of heart disease, nervous disorders, and blood pressure changes, as well as recurring headaches, fatigue, stress and chronic depression.

Today, power companies cannot avoid the EMF issue. Medical evidence has brought it to the fore. Concerned citizens have effectively organized themselves to attract the attention of the media, their public officials and, in one instance, the management of the Oakville Power Authority. Their goal is to identify the EMF problem clearly, target their objectives carefully, then make their demands known to the Public Utilities Commission. If enough reports reach the Commission, it will become clear that these are not isolated instances. Citizens must demand that utility companies prove there is a strong need to put up more power lines in residential neighborhoods.

184. Why is there concern over EMFs?

(A) They interrupt radio transmissions.
(B) They disrupt computer operations.
(C) They negatively affect one's health.
(D) They damage power lines.

185. How should a person handle an EMF problem?

(A) Determine exactly what is occurring
(B) Inform nearby power stations
(C) Have their blood pressure checked
(D) Turn off any computer equipment in the area

186. To whom should concerned citizens report their findings?

(A) Atlantic Gas & Electric
(B) The Public Utilities Commission
(C) The Omsk Power Station
(D) The Oakville Power Authority

187. How should citizens deal with the erection of new lines?

(A) Have the lines put up in isolated areas
(B) Have the company show that they are needed
(C) Have the media focus its attention on the power company
(D) Have health surveys done of nearby residents

GO ON TO THE NEXT PAGE

Questions 188–190 refer to the following memo.

MEMORANDUM

The following sales people are responsible for these territories:

Po Sau Tam – New York and New Jersey
Bob Youngs – Delaware and Pennsylvania
Art Harman – Maryland and Virginia
Bill Hoechst – North and South Carolina

Your previous territories are to be turned over to your sales assistants and the sales books for those territories are to be given to Mrs. Pliny, our accountant. Sales meetings will be held every other Monday at the corporate office instead of every Tuesday. New automobiles are being ordered for the fleet. You have a choice of either a Ford Escort or a Toyota Corolla. Please notify the office manager, John Walletti, or the receptionist, by Monday, October 2.

---

188. Who is most likely to receive this memo?

(A) The office manager
(B) The various sales people
(C) Sales assistants
(D) Automobile manufacturers

189. To whom are sales people turning over their previous territories?

(A) Sales assistants
(B) The office manager
(C) The accountant
(D) The receptionist

190. When will the sales meetings be held?

(A) Every day
(B) Every other Friday
(C) Every Tuesday
(D) Every other Monday

Jenny Lane
65 Pipeline Highway
Anchorage, Alaska 95561

May 17, 2000

Dear George,

I would like to pass on to you the results of the research I have done in determining a location for another outlet for our men's clothing store.

I am considering an enclosed mall as opposed to a downtown single address location, an outdoor strip mall, or a hotel complex. I have found that the foot traffic at the enclosed mall is 55% more than the downtown location, 35% more than the strip mall, and 75% more than the hotel.

Additionally, the rent at the enclosed mall is only 30% higher than that of the strip mall and the downtown location, and it is the same as the hotel rent. The lease at both malls is five years, whereas the downtown location is four and the hotel three.

All things considered, I think we're better off with the enclosed mall. Please drop me a line or an E-mail and let me know your thoughts on the matter.

Sincerely,

Jenny Lane

Jenny Lane

191. Which location gets the most foot traffic?

(A) The hotel complex
(B) The downtown location
(C) The strip mall
(D) The enclosed mall

192. What additional percentage of foot traffic did the enclosed mall have over the strip mall?

(A) 5%
(B) 35%
(C) 55%
(D) 75%

193. Why does Jenny recommend the enclosed mall?

(A) It has better parking.
(B) The strip mall is too long.
(C) The rent is less.
(D) The store should get more customers.

GO ON TO THE NEXT PAGE

AVAILABLE FOR IMMEDIATE SALE OR LEASE IN KHABAROVSK

This 750,000 square foot facility, of which 252,000 square feet of adjacent space is under lease to reputable tenants doing research and development, is conveniently located on the rail to Vladivostok and is ideally suited for heavy manufacturing, final assembly and distribution. The entire complex, which is situated on 129 acres, is for sale. Subdivision into two facilities is possible, one containing 450,000 square feet and the other containing 300,000 square feet. Expert assistance can also be provided for attaining local approvals,  licenses and permits. If this facility could meet your company's needs, give us a call and we'll put together an incentive package that will be too good to pass up.

194. How many square feet is for sale but currently being leased?

(A) 252,000
(B) 300,000
(C) 450,000
(D) 750,000

195. What does the ad recommend the facility be used for?

(A) Product development
(B) Market research
(C) Light manufacturing
(D) Distribution

196. What is the landlord willing to do to sell the property?

(A) Sell a portion of it
(B) Issue building permits
(C) Grant distribution licenses
(D) Meet with company representatives

Questions 197–198 refer to the following chart.

1928	The first shopping center opens in Columbus, Ohio on the outskirts of the city where the land is less expensive.
1956	The first all-indoor mall opens in Edina, Minnesota.
1976	Faneuil Hall Market is developed in downtown Boston, moving suburban malls to downtown locations.
1990	Outlet malls are currently the fastest-growing in the shopping center industry.
1989-1993	New developments see a seventy percent decrease in growth as developers turn to updating already standing shopping centers.

197. Where was the first shopping center?

(A) In the downtown area
(B) At the edge of town
(C) On a subway line
(D) Far from the city

198. What has happened most recently in shopping malls?

(A) Fewer malls are being built and more are being renovated.
(B) Outlet malls are selling more goods than strip malls.
(C) Malls are moving from the city to suburbia.
(D) Malls have lost seventy percent of their business.

GO ON TO THE NEXT PAGE

OPEN TEST
METROPOLITAN POLICE DEPARTMENT
MANHATTAN

POLICE OFFICER

STARTING SALARY: $30,740

QUALIFICATIONS:

U.S. citizen at time of application
20 years old and 6 months at time of application;
21 years at time of appointment
High school diploma or a certificate of equivalency (GED)
Valid driver's license at time of application
At least 20/60 vision correctable to 20/20 in both eyes
Background investigation which determines moral suitability
Written and physical ability tests
Medical examination, including being of proportionate weight and height
Drug screening test

TO BE SCHEDULED, CALL (817) 555-9190

199. What is the purpose of this announcement?

(A) To post a job vacancy
(B) To announce a test result
(C) To find a criminal
(D) To announce testing for a job position

200. Who isn't qualified to apply?

(A) People under twenty-one
(B) Very tall people
(C) Illiterate people
(D) People who have not graduated from college

Stop! This is the end of the test. If you finish before one hour and fifteen minutes have passed, you may go back to Parts V, VI, and VII and check your work.

Practice Test Two

LISTENING COMPREHENSION

In this section of the test, you will have the chance to show how well you understand spoken English. There are four parts to this section, with special directions for each part.

PART I

Directions: For each question, you will see a picture in your test book and you will hear four short statements. The statements will be spoken just one time. They will not be printed in your test book, so you must listen carefully to understand what the speaker says.

When you hear the four statements, look at the picture in your test book and choose the statement that best describes what you see in the picture. Then, on your answer sheet, find the number of the question and mark your answer. Look at the sample below.

Sample Answer

Now listen to the four statements.

Statement (B), "They're having a meeting," best describes what you see in the picture. Therefore, you should choose answer (B).

GO ON TO THE NEXT PAGE

1.

2.

3.

4.

GO ON TO THE NEXT PAGE ▶

5.

6.

7.

8.

GO ON TO THE NEXT PAGE ▶

9.

10.

11.

12.

GO ON TO THE NEXT PAGE

13.

14.

15.

16.

GO ON TO THE NEXT PAGE

17.

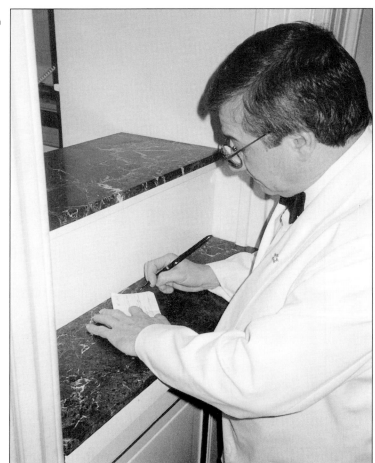

18.

19.

20.

GO ON TO THE NEXT PAGE

21.   Mark your answer on your answer sheet.

22.   Mark your answer on your answer sheet.

23.   Mark your answer on your answer sheet.

24.   Mark your answer on your answer sheet.

25.   Mark your answer on your answer sheet.

26.   Mark your answer on your answer sheet.

27.   Mark your answer on your answer sheet.

28.   Mark your answer on your answer sheet.

29.   Mark your answer on your answer sheet.

30.   Mark your answer on your answer sheet.

31.   Mark your answer on your answer sheet.

32.   Mark your answer on your answer sheet.

33.   Mark your answer on your answer sheet.

34.   Mark your answer on your answer sheet.

35.   Mark your answer on your answer sheet.

36.   Mark your answer on your answer sheet.

37.   Mark your answer on your answer sheet.

38.   Mark your answer on your answer sheet.

39.   Mark your answer on your answer sheet.

40.   Mark your answer on your answer sheet.

41.   Mark your answer on your answer sheet.

42.   Mark your answer on your answer sheet.

43.   Mark your answer on your answer sheet.

44.   Mark your answer on your answer sheet.

45.   Mark your answer on your answer sheet.

46.   Mark your answer on your answer sheet.

47.   Mark your answer on your answer sheet.

48.   Mark your answer on your answer sheet.

49.   Mark your answer on your answer sheet.

50.   Mark your answer on your answer sheet.

GO ON TO THE NEXT PAGE ▶

PART III

Directions: In this part of the test, you will hear thirty short conversations between two people. The conversations will not be printed in your test book. You will hear the conversations only once, so you must listen carefully to understand what the speakers say.

In your test book, you will read a question about each conversation. The question will be followed by four answers. You are to choose the best answer to each question and mark it on your answer sheet.

51. Why isn't the meeting date set yet?

   (A) Natalie hasn't asked Manuel about it.
   (B) Everyone is busy on Friday.
   (C) The secretary is out.
   (D) Manuel's schedule is unclear.

52. What does the man think he forgot to do?

   (A) Pay the bill.
   (B) Take his mobile phone.
   (C) Take the receipt.
   (D) Lock his car.

53. How are the speakers getting to Tokyo?

   (A) By plane.
   (B) By bus.
   (C) By train.
   (D) By car.

54. Who is the woman probably talking to?

   (A) A tailor.
   (B) A hair stylist.
   (C) A salesperson.
   (D) An artist.

55. What does the man want to buy?

   (A) A plain hamburger.
   (B) A lemonade.
   (C) A poster.
   (D) A map.

56. What does the woman do?

   (A) Breaks her fragile items.
   (B) Changes her seat.
   (C) Checks one carry-on bag.
   (D) Takes two bags on board.

57. When is the orientation?

   (A) Before lunch.
   (B) Early morning.
   (C) At noon.
   (D) After lunch.

58. What is the man's complaint?

   (A) The office needs a new printer.
   (B) The woman isn't friendly.
   (C) The office equipment is breaking down.
   (D) The printer is difficult to use.

59. What are the speakers doing?

   (A) Meeting a traveler.
   (B) Entering a building.
   (C) Shopping for a hat.
   (D) Walking down a narrow street.

60. Why are the speakers leaving soon?

   (A) Their meeting starts in twenty minutes.
   (B) There may be a lot of traffic.
   (C) The plane is arriving early.
   (D) The woman doesn't like driving.

61. Why might there be a drop in brokerage fees?

   (A) Because of new international banks.
   (B) Because new banks are opening.
   (C) Because of competition.
   (D) Because of fewer investments.

62. What does the man offer to do?

   (A) Inform everyone of the teleconference.
   (B) Rearrange the schedule.
   (C) Meet the woman at three o'clock.
   (D) Call everybody in the office.

63. What does the man want to do?

(A) Call a client.
(B) Use a room.
(C) Change his schedule.
(D) Pick up a check.

64. Why do the speakers want to get together?

(A) To participate in a demonstration.
(B) To talk with the bank manager.
(C) To have a meal together.
(D) To meet Rudy.

65. Where is the man?

(A) On vacation.
(B) In a theater.
(C) At an auto parts store.
(D) At a camera store.

66. Why will Joan be in George's office?

(A) Joan is going to work for George.
(B) Electrical work is being done near her desk.
(C) They are cutting back on office space.
(D) Joan's office is being paneled.

67. What appears to be the problem?

(A) The new boss isn't very productive.
(B) The factory needs to be renovated.
(C) There are personality conflicts.
(D) The foreman isn't experienced.

68. What will the survey try to determine?

(A) Traffic patterns.
(B) Employment rates.
(C) Elevator capacity requirements.
(D) Worker satisfaction.

69. What does the woman agree to do?

(A) Call the post office.
(B) Wait for the man.
(C) Return by four o'clock.
(D) Mail the package.

70. What does the woman's statement imply?

(A) Reducing the budget could be costly.
(B) She'll use her hard-earned money.
(C) The competition is ahead of them.
(D) They could lose employees.

71. What is the woman interested in?

(A) Renovating the office.
(B) Renting office space.
(C) Buying a card.
(D) Getting back to the office.

72. What is the problem?

(A) Workers can't get to their jobs.
(B) The sales agents lost their commissions.
(C) The service needs to be reduced.
(D) The pay raise was unacceptable.

73. Who knows about the money?

(A) Rosa.
(B) Betty.
(C) Karla.
(D) Hans.

74. What was the woman trying to do?

(A) Finish her work.
(B) Run a race.
(C) Be on time.
(D) Sharpen the pencils.

75. What is the woman suggesting?

(A) Cancelling the trip.
(B) Visiting Sweden in the summer.
(C) Taking something warm to wear.
(D) Going with friends.

76. What should the woman do?

(A) Fire her staff.
(B) Finish her meal.
(C) Join her colleagues.
(D) Plan a party.

GO ON TO THE NEXT PAGE

77. What is the problem?

(A) The driver is absent.
(B) No one can pick up Mr. Sikarda.
(C) The president is late.
(D) There's no coffee.

78. Where does this conversation take place?

(A) In a news store.
(B) In a religious building.
(C) In an immigration office.
(D) In a travel agency.

79. What had the man forgotten?

(A) That the office wasn't open.
(B) That his work schedule had changed.
(C) That the game wasn't over.
(D) That an hour had passed.

80. How long have they been waiting?

(A) A few minutes.
(B) A half-hour.
(C) An hour.
(D) All day.

Directions: In this part of the test, you will hear several short talks. Each will be spoken just one time. They will not be printed in your test book, so you must listen carefully to understand and remember what is said.

In your test book, you will read two or more questions about each short talk. The questions will be followed by four answers. You are to choose the best answer to each question and mark it on your answer sheet.

81. What will the weather be like today?

(A) Cloudy and cool.
(B) Warm and breezy.
(C) Hot and sticky.
(D) Windy and rainy.

82. On which day is this report given?

(A) Sunday.
(B) Monday.
(C) Friday.
(D) Saturday.

83. How many of the employees like the company?

(A) All of them.
(B) Very few.
(C) Less than half.
(D) Most of them.

84. How much of a raise would entice some to leave?

(A) 10%
(B) 20%
(C) 45%
(D) 80%

85. What is the story about?

(A) A new kind of cancer.
(B) How to test for cancer.
(C) A cancer-causing gene.
(D) An Asian research center.

86. Who is most likely to be affected?

(A) Scandinavians.
(B) Filipinos.
(C) Asians.
(D) Americans.

87. Where is the meeting to take place?

(A) In the new building.
(B) In one of the old offices.
(C) On the top floor.
(D) In the VIP room.

88. What is the purpose of the meeting?

(A) To organize the move.
(B) To collect all the boxes.
(C) To assign room numbers.
(D) To meet the movers.

89. What should the managers bring with them?

(A) Their files.
(B) Their books.
(C) A list of belongings.
(D) The boxes.

90. What is this meeting about?

(A) Collecting money.
(B) Swapping newsletters.
(C) Statistical analysis.
(D) Financial advice.

91. How does the speaker know the author?

(A) He's read his newsletter.
(B) He's worked with him.
(C) He is his consultant.
(D) He's listened to his speeches.

92. What does the audience have in common?

(A) They want more money.
(B) They read the same magazines.
(C) They subscribe to the same newsletters.
(D) They all have financial advisors.

GO ON TO THE NEXT PAGE

93. What is the topic of this report?

    (A) Advertising.
    (B) Consumer spending.
    (C) Labor strikes.
    (D) Economics.

94. What is causing an increase in employment opportunities?

    (A) Better working conditions.
    (B) Less classified ads being written.
    (C) Consumer confidence.
    (D) Labor union efforts.

95. What does Joe Bloomberg say about the current situation?

    (A) It's a good time for job seekers.
    (B) The labor market is slowing down.
    (C) Unemployment is up.
    (D) There's too much help-wanted advertising.

96. What is the speaker suggesting?

    (A) Hands-on experience is the best.
    (B) Being loyal to one employer.
    (C) You can't open a business without a degree.
    (D) Theory must come before practice.

97. How could one successfully learn all of the different aspects of a business?

    (A) By taking a lot of courses.
    (B) By working at different places.
    (C) By talking with other business people.
    (D) By starting one's own business.

98. Who would not be interested in this information?

    (A) Local travelers.
    (B) Airline advertisers.
    (C) Train advertisers.
    (D) Long-distance commuters.

99. How long does the train from Yamagata to Sendai take?

    (A) One hour.
    (B) One and a half hours.
    (C) Two hours.
    (D) Three hours.

100. Who or what wouldn't necessarily benefit from this news?

    (A) The airlines.
    (B) Commuters.
    (C) Train marketers.
    (D) Train stations.

This is the end of the Listening Comprehension portion of Practice Test Two. Turn to Part V in your test book.

YOU WILL HAVE ONE HOUR AND FIFTEEN MINUTES TO COMPLETE PARTS V, VI, AND VII OF THE TEST.

READING

In this section of the test, you will have a chance to show how well you understand written English. There are three parts to this section, with special directions for each part.

PART V

Directions: Questions 101–140 are incomplete sentences. Four words or phrases, marked (A), (B), (C), (D) are given beneath each sentence. You are to choose the **one** word or phrase that best completes the sentence. Then, on your answer sheet, find the number of the question and mark your answer.

You will read:

Because the equipment is very delicate, it must be handled with ....

(A) caring
(B) careful
(C) care
(D) carefully

Sample Answer
Ⓐ Ⓑ ● Ⓓ

The sentence should read, "Because the equipment is very delicate, it must be handled with care." Therefore, you should choose answer (C).

Now begin work on the questions.

101. Health care .... have been rising but so has the quality.

(A) cost
(B) costs
(C) costing
(D) costly

102. We are restocking the warehouse now that the transport strike is over .... that customers get what they need right away.

(A) to ensure
(B) ensured
(C) for ensuring
(D) ensure

103. Electrical services will be restored more .... if we call in some of the part-timers.

(A) quicker
(B) quickly
(C) quickest
(D) quick

104. Assembly lines in car manufacturing plants .... for countless jobs.

(A) supply
(B) create
(C) account
(D) look

105. .... spending is probably going to maintain this upward trend throughout the year.

(A) Consume
(B) Consumer
(C) Consuming
(D) Consumed

106. If you go .... your travel agent, you're likely to get a much better fare.

(A) after
(B) over
(C) about
(D) through

107. Whereas the language barrier, in .... times, was once an obstacle to trade, that is no longer the case.

(A) earliness
(B) earlier
(C) early on
(D) early to

108. The trade show has always been in Oslo, ... this year the directors have decided to hold it in Stockholm.

(A) but
(B) nor
(C) during
(D) when

109. The architecture of New York .... its importance as a center of world trade.

(A) realizes
(B) inscribes
(C) remembers
(D) reflects

110. Not one of our representatives .... to participate in the final draft

(A) chosen
(B) were choosing
(C) have been chosen
(D) has been chosen

111. If John had found the wallet, we .... you right away.

(A) called
(B) would call
(C) would have called
(D) would be calling

112. He bought an air conditioner and installed .... himself.

(A) them
(B) it
(C) him
(D) your

113. Patrick didn't realize .... his promotion also pushed him into a higher tax bracket.

(A) that
(B) then
(C) when
(D) since

114. Many stockholders didn't even notice when their shares went ....

(A) out
(B) down
(C) way
(D) to

115. The prime minister will impose a tariff .... domestic interests are being threatened by a flood of imports.

(A) in spite of
(B) despite
(C) ever since
(D) as

116. The professor praised him for his .... the class when she was sick.

(A) assist
(B) to assist
(C) assisting
(D) assisted

117. According to the *Financial Times*, the prime rate .... up slightly even without the housing boom.

(A) would have gone
(B) will have gone
(C) were to go
(D) was going

118. I am honored to accept this award .... our departed director.

(A) in light of
(B) because of
(C) on account of
(D) on behalf of

119. Economists watch the business cycle as it goes through its various ....

(A) segments
(B) phases
(C) sectors
(D) divisions

120. Studies .... that these new policies have done nothing to boost the economy.

(A) have shown
(B) shown
(C) has shown
(D) are shown

121. The water department has warned that the water may not be potable, ... the residents shouldn't even use it to brush their teeth.

(A) but
(B) so
(C) because
(D) nor

122. The telephone lines of the United States are .... than those of any country in the world.

(A) longer
(B) longest
(C) long
(D) longs

123. These amendments will be ratified by a majority before they .... presented to the legislative body.

(A) will be
(B) would be
(C) are
(D) were

124. Please report .... the engineering department.

(A) directly
(B) to
(C) forward
(D) aside

125. If you wait until the twelfth, the president .... for two days by then.

(A) has been waiting
(B) has waited
(C) will have been waiting
(D) was waiting

126. I'm sorry, but he is not .... to his trust fund yet.

(A) authorized
(B) allowed
(C) accessed
(D) entitled

127. The banks are very willing to give loans for home ....

(A) impropriety
(B) improvements
(C) improvisation
(D) impulse

128. She will neither .... the terms nor give in to your badgering.

(A) acceptable
(B) accepts
(C) accepting
(D) accept

129. The Malaysian Peninsula is .... Burma.

(A) fastened with
(B) connected to
(C) put together
(D) combined with

130. .... we invested in the telecommunications industry, we would be rich by now.

(A) Shall
(B) Should
(C) Will
(D) Had

GO ON TO THE NEXT PAGE

131. The presiding officials took off their hats
.... the slain leader.

    (A) in charge of
    (B) because of
    (C) in deference to
    (D) in light of

132. This prestigious award is not given to just
....

    (A) anyone
    (B) someone
    (C) somebody
    (D) many

133. Marine biologists want to reduce industrial
....

    (A) pollution
    (B) environment
    (C) pollutes
    (D) environmental

134. One of the things they will be .... is
whether or not you are a team player.

    (A) finding
    (B) looking for
    (C) inquiring
    (D) seeking

135. I was told that the maître d', who .... us
so much, had just been fired.

    (A) helping
    (B) had been helped
    (C) helped
    (D) are being helped

136. Since most of the business meetings were at
night we were able to spend the day............. .

    (A) to sightsee
    (B) to enjoy sightseeing
    (C) going to sightsee
    (D) sightseeing

137. These stocks have done very .... since
the company changed management.

    (A) slowly
    (B) weakly
    (C) poorly
    (D) steadily

138. She wasn't able to identify the man she
.... that night.

    (A) sees
    (B) was seen
    (C) will see
    (D) had seen

139. We were told we .... be able to reserve
a seat on the mailboat that passes through
the Arctic Circle.

    (A) might
    (B) must
    (C) can
    (D) could

140. The lower cost of doing business overseas is
enticing .... many of our local
manufacturers.

    (A) to
    (B) on
    (C) with
    (D) by

PART VI

Directions: In **Questions 141–160**, each sentence has four words or phrases underlined. The four underlined parts of the sentence are marked (A), (B), (C), (D). You are to identify the **one** underlined word or phrase that should be corrected or rewritten. Then, on your answer sheet, find the number of the question and mark your answer.

Example:

Sample Answer
● Ⓑ Ⓒ Ⓓ

All employee are required to wear their
   A   B
identification badges while at work.
      C   D

The underlined word "employee" is not correct in this sentence. This sentence should read, "All employees are required to wear their identification badges while at work." Therefore, you should choose answer (A).

Now begin work on the questions.

---

141. The deputy officer was charged with
                          A
looking at over the files to find other evidence
   B   C
of wrongdoing.
   D

142. Initial we were very anxious to start the
        A
computer seminar, but we found it so difficult
                        B   C
that we eventually withdrew.
              D

143. Gone through the folders one by one, we were
        A   B
able to find the missing invoice in the
   C
storage drawer.
   D

144. All things considered, the inclement weathers
                                        A   B
this month hasn't significantly decreased
              C
productivity of the staff.
        D

145. Having been to Barcelona twice himself, Bob
                          A
told us last week that aquatics sports are
   B   C
becoming increasingly popular there.
              D

146. She repeated because she did not want any of
              A   B
her money invested in the heavily advertised,
              C
but high-risk companies.
        D

147. We will be traveling with the vice president and
              A
his wife they are members of the
          B
finance committee for the new arts center.
        C   D

148. The staff worked throughout night to meet the
        A   B   C
client's deadline.
        D

GO ON TO THE NEXT PAGE

149. Biologists are always search for insights into
    A   B
    the nature of the human cell.
        C   D

150. The museum director was neither friendly or
                              A
    professional in his approach to the
                 B
    interested students and their teacher.
        C   D

151. Remembered the backlog from last year,
        A
    the staff decided to work a little overtime every
        B   C
    day to avoid a recurrence.
        D

152. Jeff and Gloria went to pick out carpeting and
                    A
    decoration, including furnitures, for the new VIP
                 B
    lounge that was opening on the third floor.
        C   D

153. Did you know that you can save
        A
    up to 25 percent in disabled insurance
        B   C
    if you are a non-smoker?
        D

154. The computer has mistakenly canceled your
                    A
    club membership but it can be reinstate by
        B   C
    tonight or tomorrow at the latest.
                    D

155. Copyright law clearly stated that you have
                        A
    to have the permission of the authors or the
        B   C
    publishers before copying their work.
                    D

156. Your paycheck for last week given to the
        A   B
    head of your department to pass on to you.
        C   D

157. These interested paintings were donated to the
            A   B
    library by the Gilmore Foundation
            C
    over twenty years ago.
        D

158. When you show him your
            A
    letters of recommendation, I'm sure he
                B
    will not hesitant to give you the salary
                C
    that you want.
        D

159. When we entering Tokyo proper, we drove right
                A   B
    through a tunnel that opened into the
            C   D
    Royal Gardens.

160. I think it would be easier to hold the
                A
    audience's attention if you had a slide show
                B   C
    along to the lecture.
        D

PART VII

Directions: Questions 161–200 are based on a selection of reading materials, such as notices, letters, forms, newspaper and magazine articles, and advertisements. You are to choose the **one** best answer (A), (B), (C), or (D) to each question. Then, on your answer sheet, find the number of the question and mark your answer. Answer all questions following each reading selection on the basis of what is **stated** or **implied** in that selection.

Read the following example.

> The Museum of Technology is a "hands-on" museum, designed for people to experience science at work. Visitors are encouraged to use, test, and handle the objects on display. Special demonstrations are scheduled for the first and second Wednesdays of each month at 13:30. Open Tuesday–Friday 12:00–16:30, Saturday 10:00–17:30, and Sunday 11:00–16:30.

When during the month can visitors see special demonstrations?

Sample Answer
Ⓐ ● Ⓒ Ⓓ

(A)   Every weekend
(B)   The first two Wednesdays
(C)   One afternoon a week
(D)   Every other Wednesday

The reading selection says that the demonstrations are scheduled for the first and second Wednesdays of the month. Therefore, you should choose answer (B).

Now begin work on the questions.

Questions 161–162
refer to the following classified advertisement.

NARRAGANSETT HOMES, INC.,

a major regional homebuilder, is looking for a marketing professional who is highly energetic and has a team player attitude to develop and implement marketing and sales programs. This is a highly visible position which reports directly to the president. The individual will oversee merchandising and marketing in several states.

A minimum of six years' experience in a similar position is required.
Send résumé and salary requirements to:

Human Resources
Narragansett Homes
2321 Rightward Road
Marlboro, NV 55461

161.   What kind of employee are they looking for?

(A)   Athletic
(B)   Diplomatic
(C)   Motivated
(D)   Strong

162.   In what area should the person be experienced?

(A)   Home construction
(B)   Computer programming
(C)   Demographics
(D)   Product promotion

GO ON TO THE NEXT PAGE ➤

Questions 163–164 refer to the following form.

JOIN THE SYDNEY NATIONAL FILM THEATER

$25 Sydney National Film Theater Patron

- One year subscription to *Forecast*, the National Film Theater's monthly program guide
- Discount tickets (for you and a guest) to the more than 700 films presented annually at the Sydney Theater
- First chance at tickets to meet filmmakers for discussions
- Advance ticket purchase and reservations privileges

For more information on **National Membership**
call the Sydney National Member Hotline 1-800-645-8976

Name _____

Address _____

City _____ State _____ Postal Code _____

Telephone # (home) _____ (work) _____

___ Check enclosed   ___ Bill me   Is this a renewal? __Y __N

163. What do patrons receive?

(A) A discount on a subscription to *Forecast*
(B) Invitations to meet filmmakers
(C) An opportunity to buy tickets ahead of time
(D) Special reserved seats at all shows

164. What information is requested in the form?

(A) Country
(B) Workplace
(C) Renewal code number
(D) Type of payment

There are two companies hoping to be selected as the builders of the new international terminal at Singapore Airport in Changi. Both have been given approval to begin feasibility studies for the project. The State Board for Project Evaluation has selected Great Britain's Dar Handash and Germany's Dywidag Euromill to conduct the studies. Pending the completion of the Civil Aviation Authority of Singapore's financial analysis of the project, a decision could be reached as early as September.

165. What is the topic of the article?

(A) Plans to construct an international terminal
(B) Public relations between Germany and Singapore
(C) A new training program for pilots
(D) Investments in Great Britain

166. When can a decision be made?

(A) After completion of preparations in Changi
(B) After comparing results of the feasibility studies
(C) After the meeting meeting between Dar Handash and Dywidag Euromill
(D) After financial review by Singapore aviation officials

167. What is Dar Handash going to do?

(A) Find out what can and can't be done
(B) Build at Singapore Airport
(C) Conduct an evaluation of Euromill
(D) Send its reports to the Civil Aviation Authority of Singapore

GO ON TO THE NEXT PAGE

RACE TRACK REVIEWS
By Stefan Mueller
Illustrated. 165 pp. New York:
Litton Publishing Company. $8.95

Race Track Reviews not only gives insight into what's under the hood of the winning cars but also who's behind the wheel.This collection of twenty-six biographical sketches is both informative and entertaining. For the more serious racer, Mueller includes in-depth coverage of the only car to break the sound barrier, as well as a battery of illustrations revealing the effects on the body of the car. It is noteworthy that the author has taken steps to minimize the use of technical jargon, making the subject more inviting to lay readers.

168. Who would most likely buy this publication?

(A) Collectors of antique cars
(B) People interested in car racing
(C) People who bet on horse races
(D) Technicians

169. What information is in this book?

(A) How to build a car
(B) Body repair techniques
(C) Data about engines
(D) Locations of car races

170. How has the author broadened the book's appeal?

(A) By using sketches
(B) By using fewer technical terms
(C) By using an entertaining style
(D) By using personal stories

A French cosmetics giant announced that it has applied for a license to construct a $7.5 million cosmetics factory in the Dietaka Industrial Park in Cong Tum. The factory will be similar in design to one they built five years ago outside Malacca in Malaysia. The completely foreign-owned enterprise will produce skin care products, cosmetics and perfume. According to a study done by the company, 75% of the raw materials will be sourced locally and the plant will employ up to 450 workers from Cong Tum and neighboring Qui Nohn and Play Cu. The new Vietnamese factory is expected to enjoy sales totaling $2 million dollars within the first year, with an additional million the year after.

171. Where will the new factory be located?

(A) Malacca
(B) Cong Tum
(C) Play Cu
(D) Qui Nohn

172. What does the company need to begin building?

(A) At least 450 workers
(B) A lease agreement with Dietaka Industrial Park
(C) A license to start
(D) Foreign capital

173. Where will most of the factory's production resources come from?

(A) France
(B) Overseas
(C) Malaysia
(D) The Cong Tum region

174. What will be the expected sales in the second year?

(A) 1 million dollars
(B) 2 million dollars
(C) 3 million dollars
(D) 7.5 million dollars

GO ON TO THE NEXT PAGE

Questions 175–178 refer to the following notice.

KEEP YOUR VOTER FILE UP-TO-DATE!

If we don't have your current name or address, you might not be on the voters' list.
You will not be able to vote in the next election unless you are listed.

Use the attached Form VRR 188 to register.
This form can also be used to report a change of name or address. Additional VRR 188 forms
may be obtained at Town Hall on Dorsey Street or by calling 885-1254.

To vote in a primary election, you must be registered with a party that is holding a primary
election: the Democratic, Republican or Umoja Party. If you register with the Liberal Party or any
other party, or with no particular party at all, you may only vote in special or general elections.
Use Form VRH 189 to register with a party or to change parties.

Your social security number will only be used for identification purposes when registering.
As per the Federal Privacy Act, it cannot be made available to the public or used in any reports.

175. What would prevent someone from voting?

(A) An outdated file
(B) Failure to appear
(C) Appearing on the voters' list
(D) Affiliation with the Democratic Party

176. What must one do to sign up for a particular party?

(A) Use Form VRR 188
(B) Call 885-1254
(C) Use Form VRH 189
(D) Vote in a primary election

177. What is the restriction for voters with no party affiliation?

(A) They must provide their social security numbers.
(B) They can only vote in primaries.
(C) They must register as Liberals.
(D) They cannot vote in primary elections.

178. Why is a voter's social security number asked for?

(A) To establish identity
(B) Because of Federal Privacy Act requirements
(C) To update public records
(D) To use in reports

Citizens Action Coalition
76 Ansolm Street
Cork, Ireland

March 21, 2000

Dear Jeanne,

Let me take this opportunity to congratulate and welcome you to the Executive Board of the Citizens Action Coalition. I look forward to working with you.

Our bylaws require a minimum of three board meetings per year, however, sometimes the need arises to convene more than three times. Our meetings are scheduled on Friday evenings. Minutes and agendas will be provided for you prior to the board meetings. You will need to bring them to the meetings with you as additional ones are not provided. I am enclosing a brochure which covers the various committees in our organization and their purposes. Committee meetings are generally scheduled during the day on the Friday of the board meeting. (Last week's Monday meeting was an exception.) Emergency committee meetings are usually held on the weekend during the day.

Starting July you will receive a stipend each month of £500 to defray expenses of the board and related meetings. Expenses that go beyond the £500 may be reimbursed, but only if accompanied by Form 113 and approved by the treasury secretary.

Again, congratulations and welcome!

Sincerely yours,

Margaret Kohl

Margaret Kohl
Library Director

---

179. Why was this letter written?

(A) To raise contributions
(B) To acknowledge a new board member
(C) To inquire about availability for meetings
(D) To suggest a change in work schedules

180. What should Jeanne bring to the board meetings?

(A) A brochure
(B) Her personal agenda
(C) A watch or clock
(D) A schedule for the meeting

181. When would the committees normally meet?

(A) When the board deems it necessary
(B) On the day of the Friday board meeting
(C) On Mondays
(D) On Friday evenings

182. How would Jeanne get reimbursed for £600 of board related expenses?

(A) She would use her stipend.
(B) She would see the cashier in the treasury office.
(C) She would submit Form 113.
(D) She would apply to the finance committee.

GO ON TO THE NEXT PAGE

The Ministry of Foreign Commerce and Economic Progress has issued a business license to the Qua Ping Trading Corporation, Thailand's first joint-venture foreign trade company. The Bangkok-based venture was set up through an agreement between the Eastern Trading Company of Bangkok, which holds a 52% share in the new venture; the Fidushi Corporation of Taegu, a 27% share; and the Detroit-based Global Agro Company, 21%.

The new venture is being capitalized at $11.5 million and will trade in consumer and industrial electronics and machinery for both light and heavy manufacturing.

This venture company is a direct result of a pledge made by Thailand's Minister of Finance in Seoul at the Asian-Pacific Economic Cooperation forum in 1961. According to one economic analyst, foreign companies will benefit from this new venture company because of a 3% lowering of tariffs on goods exported to Thailand, while Thailand will have an opportunity to learn from foreign management styles.

183. What is special about the Qua Ping Trading Corporation?

(A) It's a joint venture.
(B) It's foreign-owned.
(C) It is worthwhile.
(D) It will trade in both electronics and machinery.

184. Which company has the smallest stake?

(A) Eastern Trading Company
(B) Fidushi Corporation
(C) Global Agro Company
(D) An Asian-Pacific conglomerate

185. What is one benefit of the deal?

(A) Ease of obtaining business licenses
(B) Inclusion in more conferences
(C) Superior foreign management
(D) Lowered taxes on exports to Thailand

186. What occurred in 1961?

(A) Presidents of several joint ventures convened.
(B) A promise was made for economic cooperation.
(C) Tariffs in Thailand were lowered.
(D) The Qua Ping Trading Corporation received approval in Asia.

The state of California plans to build a nuclear waste disposal site in the California desert. This proposed plan is being met with challenges on all sides. Economist Lisa Shue thinks the site is unnecessary. "With the advances in recycling and new compacting technologies, our other waste sites are not even in full use." Shue argues that existing sites should be developed before new ones are built. Furthermore, environmentalists are asking that all waste sites be tested for leaks and other safety tests be carried out. Developers in the California desert also resist the plans for the site. Most builders in the area would prefer to have the land developed for homes.

187. What is the subject of this article?

    (A) Environmental effects of nuclear waste disposal sites

    (B) Growth in the California desert

    (C) Opposition to a planned nuclear waste disposal site

    (D) Advancements in recycling and compacting technologies

188. Why does Lisa Shue think this site is unnecessary?

    (A) There are already too many waste sites in California.

    (B) The existing waste sites are not being used to their capacity.

    (C) It will be an economic burden on the State of California.

    (D) Now that people recycle, California doesn't need waste sites.

189. What do developers envision for the land?

    (A) Residential construction

    (B) A theme park

    (C) Major resistance

    (D) Multiple sites

GO ON TO THE NEXT PAGE

"Too many consumers are buying high octane gas thinking it is a 'treat' or a 'treatment' for their cars," said Karen Finkelstein, Assistant Director of the Consumer Protection Agency. "But, the fact is, the consumers are the ones getting the treatment, not the cars," she added. "Now, Ready Gas will join the Consumer Protection Agency to get the word out to consumers: Unless the owner's manual for your car calls specifically for high octane fuel or your engine is knocking, there's no reason to pay for premium gasoline," she advised.

In June of this year, the Consumer Protection Agency filed a complaint charging Ready Gas with making unfounded advertising claims about the ability of Ready Gas gasoline to clean engines and reduce automobile maintenance costs. As part of an agreement to settle the charges, Ready Gas agreed to air a twenty second television ad featuring a Ready Gas official saying, "Normally cars run properly on regular octane, so check your owner's manual and stop by Ready Gas for this informative pamphlet." This law enforcement remedy will not only set a precedent but will also save consumers money.

190. What is the purpose of this bulletin?

(A) To endorse Ready Gas gasoline
(B) To promote high octane fuel
(C) To show that a wrong has been righted
(D) To encourage regular auto maintenance

191. Why should someone buy high octane fuel?

(A) To get better mileage
(B) Because it's indicated by the car manufacturer
(C) Because it cleans the engine
(D) To reduce costs

192. How is Ready Gas addressing the issue?

(A) By educating the public
(B) By giving discounts on high octane fuel
(C) By changing their advertising agency
(D) By issuing new, updated owner's manuals

A survey done by the University of Tokyo for Oriental Agriculture regarding business people revealed the following: A study involving the health claims of 4,000 staff indicated that men who traveled made 80% more health claims than those who didn't, whereas women who traveled made only 18% more claims than those who didn't.

In a separate survey of 400 business travelers by Sarim Consultants for Asian Imports, however, it was found that women reported feeling more stress than men when they travel. Women are more concerned about personal obligations they've left behind (60% women; 35% men) and about work not getting done at the office (85% women; 65% men). Women also feel more pressured to perform their jobs while on the road (58% women; 44% men).

193. Who took part in these surveys?

(A) Health insurance agents
(B) University of Tokyo students
(C) Traveling and non-traveling business people
(D) Travel agents

194. How many people were surveyed altogether?

(A) 400
(B) 4,000
(C) 4,400
(D) 4,800

195. What distinguishes male travelers from female travelers?

(A) They claim higher expenses.
(B) They travel more.
(C) Their blood pressure is lower than that of women travelers.
(D) They have proportionately more travel-related health complaints.

196. What concerns the most women travelers?

(A) Unfinished personal matters back home
(B) Work falling behind at the office
(C) Performance pressures
(D) Stress in the lives of their husbands

GO ON TO THE NEXT PAGE

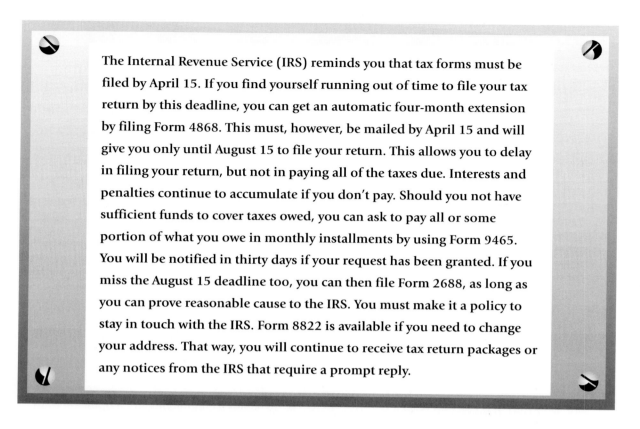

The Internal Revenue Service (IRS) reminds you that tax forms must be filed by April 15. If you find yourself running out of time to file your tax return by this deadline, you can get an automatic four-month extension by filing Form 4868. This must, however, be mailed by April 15 and will give you only until August 15 to file your return. This allows you to delay in filing your return, but not in paying all of the taxes due. Interests and penalties continue to accumulate if you don't pay. Should you not have sufficient funds to cover taxes owed, you can ask to pay all or some portion of what you owe in monthly installments by using Form 9465. You will be notified in thirty days if your request has been granted. If you miss the August 15 deadline too, you can then file Form 2688, as long as you can prove reasonable cause to the IRS. You must make it a policy to stay in touch with the IRS. Form 8822 is available if you need to change your address. That way, you will continue to receive tax return packages or any notices from the IRS that require a prompt reply.

197. What is being advised as a general policy towards the IRS?

(A) Informing yourself of your options
(B) Paying all penalties and interest payments on time
(C) Staying in communication
(D) Being sure to use the form that applies to your situation

198. If you miss the first extension deadline, what is minimally required?

(A) A good excuse
(B) Monthly installments
(C) Sending in Form 4868
(D) Immediate filing of the tax return

199. What should you do if you owe but have no money?

(A) File Form 2688
(B) File Form 4868
(C) File Form 8822
(D) File Form 9465

200. What is the purpose of Form 8822?

(A) To notify the IRS of revised contact information
(B) To ask for a tax return package
(C) To demand a prompt reply
(D) To request permission to move

Stop! This is the end of the test. If you finish before one hour and fifteen minutes have passed, you may go back to Parts V, VI, and VII and check your work.

Practice Test Three

LISTENING COMPREHENSION

In this section of the test, you will have the chance to show how well you understand spoken English. There are four parts to this section, with special directions for each part.

PART I

Directions: For each question, you will see a picture in your test book and you will hear four short statements. The statements will be spoken just one time. They will not be printed in your test book, so you must listen carefully to understand what the speaker says.

When you hear the four statements, look at the picture in your test book and choose the statement that best describes what you see in the picture. Then, on your answer sheet, find the number of the question and mark your answer. Look at the sample below.

Sample Answer
Ⓐ ● Ⓒ Ⓓ

Now listen to the four statements.

Statement (B), "They're having a meeting," best describes what you see in the picture. Therefore, you should choose answer (B).

GO ON TO THE NEXT PAGE

1.

2.

3.

4.

GO ON TO THE NEXT PAGE ➤

5.

6.

7.

8.

GO ON TO THE NEXT PAGE

9.

10.

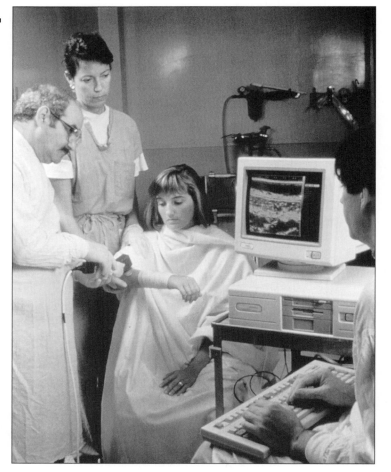

11.

12.

GO ON TO THE NEXT PAGE

13.

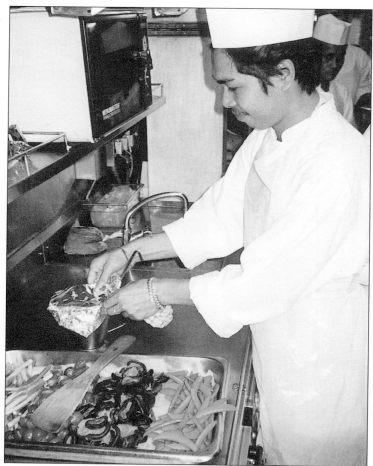

14.

15.

16.

GO ON TO THE NEXT PAGE ▶

17.

18.

19.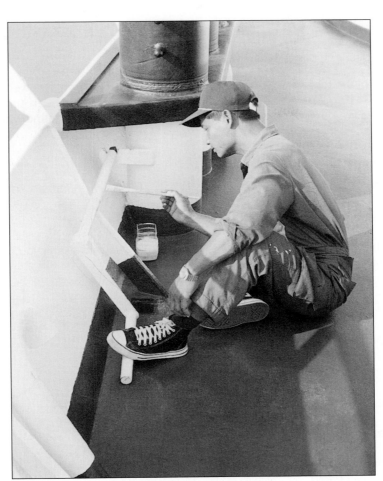

20.

GO ON TO THE NEXT PAGE

PART II

Directions: In this part of the test, you will hear a question spoken in English, followed by three responses, also spoken in English. The question and the responses will be spoken just one time. They will not be printed in your test book, so you must listen carefully to understand what the speakers say. You are to choose the best response to each question.

Now listen to a sample question.

You will hear:

You will also hear:

Sample Answer

The best response to the question "How are you?" is choice (A), "I am fine, thank you." Therefore, you should choose answer (A).

21.   Mark your answer on your answer sheet.

22.   Mark your answer on your answer sheet.

23.   Mark your answer on your answer sheet.

24.   Mark your answer on your answer sheet.

25.   Mark your answer on your answer sheet.

26.   Mark your answer on your answer sheet.

27.   Mark your answer on your answer sheet.

28.   Mark your answer on your answer sheet.

29.   Mark your answer on your answer sheet.

30.   Mark your answer on your answer sheet.

31.   Mark your answer on your answer sheet.

32.   Mark your answer on your answer sheet.

33.   Mark your answer on your answer sheet.

34.   Mark your answer on your answer sheet.

35.   Mark your answer on your answer sheet.

36.   Mark your answer on your answer sheet.

37.   Mark your answer on your answer sheet.

38.   Mark your answer on your answer sheet.

39.   Mark your answer on your answer sheet.

40.   Mark your answer on your answer sheet.

41.   Mark your answer on your answer sheet.

42.   Mark your answer on your answer sheet.

43.   Mark your answer on your answer sheet.

44.   Mark your answer on your answer sheet.

45.   Mark your answer on your answer sheet.

46.   Mark your answer on your answer sheet.

47.   Mark your answer on your answer sheet.

48.   Mark your answer on your answer sheet.

49.   Mark your answer on your answer sheet.

50.   Mark your answer on your answer sheet.

GO ON TO THE NEXT PAGE ▶

Directions: In this part of the test, you will hear thirty short conversations between two people. The conversations will not be printed in your test book. You will hear the conversations only once, so you must listen carefully to understand what the speakers say.

In your test book, you will read a question about each conversation. The question will be followed by four answers. You are to choose the best answer to each question and mark it on your answer sheet.

51. Where are the speakers?

    (A) At a hospital.
    (B) In a restaurant.
    (C) At an ice rink.
    (D) In a bank.

52. Where is the hotel restaurant?

    (A) On the second floor.
    (B) Downstairs.
    (C) Next to the reading room.
    (D) On the left-hand side of the corridor.

53. What does the man need to do?

    (A) Send a fax.
    (B) Talk to his secretary.
    (C) Charge more money.
    (D) Lease a fax machine.

54. What is the woman trying to do?

    (A) Start a construction company.
    (B) Find a job for her brother.
    (C) Learn carpentry skills.
    (D) Locate a summer home.

55. What's the weather like today?

    (A) Sunny.
    (B) Foggy.
    (C) Raining.
    (D) Snowing.

56. Why is there no paper?

    (A) The man used it up himself.
    (B) Some was given to another department.
    (C) None was ordered.
    (D) They couldn't find it.

57. How often does the woman buy the *New York Times*?

    (A) Every day.
    (B) Once a month.
    (C) Twice a week.
    (D) Never.

58. How are they going to the movies?

    (A) By train.
    (B) By car.
    (C) By bus.
    (D) By taxi.

59. What does the woman want?

    (A) A new printer.
    (B) Current price lists.
    (C) More time.
    (D) A lower sales quota.

60. To whom is the woman talking?

    (A) A waiter.
    (B) A travel agent.
    (C) An airline attendant.
    (D) A train conductor.

61. What is the man implying?

    (A) All the information is there.
    (B) There are lots of problems.
    (C) The president won't approve the proposals.
    (D) The president will prove his point.

62. Who is Mr. Samo talking to?

    (A) A town clerk.
    (B) A car salesman.
    (C) A test administrator.
    (D) A chauffeur.

63. What are they discussing?

(A) Ordering more computers.
(B) Selling very large furniture.
(C) Displaying more computer furniture.
(D) Making the bedroom smaller.

64. How does the woman solve the problem?

(A) By calling a courier.
(B) By doing it herself.
(C) By renting a car.
(D) By shipping it.

65. What is the man's occupation?

(A) Flight attendant.
(B) Travel agent.
(C) Security guard.
(D) Housekeeper.

66. Why does the woman prefer the mystery section?

(A) It is less noisy.
(B) It is nicely decorated.
(C) It has padded seats.
(D) It has long tables.

67. How much time do the local deliveries usually take?

(A) About 2 hours.
(B) About 6 hours.
(C) About 12 hours.
(D) About a week.

68. What is the problem?

(A) There aren't enough chairs.
(B) The rent is expensive.
(C) The store is closed.
(D) The meeting is too long.

69. What do they need help with?

(A) Serving lunch.
(B) Talking to Sam and David.
(C) Moving furniture.
(D) Counting the tables.

70. Who is talking to the woman?

(A) An optician.
(B) A librarian.
(C) A typesetter.
(D) A pharmacist.

71. Why might the company file for bankruptcy?

(A) Its situation is unknown.
(B) It needs more staff.
(C) It is being sued by the bank.
(D) It can't meet the payroll.

72. Where are they going in the afternoon?

(A) To a supermarket.
(B) To a car wash.
(C) To a restaurant.
(D) To a friend's house.

73. What are they looking for?

(A) A snow shovel.
(B) A book.
(C) A telephone.
(D) A job.

74. What is being sent to Cairo?

(A) More telephones.
(B) A new fax machine.
(C) Electrical equipment.
(D) Incoming orders.

75. What does the woman want to do?

(A) Sell a ticket.
(B) Enjoy a performance.
(C) Wait for a bus.
(D) Get a refund.

76. Where are the people from the media?

(A) Outdoors.
(B) On their way.
(C) At their magazine headquarters.
(D) In the waiting room.

GO ON TO THE NEXT PAGE ➤

77. What are the speakers talking about?

(A) The desert they visited.
(B) The birds they saw.
(C) A meal they ate.
(D) A table they purchased.

78. Who is the woman talking to?

(A) A doorman.
(B) A neighbor.
(C) An architect.
(D) A real estate agent.

79. What is being referred to?

(A) A power cut.
(B) An emergency operation.
(C) An automatic transmission.
(D) A new patient.

80. Why was Tom given another job?

(A) He wanted to work closer to home.
(B) He was promoted.
(C) He wasn't working hard enough.
(D) His hearing wasn't very good.

Directions: In this part of the test, you will hear several short talks. Each will be spoken just one time. They will not be printed in your test book, so you must listen carefully to understand and remember what is said.

In your test book, you will read two or more questions about each short talk. The questions will be followed by four answers. You are to choose the best answer to each question and mark it on your answer sheet.

81. What is Mr. Makowitz's job in the company?

    (A) Personnel Director.
    (B) Fund-raiser.
    (C) Children's tutor.
    (D) Board member.

82. What is the purpose of the gathering?

    (A) To tutor children.
    (B) To raise money.
    (C) To acknowledge Mr. Makowitz.
    (D) To form the Literacy Crusade.

83. Which staff must report to work?

    (A) Everyone but management.
    (B) Only housekeeping.
    (C) Only management.
    (D) All personnel.

84. When will the hotel open its doors?

    (A) In November.
    (B) In February.
    (C) In March.
    (D) In April.

85. What will the staff be given at the re-opening?

    (A) Their paychecks.
    (B) New outfits.
    (C) A banquet.
    (D) A revised work schedule.

86. What is the announcement about?

    (A) A fire drill.
    (B) Office renovations.
    (C) An accounting procedure.
    (D) New stairs.

87. Where should everyone gather?

    (A) In the stairwell.
    (B) In the parking lot.
    (C) At the elevator.
    (D) At the front office.

88. What will the fire marshal talk about?

    (A) Elevators.
    (B) Speed.
    (C) New equipment.
    (D) Parking.

89. Where is the office?

    (A) At the university.
    (B) In a hospital.
    (C) On a quiet back street.
    (D) Near two main roads.

90. What kind of office has been contacted?

    (A) A highway department.
    (B) A dentist's office.
    (C) A hospital emergency room.
    (D) A cleaning service.

91. How does one get help right away?

    (A) By staying on the line.
    (B) By calling during regular office hours.
    (C) By calling Dr. Malcolm's beeper.
    (D) By pressing 9.

92. What are listeners encouraged to do?

    (A) Read a publication.
    (B) Invest quickly.
    (C) Talk to a columnist.
    (D) Be conservative.

GO ON TO THE NEXT PAGE

93. For what reason are new strategies necessary?

    (A) Temporary conditions.
    (B) Fear of failure.
    (C) Short-term inflation.
    (D) Worldwide economic change.

94. What is the purpose of the talk?

    (A) To reiterate a policy.
    (B) To explain expense reports.
    (C) To collect money.
    (D) To create new policies.

95. Why is there a problem?

    (A) Computers are breaking down.
    (B) Paychecks are missing.
    (C) People are disregarding company policy.
    (D) Receipts are being misplaced.

96. What is the accounting department busy with?

    (A) Writing paychecks.
    (B) New computers.
    (C) Handling complaints.
    (D) Revising policy.

97. What is the advantage of this new design?

    (A) Low maintenance.
    (B) Streamlined look.
    (C) Cost-effectiveness.
    (D) High speed.

98. How does the new train move?

    (A) By riding on the track.
    (B) By spinning its wheels.
    (C) By floating on magnetic fields.
    (D) By sliding on the steel rail.

99. Who is the announcement directed at?

    (A) Elderly and disabled customers.
    (B) Small children.
    (C) Subway personnel.
    (D) Passengers.

100. When does the bell sound?

    (A) Before the doors close.
    (B) When the elevator arrives.
    (C) Before the train arrives.
    (D) When the red button is pressed.

This is the end of the Listening Comprehension portion of Practice Test Three. Turn to Part V in your test book.

YOU WILL HAVE ONE HOUR AND FIFTEEN MINUTES TO COMPLETE PARTS V, VI, AND VII OF THE TEST.

READING

In this section of the test, you will have a chance to show how well you understand written English. There are three parts to this section, with special directions for each part.

PART V

Directions: Questions 101–140 are incomplete sentences. Four words or phrases, marked (A), (B), (C), (D) are given beneath each sentence. You are to choose the **one** word or phrase that best completes the sentence. Then, on your answer sheet, find the number of the question and mark your answer.

You will read:

Because the equipment is very delicate, it must be handled with ....

(A) caring
(B) careful
(C) care
(D) carefully

Sample Answer

Ⓐ Ⓑ ● Ⓓ

The sentence should read, "Because the equipment is very delicate, it must be handled with care." Therefore, you should choose answer (C).

Now begin work on the questions.

---

101. The doctor advised her .... more often.

(A) swimming
(B) swam
(C) to swim
(D) to have swum

102. This year the company has .... heavily in research and development.

(A) was invested
(B) invest
(C) investing
(D) invested

103. We found them .... down at the beach.

(A) playing
(B) to go play
(C) play
(D) to play

104. The negotiations cannot be .... because of the disagreements.

(A) concurred
(B) continued
(C) contoured
(D) confounded

105. The buying and selling of stocks and bonds is .... I would like to learn more about.

(A) something
(B) somewhere
(C) somehow
(D) somewhat

106. Income-producing stocks will .... healthy dividends.

(A) order
(B) cause
(C) generate
(D) develop

GO ON TO THE NEXT PAGE

107. If the treasurer .... here, he would sign your check.

(A) will be
(B) is
(C) has been
(D) were

108. It is better to hold the vote .... than later.

(A) sooner
(B) soonest
(C) soon
(D) some soon

109. Only .... families were invited to the gala event.

(A) opulent
(B) affluent
(C) abundant
(D) expensive

110. It is common practice to look .... someone when they talk to you.

(A) at
(B) to
(C) on
(D) by

111. Three-piece suits are back .... style.

(A) around
(B) through
(C) in
(D) unto

112. Before you can drive, you must have a ....

(A) presence
(B) ticket
(C) diploma
(D) license

113. Rewiring the office to accommodate the new air conditioning units was .... as expensive as the units themselves.

(A) just
(B) quite
(C) moreover
(D) same

114. .... employees in the postal service has meant slower service in the last two years.

(A) Less
(B) Fewer
(C) Few
(D) Least

115. Does the tide always come .... at this hour?

(A) in
(B) over
(C) out
(D) down

116. The trainees had a .... time filling out the application after they learned it was the sole assessment tool.

(A) harder
(B) hardly
(C) hardest
(D) harden

117. We have .... nothing left in the bank.

(A) because of
(B) by way of
(C) next to
(D) closest to

118. These pension .... have been carefully worked out.

(A) plan
(B) plans
(C) planning
(D) planned

119. He wasn't able to .... my point of view.

(A) think
(B) mind
(C) see
(D) reckon

120. The manufacture of textiles is considered a labor .... industry.

(A) intensive
(B) involved
(C) indicative
(D) incisive

121. .... in the accounting department was required to become familiar with the new software.

(A) Anyone
(B) All
(C) One another
(D) Everyone

122. Job seekers talked to recruiters who were ....

(A) employing
(B) analyzing
(C) specifying
(D) hiring

123. The tax authorities will soon .... new guidelines.

(A) having issued
(B) issuing
(C) to issue
(D) be issuing

124. Not just .... is allowed to enter certain government buildings.

(A) no one
(B) anyone
(C) someone
(D) each one

125. The dealerships outdo each other in advertising .... they can attract customers.

(A) because
(B) but
(C) so
(D) for

126. The color illustrations included in the new edition of the book made it .... attractive.

(A) much more
(B) many more
(C) that more
(D) the more

127. He wanted to talk to someone knowledgeable in computers before purchasing ....

(A) any
(B) ones
(C) many
(D) other

128. All financial aid to the country was .... after our ambassador was dismissed.

(A) shut off
(B) closed off
(C) sealed off
(D) cut off

129. The prospective buyer grew .... when the seller tried to rush the sale.

(A) suspects
(B) suspicious
(C) suspicion
(D) suspected

130. Had we monitored the profit trends, we could have predicted this drop well ....

(A) sooner
(B) faster
(C) in advance
(D) previous

GO ON TO THE NEXT PAGE

131. .... first-aid training is precautionary, often going unused in real life.

(A) Less
(B) Many
(C) Few
(D) Much

132. If we had proven that the diamonds .... to the Crown, they would be in the national museum today.

(A) would belong
(B) belong
(C) belonged
(D) were belonging

133. The accountants did not find .... many errors in the spreadsheet.

(A) too
(B) any
(C) few
(D) hardly

134. The alarm system of a car must .... reliably.

(A) function
(B) to function
(C) functioned
(D) functioning

135. They think so highly of you, that promotion is yours for ....

(A) the asking
(B) to ask
(C) the ask
(D) you asked

136. Please hold while I .... you to the parts department.

(A) am connected
(B) to connect
(C) connect
(D) connected

137. When you .... the audience, don't look at any one person.

(A) address
(B) talk
(C) focus
(D) communicate

138. Tickets for tonight's concert can be purchased .... the box office.

(A) between
(B) at
(C) around
(D) by

139. Several crops .... by the government.

(A) will have been subsidizing
(B) being subsidized
(C) are subsidizing
(D) are being subsidized

140. Do you feel I was too friendly .... the applicants?

(A) with
(B) at
(C) on
(D) across

PART VI

Directions: In **Questions 141–160**, each sentence has four words or phrases underlined. The four underlined parts of the sentence are marked (A), (B), (C), (D). You are to identify the **one** underlined word or phrase that should be corrected or rewritten. Then, on your answer sheet, find the number of the question and mark your answer.

Example:

Sample Answer
● Ⓑ Ⓒ Ⓓ

All <u>employee</u> are required <u>to wear</u> their
　　　 A　　　　　　　　　 B

<u>identification</u> badges <u>while</u> at work.
　　　 C　　　　　　　 D

The underlined word "employee" is not correct in this sentence. This sentence should read, "All employees are required to wear their identification badges while at work." Therefore, you should choose answer (A).

Now begin work on the questions.

---

141. The <u>wooden</u> fence <u>surrounded</u> the factory
　　　　　　 A　　　　　 B
<u>is beginning</u> to deteriorate <u>from rain</u>.
　　 C　　　　　　　　　　 D

142. The <u>head</u> lawyer resigned <u>from</u> the case <u>when</u>
　　　　 A　　　　　　　 B　　　　　 C
the conflict of interest <u>becomes obvious</u>.
　　　　　　　　　　 D

143. The <u>tire industry</u> is constantly searching <u>to</u>
　　　　 A　　　　　　　　　　　 B
alternative rubber sources <u>as</u> conventional
　　　　　　　　 C
sources <u>are dwindling</u>.
　　　 D

144. It was <u>apparent</u> that our advice <u>to expand</u>
　　　　　 A　　　　　　　　　 B
<u>into</u> the Asian markets was <u>ignore</u>.
　 C　　　　　　　　　　 D

145. Since Mrs. Papin <u>herself</u> initiated the trade
　　　　 A　　　　　 B
negotiations, <u>it was assumed</u> that the decrease
　　　　　　 C
in tariffs was done <u>from</u> her blessing.
　　　　　　　 D

146. After our <u>discussion</u>, we decided <u>to take</u> a later
　　　　　 A　　　　　　　 B
flight <u>and so that</u> we <u>could spend more time</u>
　　 C　　　　　　 D
with the clients.

147. If you <u>like to traveling</u> a lot, you <u>should consider</u>
　　　 A　　　　　　　　　 B
career opportunities <u>in</u> the cruise industry or
　　　　　　　 C
in other <u>travel-related fields</u>.
　　　　 D

148. I drove for <u>almost an hour</u> before <u>realizing</u> that
　　　　　 A　　　　　　 B
I <u>had forgotten</u> my suitcase with the important
　　 C
things in <u>them</u>.
　　　 D

GO ON TO THE NEXT PAGE ▶

149. In order to finish the project
$\overline{}$
A

according to schedule, we will have to work
$\overline{}$ $\overline{}$
B C

in advance on the steps what require
$\overline{}$
D

contractors' work.

150. The native population of Alaska has begun
$\overline{}$ $\overline{}$
A B

documenting it's wildlife's migratory patterns.
$\overline{}$ $\overline{}$
C D

151. Every departments from shoes to furniture
$\overline{}$ $\overline{}$
A B

will be inspected by the fire marshal
$\overline{}$
C

for compliance.
$\overline{}$
D

152. The results of our marketing survey show that
$\overline{}$ $\overline{}$
A B

there will be quite a demand for electric cars
$\overline{}$
C

in the ahead years.
$\overline{}$
D

153. From this bill of sale, we can see that she
$\overline{}$ $\overline{}$
A B

had sold the computer about six months after
$\overline{}$ $\overline{}$
C D

she bought it.

154. The building manager is having all the windows
$\overline{}$
A

and doors replace on the second and third
$\overline{}$ $\overline{}$
B C

floors as well as in the restaurant.
$\overline{}$
D

155. The recent developments in the field of robotics
$\overline{}$ $\overline{}$
A B

has been extremely beneficial to those who are
$\overline{}$ $\overline{}$
C D

physically handicapped.

156. Initially, your loan application sent to the loan
$\overline{}$ $\overline{}$
A B

officer, who must check your credit standing
$\overline{}$
C

before making any preliminary decision.
$\overline{}$
D

157. Reports on the rise in hotel costs come from
$\overline{}$ $\overline{}$
A B

authority sources in the industry.
$\overline{}$ $\overline{}$
C D

158. Laboratory tests revealed that the metal
$\overline{}$
A

using in this particular model was actually an
$\overline{}$ $\overline{}$
B C

alloy of inferior quality.
$\overline{}$
D

159. When the archeological findings have been first
$\overline{}$ $\overline{}$
A B

released, many scholars were dumbfounded.
$\overline{}$ $\overline{}$
C D

160. After analyzing the steep rise in profits
$\overline{}$ $\overline{}$
A B

according to your explanation, we

were convinced that your analyses was correct.
$\overline{}$ $\overline{}$
C D

PART VII

Directions: Questions 161–200 are based on a selection of reading materials, such as notices, letters, forms, newspaper and magazine articles, and advertisements. You are to choose the **one** best answer (A), (B), (C), or (D) to each question. Then, on your answer sheet, find the number of the question and mark your answer. Answer all questions following each reading selection on the basis of what is **stated** or **implied** in that selection.

Read the following example.

> The Museum of Technology is a "hands-on" museum, designed for people to experience science at work. Visitors are encouraged to use, test, and handle the objects on display. Special demonstrations are scheduled for the first and second Wednesdays of each month at 13:30. Open Tuesday–Friday 12:00–16:30, Saturday 10:00–17:30, and Sunday 11:00–16:30.p.m.

When during the month can visitors see special demonstrations?

Sample Answer
Ⓐ ● Ⓒ Ⓓ

- (A)   Every weekend
- (B)   The first two Wednesdays
- (C)   One afternoon a week
- (D)   Every other Wednesday

The reading selection says that the demonstrations are scheduled for the first and second Wednesdays of the month. Therefore, you should choose answer (B).

Now begin work on the questions.

GO ON TO THE NEXT PAGE

WHAT SUBSCRIBERS SAY ABOUT
THE HANDYMAN'S GUIDE:

"By checking with ***THE HANDYMAN'S GUIDE*** before I built my deck, I was able to save countless dollars by knowing which tools were best for the job. I was also able to avoid any of a dozen pitfalls by studying the excellent illustrations it provides. It definitely kept me on the right course."

"I find that I can service my customers more efficiently. My costs and theirs have gone down due to all the time-saving tips that ***THE HANDYMAN'S GUIDE*** has to offer. My reputation is spreading and my income is rising."

Order today and get a full money-back guarantee for the entire length of your subscription.

---

161. Why would someone subscribe to this magazine?

(A) To get job offers
(B) To learn and earn more
(C) To get discounts
(D) To understand finances

162. What does this magazine provide its readers?

(A) Useful, practical tips
(B) A free CD
(C) Guaranteed income
(D) Free services

163. Who would most likely subscribe to this guide?

(A) A cook
(B) A customer
(C) A builder
(D) An electrician

About nine thousand years ago, almost forty percent of the land surface of Earth was covered by forests. Today, thanks to the ax and the mighty power of bulldozers and chain saws, about half of these forests have vanished.

Few forests remain which are still ecologically intact. It is difficult to measure the extent of the loss, because forests are so central to life on Earth. They tend to stabilize climate, foster and maintain bio-diversity and prevent flooding and erosion.

The effects of a forest which has been denuded by logging are more deadly than may first appear. Erosion begins, hunters and miners move in as the land becomes more accessible, and then farming takes over as the last trees are cleared away. Once farming establishes itself, there is little hope for reforestation.

164. What is the author's purpose?

(A) To hold a controversial position
(B) To release new scientific research
(C) To sell forests to developers
(D) To warn readers of a dangerous situation

165. Why are the effects of logging so hard to gauge?

(A) Forests are so vast.
(B) They appear late.
(C) The hope of reforestation remains.
(D) They are so widespread.

166. What is a common order of events for forests that are cut?

(A) They are reforested and re-cut.
(B) They stabilize the climate, foster bio-diversity, and stop flooding.
(C) They are cut down and die.
(D) They are cleared by loggers and exploited by others.

GO ON TO THE NEXT PAGE

Questions 167–168 refer to the following advertisement.

MORE MONEY!

With our user-friendly financial software package, you can anticipate your

- net income for the coming year
- optimal deductions claim
- tax bracket
- health insurance costs
- savings potential

Available now in your local bookstores.

167. According to this advertisement, what can the buyer expect to get?

(A) A better understanding of one's income
(B) Lower health insurance costs
(C) Additional tax shelters
(D) Fewer deductions

168. What is implied in this ad?

(A) Pay raises are predictable.
(B) Most people don't claim finance deductions.
(C) Personal finances are complex.
(D) Saving money takes time.

Questions 169–171 refer to the following label instructions.

> **WARNING!** Do not take this medication while driving or while operating machinery. If taking other medication, see your doctor or pharmacist beforehand. Please note the following side effects: nausea, dryness of the mouth, headaches and drowsiness.
> If a rash appears, discontinue use and notify your physician.

169. Who should avoid taking this medication while working?

(A) A writer
(B) A chauffeur
(C) A waitress
(D) A clerk

170. What is one of the negative effects of this medication?

(A) Dry skin
(B) Upset stomach
(C) Hunger
(D) Light-headedness

171. Who should see a doctor?

(A) People with nausea
(B) People who take this medication
(C) People who discontinue use
(D) People who get skin irritation

Questions 172–174 refer to the following report.

TRANSMISSION VERIFICATION REPORT

DATE & TIME OF TRANSMISSION	06/18 06:19
FAX NO./NAME	181 344 18849
DURATION	00:00:38
PAGE(S)	01
RESULT	OK
MODE	STANDARD

---

172. What kind of report is this?

(A) Express mail transmission
(B) Serial number record
(C) Proof of a sent facsimile
(D) Arrival record

173. How long did this event take?

(A) 6 hours and 18 minutes
(B) 6 hours and 19 minutes
(C) 1 minute
(D) 38 seconds

174. How many sheets were sent?

(A) 1
(B) 6
(C) 11
(D) 38

Questions 175–176 refer to the following Order Form.

ORDER TOLL FREE 800-224-7100

8AM–MIDNIGHT, Monday–Friday

1. Your electronic testing equipment order will be shipped and billed to the address shown below unless you indicate otherwise. Make any corrections in the area on the right.

**Electrical Dynamics
Attn: George Bingham
Dept. 65 Supervisor
1867 Carriage Road
Los Angeles, CA 91926**

Note: A street address is required for shipment.
Deliveries cannot be made to P.O. boxes.

2. Items ordered:
When ordering, be sure to include the product numbers from the catalogue. Overnight shipping is available. Check form of payment.

_ Bill Me
_ Credit Card _____
_ Check or Money Order Enclosed

3. We will bill you or you can pay with a Credit Card, Check or Money Order.

---

175. What is the purpose of this form?

(A) To describe electronic equipment
(B) To place an order
(C) To make a refund
(D) To make corrections

176. What is needed for shipment?

(A) A post office box
(B) A credit card
(C) Advance payment
(D) A street address

GO ON TO THE NEXT PAGE

Questions 177–181 refer to the following memo.

MEMORANDUM

ATTENTION ALL HOURLY EMPLOYEES

Effective immediately, paychecks will no longer be handed out on Fridays. Due to changes in payroll, we will now have paychecks available on the first and third Monday of each month. You can either pick your check up on these days in the Human Resources office (on floor 11) before 5:00 p.m., or you can sign up for automatic deposit.

For those of you who are unfamiliar with automatic deposit, this means that your check will be put directly into your checking account and you will receive a receipt of deposit from the bank each month in the mail. If you are interested in automatic deposit, you must sign up before February 23. The sign-up sheet is posted on the door of Human Resources.

For those who pick up their checks directly, remember that if you do not sign for your check on the first or third Monday, it will automatically be sent to you in the mail. Please be aware that we do not take responsibility for checks that are lost in the mail, and stop-payment fees are paid by the employee.

---

177. When will this change in payroll take place?

(A) Right away
(B) On February 23
(C) On Friday
(D) The first Monday of the month

178. What is automatic deposit?

(A) Payment goes into a bank account.
(B) Payment is automatically sent to you in the mail.
(C) Checks are handed out directly on Fridays.
(D) Taxes are withheld regardless of payment method.

179. What do hourly employees need to do to pick up their check?

(A) Provide an employee number and photo I.D.
(B) They must work on the Monday that they pick up their check.
(C) They must sign up by February 23.
(D) They must sign their name.

180. What would be likely to happen if a check got lost in the mail?

(A) The employee would pick it up on the next Monday.
(B) The company would pay for a stop payment.
(C) A deposit slip would be automatically sent to the employee.
(D) The employee would report the loss and cover the fee.

181. Who would need to read this memo?

(A) Any worker who goes to Human Resources for their check
(B) Any worker who is paid by the hour
(C) All employees who want to learn about automatic deposit
(D) Employees interested in becoming paid by the hour

Questions 182–185 refer to the following instructions.

IN-FLIGHT INSTRUCTIONS:

In the event of an emergency, please go to your seat and fasten your seatbelt. Attendants will be on hand to assist you.

All electronic devices should be turned off, as these could interfere with the pilot's radio transmissions.

Should the cabin lose pressure, an oxygen mask will automatically fall from the overhead compartment. Simply slide the plastic cord over your head, fit the mask to your face and then breathe through the mask. If you are with a child, first put on your own mask. This will help you to assist your child.

In the unlikely event that the plane is forced to make a water landing, the seat on which you are sitting is also a flotation device. Simply pull it up and out.

Exit ramps from the plane are clearly marked.

---

182. Where would someone most likely read this?

(A) At an airport
(B) On a boat
(C) In a hospital
(D) On a plane

183. Where should one go at the first sign of an emergency?

(A) To the pilot
(B) To the flight attendant
(C) To one's seat
(D) To the exit ramp

184. Where are the oxygen masks stored?

(A) Under the seats
(B) In overhead compartments
(C) Next to the exit ramps
(D) In the rear of the cabin

185. What should a parent with a child do if the plane loses pressure?

(A) Put on their own mask first
(B) Call the attendant
(C) Put on the child's mask first
(D) Go to the exit

GO ON TO THE NEXT PAGE

House History Researched

Do you know the history of the house you are considering buying or selling? Let us research the owners, builders and architects associated with your home. Find out who they were and where they worked. We will provide you with photographs, maps and written research.

For more information or a free estimate, call Thorndike and Company at 312/589-9812, or stop by our offices at 14th Street and J. You will learn the histories of many local homes, from those on K Street built during the Civil War, to the luxury homes that fill the entire city block between 8th and 9th Avenues.

186. Who would be most interested in this ad?

(A) Photographers
(B) Architects
(C) Homeowners
(D) Construction engineers

187. Where could one go to learn the histories of some of the researched homes?

(A) J Street
(B) 8th Avenue
(C) K Street
(D) 9th Avenue

LS
Levine & Schmidt
88 Jhansi Street
District 2
Delhi, India
Tel: (83-8) 744 7923
Fax: (83-8) 743 7924

January 5th

Dr. Nguyen Luc
Bio-Chem Industries
86 Musang Street
Kuala Lumpur
Malaysia

Dear Dr. Luc,

Thank you for your request for information about this year's convention.
Enclosed you will find convention information as well as several brochures about accommodations in the area.

Our special events coordinator has told me that the Maxton Hotel is offering sizable group discounts this year – up to 40%. Maybe this year your entire staff could join you.

If you have any further questions about the convention or need any help with accommodations, please don't hesitate to call me at the above number.

I look forward to seeing you at this gathering and I'm hoping that you and I and Dr. Jean Delois will be able to have dinner together.

Sincerely,

Langh Thien

Langh Thien
Vice President

188. What is the main purpose of this letter?

(A) To find the location of the convention
(B) To promote the Maxton Hotel
(C) To send convention information
(D) To ask about accommodations

189. What accompanies the letter?

(A) Hotel discount coupons
(B) Information about the convention
(C) Reports about last year's convention
(D) A letter from Dr. Jean Delois

190. What does Langh Thien suggest?

(A) Using the special events coordinator
(B) Visiting Levine & Schmidt
(C) Contacting Dr. Delois
(D) Bringing the whole Bio-Chem Staff

GO ON TO THE NEXT PAGE

What mosquitos do and why their bites itch!

When a mosquito lands on you, its first task is to find a blood vessel. As blood vessels make up less than five percent of your skin, this is no small task. Once a mosquito has succeeded with its probing, it begins the extraction. To keep the blood flowing and the vessel dilated, mosquitos pump in chemicals which thin the blood and expand the vessel. Our allergic reaction to these chemicals is what causes the itch.

191. What is this article about?

(A) Mosquito nesting habits
(B) The diet of a mosquito
(C) Why mosquito bites itch
(D) How mosquitos find blood vessels

192. Where do the chemicals originate?

(A) Human skin
(B) The mosquito
(C) The blood vessels
(D) The blood

Questions 193–196 refer to the following investment information.

One out of every six Americans invests in stocks and bonds. And every single one of them is trying to find out which investment is best. Ideally speaking, the best advice would come from a person who knew everything about every company: what the products are, how big the demand is, how big the demand will be, what the overhead is, etc. The list could go on for pages.

That would be the ideal picture. The other end of the spectrum would be advice based on hearsay.

The truth is, if you're going to take control of your financial investments, then either you have to do the research yourself, or find someone else you can rely on. Chances are you don't really have time to do the research. You're too busy making the money to invest. So how do you know which person or company to trust? How do you know if *they* are doing their homework?

Do some research. Ask some questions. You see, a good financial advisor will tell you *how* he comes up with his conclusions. He digs for the data. He finds out about a company's management. He visits factories. He looks at the potential for demand, watches the local political climate, etc.

So, if you really want to take control, you can, but you have to be willing to ask the questions. A good financial advisor is more than willing to tell you why he makes the decisions he does.

193. What is the topic of this passage?

(A) Which companies to invest in
(B) How to choose a financial advisor
(C) How politics affect company profits
(D) How to research stocks and bonds

194. What is the purpose of this notice?

(A) To warn stockholders
(B) To encourage investment
(C) To advise investors
(D) To support independent businesses

195. What makes a good financial advisor?

(A) Access to multiple stocks and bonds
(B) A background in politics
(C) A master's degree in economics
(D) Knowledge of internal and external factors

196. How could someone manage their investments?

(A) Do research
(B) Get advice from another investor
(C) Find a company with a good name
(D) Follow demand carefully

GO ON TO THE NEXT PAGE

THE RESULTS of a Westchester real estate survey reveal that although 50% of those interviewed would prefer not to make monthly rental payments or deal with landlords, the biggest reason people buy a house is so that they can have a place they can call their own. Only 10% were motivated by financial reasons – buying the house to sell later at a profit. Twenty-five percent of those interviewed did so because they wanted property for their children to play on. Of that, 5% were concerned about room for pets. Oddly enough, next to "having your own place," the greatest motivating factor was the urge to build, remodel, and choose design interiors. And although owning a home puts one in a certain social station, that consideration had almost no influence in the decision to buy (less than 1%). Now, more than anything else, people want to have a place of their own to do with as they wish.

197. Why do most people want to buy a home?

(A) They don't want to pay rent.
(B) They want to have their own yard.
(C) They want to have a place of their own.
(D) They don't want to have a landlord.

198. What percentage of people see their home as an investment?

(A) 5%
(B) 10%
(C) 25%
(D) 50%

199. What is the second greatest reason for buying a home?

(A) Wanting to renovate and decorate
(B) Seeing it as an investment
(C) Having a place for the cats and dogs
(D) Impressing others

200. What is the least common reason for buying a home?

(A) Having a yard for animals
(B) Wanting to build equity
(C) Wanting to have their own place
(D) A matter of prestige

Stop! This is the end of the test. If you finish before one hour and fifteen minutes have passed, you may go back to Parts V, VI, and VII and check your work.

Practice Test Four

LISTENING COMPREHENSION

In this section of the test, you will have the chance to show how well you understand spoken English. There are four parts to this section, with special directions for each part.

PART I

Directions: For each question, you will see a picture in your test book and you will hear four short statements. The statements will be spoken just one time. They will not be printed in your test book, so you must listen carefully to understand what the speaker says.

When you hear the four statements, look at the picture in your test book and choose the statement that best describes what you see in the picture. Then, on your answer sheet, find the number of the question and mark your answer. Look at the sample below.

Sample Answer
 Ⓐ ● Ⓒ Ⓓ

Now listen to the four statements.

Statement (B), "They're having a meeting," best describes what you see in the picture. Therefore, you should choose answer (B).

GO ON TO THE NEXT PAGE

1.

2.

3.

4.

GO ON TO THE NEXT PAGE

5.

6.

7.

8.

GO ON TO THE NEXT PAGE ➤

9.

10.

11.

12.

GO ON TO THE NEXT PAGE

13.

14.

15.

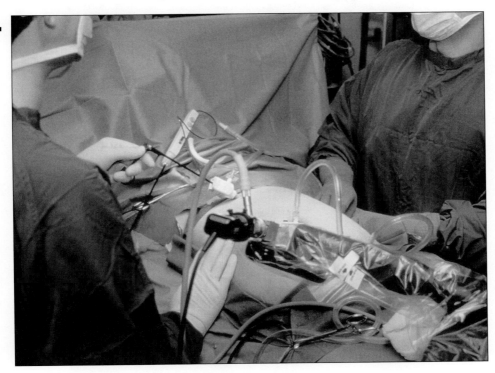

16.

GO ON TO THE NEXT PAGE

17.

18.

19.

20.

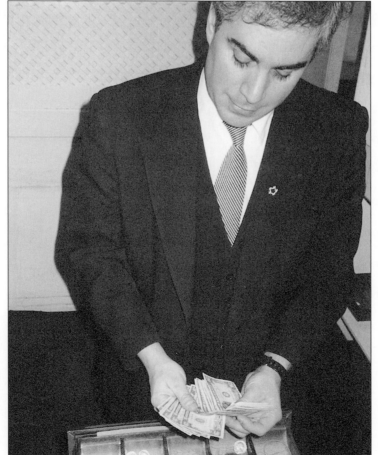

GO ON TO THE NEXT PAGE

PART II

Directions: In this part of the test, you will hear a question spoken in English, followed by three responses, also spoken in English. The question and the responses will be spoken just one time. They will not be printed in your test book, so you must listen carefully to understand what the speakers say. You are to choose the best response to each question.

Now listen to a sample question.

You will hear:

You will also hear:

Sample Answer

The best response to the question "How are you?" is choice (A), "I am fine, thank you." Therefore, you should choose answer (A).

21. Mark your answer on your answer sheet.

22. Mark your answer on your answer sheet.

23. Mark your answer on your answer sheet.

24. Mark your answer on your answer sheet.

25. Mark your answer on your answer sheet.

26. Mark your answer on your answer sheet.

27. Mark your answer on your answer sheet.

28. Mark your answer on your answer sheet.

29. Mark your answer on your answer sheet.

30. Mark your answer on your answer sheet.

31. Mark your answer on your answer sheet.

32. Mark your answer on your answer sheet.

33. Mark your answer on your answer sheet.

34. Mark your answer on your answer sheet.

35.   Mark your answer on your answer sheet.

36.   Mark your answer on your answer sheet.

37.   Mark your answer on your answer sheet.

38.   Mark your answer on your answer sheet.

39.   Mark your answer on your answer sheet.

40.   Mark your answer on your answer sheet.

41.   Mark your answer on your answer sheet.

42.   Mark your answer on your answer sheet.

43.   Mark your answer on your answer sheet.

44.   Mark your answer on your answer sheet.

45.   Mark your answer on your answer sheet.

46.   Mark your answer on your answer sheet.

47.   Mark your answer on your answer sheet.

48.   Mark your answer on your answer sheet.

49.   Mark your answer on your answer sheet.

50.   Mark your answer on your answer sheet.

GO ON TO THE NEXT PAGE ➤

PART III

Directions: In this part of the test, you will hear thirty short conversations between two people. The conversations will not be printed in your test book. You will hear the conversations only once, so you must listen carefully to understand what the speakers say.

In your test book, you will read a question about each conversation. The question will be followed by four answers. You are to choose the best answer to each question and mark it on your answer sheet.

51. Where does this conversation take place?

    (A) In a store.
    (B) In a restaurant.
    (C) In a theater.
    (D) In a train station.

52. What does the new accountant want to do?

    (A) Inspect former records.
    (B) Taste some food.
    (C) Purchase new storage space.
    (D) Pack up the files.

53. What is the problem?

    (A) Several managers are sick.
    (B) Unemployment is rising.
    (C) Stefan reprimands everybody.
    (D) Stefan hasn't been doing his job.

54. Who is the woman talking to?

    (A) A carpet installer.
    (B) An office manager.
    (C) A janitor.
    (D) A restaurant manager.

55. What might the speakers be working with?

    (A) Wood.
    (B) Stone.
    (C) Gas.
    (D) Water.

56. What is the woman doing?

    (A) Learning a language.
    (B) Ordering French bread.
    (C) Studying Spanish.
    (D) Applying for a job.

57. Who is the man talking to?

    (A) A lifeguard.
    (B) A travel agent.
    (C) A gift wrapper.
    (D) A gymnasium manager.

58. What does the woman want the man to do?

    (A) Ask her about the evening before.
    (B) Telephone the police.
    (C) Give her some information about cars.
    (D) Look to see what was taken.

59. What was the goal of the meeting?

    (A) To organize a protest.
    (B) To work out a good schedule.
    (C) To learn about computers.
    (D) To reach a purchasing decision.

60. Who is the man talking to?

    (A) A banker.
    (B) An accountant.
    (C) A travel agent.
    (D) A librarian.

61. What does the man want to do?

    (A) Visit Indonesia.
    (B) Pay his taxes.
    (C) Sell computers abroad.
    (D) Start a consulting business.

62. What does the woman agree to do?

    (A) Go to an earlier show.
    (B) See a boxing match.
    (C) Call George.
    (D) Go by cab.

63. What is wrong with the fax machine?

   (A) The print is too light.
   (B) The paper inside is jammed.
   (C) The supply tray is askew.
   (D) The printer is broken.

64. What is the problem?

   (A) The man doesn't want to transfer to the other office.
   (B) The inventory has not been kept up-to-date.
   (C) There are no chairs in stock.
   (D) The man can't access the inventory records.

65. What kind of rooms are being referred to?

   (A) Offices.
   (B) Bathrooms.
   (C) Dining rooms.
   (D) Bedrooms.

66. What is Sonya responsible for?

   (A) Selecting a suitable projector.
   (B) Product presentation.
   (C) Calling those attending the meeting.
   (D) Training the sales staff.

67. What is the man asking Maria to do?

   (A) Work faster.
   (B) Purchase some office equipment.
   (C) Get travel brochures about Hong Kong.
   (D) Take down some numbers.

68. When will the speakers meet again?

   (A) Monday.
   (B) Tuesday.
   (C) Thursday.
   (D) Friday.

69. Where are the speakers?

   (A) At a church ceremony.
   (B) In a clothing store.
   (C) In an office.
   (D) At a dinner.

70. What is Ms. Carreras' job?

   (A) Copy machine mechanic.
   (B) Course lecturer.
   (C) Printer.
   (D) Advertiser.

71. What does the woman want to do?

   (A) Visit Korea.
   (B) Find her luggage.
   (C) Book an international flight.
   (D) Purchase a newspaper.

72. What is the man suggesting to Rita?

   (A) Buying a bigger bowl.
   (B) Practising more.
   (C) Joining the team.
   (D) Trying to win an award.

73. Why was the man impressed?

   (A) Because the woman used the same software.
   (B) Because the woman wrote the program.
   (C) Because the woman solved the problem.
   (D) Because the woman had an expensive computer.

74. What is the purpose of the contribution?

   (A) To help clean up pollution.
   (B) To design security systems.
   (C) To promote the arts.
   (D) To research lubricants.

75. Where are the speakers?

   (A) At a bus station.
   (B) In an airport.
   (C) In an office.
   (D) At a theater.

76. To whom is the man talking?

   (A) A travel agent.
   (B) A bus driver.
   (C) A taxi driver.
   (D) A tour guide.

GO ON TO THE NEXT PAGE

77. What are the speakers discussing?

    (A) New marketing strategies.
    (B) Possible lay-offs.
    (C) Replacing the copier.
    (D) Their finances.

78. What is the man concerned about?

    (A) Having a larger car.
    (B) Meeting his family.
    (C) Buying a sofa.
    (D) Getting home quickly.

79. What does the man want to buy?

    (A) A printer.
    (B) Some socks.
    (C) Some paint.
    (D) An ink cartridge.

80. What is the problem?

    (A) Someone hit a customer.
    (B) Orders are being lost.
    (C) The meeting had to be canceled.
    (D) Nobody called the representatives.

PART IV

Directions: In this part of the test, you will hear several short talks. Each will be spoken just one time. They will not be printed in your test book, so you must listen carefully to understand and remember what is said.

In your test book, you will read two or more questions about each short talk. The questions will be followed by four answers. You are to choose the best answer to each question and mark it on your answer sheet.

81. Who is making this report?

    (A) A radio announcer.
    (B) Blair County residents.
    (C) A newspaper reporter.
    (D) The police.

82. What is being advised?

    (A) Canceling the baseball game.
    (B) Cleaning up the streets.
    (C) Avoiding driving if possible.
    (D) Reporting any changes.

83. When is this message sent?

    (A) Friday.
    (B) Saturday.
    (C) Sunday.
    (D) Monday.

84. Where was John over the weekend?

    (A) In the hospital.
    (B) At the airport.
    (C) With the company president.
    (D) In a delivery truck.

85. What is the name of the theater?

    (A) Bernstein Movies.
    (B) Northstar Movies.
    (C) Crown Movies.
    (D) Gemstone Movies.

86. What is the purpose of this recording?

    (A) To give directions to the theater.
    (B) To give movie names and show times.
    (C) To inform movie-goers about coming attractions.
    (D) To advertise in the shopping center.

87. What is the speech about?

    (A) Increasing the proposed budget.
    (B) The history of the Treasury Department.
    (C) Protecting the country's waterways.
    (D) How laws are made.

88. Why are some groups opposed?

    (A) Increased government intervention.
    (B) Restricted water use.
    (C) Higher land prices.
    (D) Lack of careful research.

89. Who is resisting the plan?

    (A) Local residents.
    (B) The shipping industry.
    (C) Environmentalists.
    (D) Western lawmakers.

90. What is the speaker discussing?

    (A) Childbearing versus lifespan.
    (B) Female hormones.
    (C) Child behavior.
    (D) Styles at the turn of the century.

91. How many groups of women were involved in the study?

    (A) One.
    (B) Two.
    (C) Three.
    (D) Five.

92. What are women who live longer four times more likely to have done?

    (A) Been born in the nineteenth century.
    (B) Come from large families.
    (C) Borne children in their forties.
    (D) Had older parents.

GO ON TO THE NEXT PAGE

93. How do people feel about the economy?

    (A) Worried.
    (B) Pessimistic.
    (C) Confident.
    (D) Upset.

94. What makes Europeans upset with their personal wages?

    (A) Heavy taxes.
    (B) Inflation.
    (C) Changes in corporate policy.
    (D) Economic instability.

95. What is one of the main problems?

    (A) Companies relocating out-of-state.
    (B) The speed of economic growth.
    (C) Workers can't meet production demands.
    (D) Wasteful use of taxes.

96. Who is the announcement directed at?

    (A) Law enforcement officials.
    (B) People who drink alcoholic beverages.
    (C) People who don't drink alcoholic beverages.
    (D) Park officials.

97. Where is drinking alcohol allowed?

    (A) Outside the fairgrounds.
    (B) Only in the park restaurants.
    (C) In designated areas.
    (D) Only at the park refreshment stands.

98. What is this announcement mainly concerned with?

    (A) Assigning work areas.
    (B) Fixing individual work times.
    (C) Clarifying scheduling policy.
    (D) Letting people go.

99. By what time does everyone have to be at work in the morning?

    (A) Eight o'clock.
    (B) Nine o'clock.
    (C) Ten o'clock.
    (D) Eleven o'clock.

100. What is the maximum amount of overtime allowed?

    (A) Three hours.
    (B) Four hours.
    (C) Seven hours.
    (D) Ten hours.

This is the end of the Listening Comprehension portion of Practice Test Four. Turn to Part V in your test book.

READING

In this section of the test, you will have a chance to show how well you understand written English. There are three parts to this section, with special directions for each part.

PART V

Directions: Questions 101–140 are incomplete sentences. Four words or phrases, marked (A), (B), (C), (D) are given beneath each sentence. You are to choose the **one** word or phrase that best completes the sentence. Then, on your answer sheet, find the number of the question and mark your answer.

You will read:

Because the equipment is very delicate, it must be handled with ....

(A) caring
(B) careful
(C) care
(D) carefully

Sample Answer

Ⓐ Ⓑ ● Ⓓ

The sentence should read, "Because the equipment is very delicate, it must be handled with care." Therefore, you should choose answer (C).

Now begin work on the questions.

---

101. Another four inches of snow will .... overnight.

(A) heighten
(B) accumulate
(C) develop
(D) raise

102. The retired colonel has decided to take .... residence in Morocco.

(A) in
(B) out
(C) up
(D) with

103. A chart .... the employees' wages was found posted on the lobby bulletin board.

(A) lists
(B) listed
(C) listing
(D) to list

104. Nothing the workers did was able to .... the new foreman.

(A) satisfactorily
(B) satisfaction
(C) satisfy
(D) satisfies

105. We should have been at the office several hours ....

(A) earliest
(B) previous
(C) sooner
(D) past

106. His evaluation of the marketing department was right .... the mark.

(A) over
(B) on
(C) against
(D) into

GO ON TO THE NEXT PAGE

107. The secretary knew exactly where to look for the documents .... who to blame for their absence.

(A) but
(B) above
(C) beyond
(D) and

108. After examining my account, I was surprised to find out that I only had $385 in ....

(A) them
(B) that
(C) those
(D) it

109. Many an illustrator has .... himself to learning computer graphics.

(A) given up
(B) admitted
(C) relinquished
(D) resigned

110. This tractor is a good value but .... one over there has the features I need.

(A) it
(B) those
(C) these
(D) that

111. Genetic makeup .... one's hair and eye color.

(A) determined
(B) had been determined
(C) determining
(D) determines

112. I found that the shop steward put forth some very ...., down-to-earth arguments.

(A) scented
(B) sensational
(C) sensible
(D) sensuous

113. The crew worked so hard, they finished the entire project three days .... of schedule.

(A) forward
(B) ahead
(C) onward
(D) atop

114. Records of tourism in Puerto Rico .... lost in the hurricane.

(A) were
(B) are
(C) was
(D) has been

115. My company called us on Monday and told us that they had already booked the flight .... us that day.

(A) to
(B) with
(C) for
(D) by

116. He is simply biding his .... until the prices go down.

(A) time
(B) activity
(C) wherewithal
(D) wait

117. I am writing .... regard to the job of administrative assistant listed in Sunday's paper.

(A) in
(B) as
(C) for
(D) from

118. Many layers of ignorance had to be stripped away if we .... to bring women to the voting polls.

(A) want
(B) had wanted
(C) wanted
(D) wanting

119. We are hoping that the community will .... in the waterfront clean-up efforts.

(A) involve
(B) associate
(C) concern
(D) participate

120. Putting a new transmission in was .... of the question.

(A) above
(B) out
(C) overhead
(D) outside

121. There was no .... to call an emergency meeting over such a trivial matter.

(A) need
(B) dire
(C) must
(D) responsibility

122. The diamond is .... durable than crystal.

(A) most
(B) more
(C) many
(D) much

123. It was her .... with the language that impressed us.

(A) fertility
(B) facility
(C) compatability
(D) potentiality

124. .... representatives agreed to speak in a televised broadcast.

(A) Neither
(B) Both
(C) None of
(D) Each

125. Nothing could divert him .... his goals.

(A) over
(B) into
(C) from
(D) throughout

126. Payments will only be made after you reach retirement age, ... you notify the company of your whereabouts.

(A) while
(B) or
(C) because
(D) if

127. Bali is a favorite stop for tourists .... in the Far East.

(A) vacationed
(B) vacationing
(C) vacation
(D) vacations

128. If you expect to stay in business .... you'll have to advertise regularly.

(A) because
(B) then
(C) for
(D) since

129. The Prime Minister gave .... of his attention to the visiting dignitaries.

(A) everything
(B) about
(C) fourth
(D) all

130. The new CEO asked that all inter-office communications be made in writing rather than in person, whenever ....

(A) available
(B) present
(C) aboard
(D) possible

GO ON TO THE NEXT PAGE ▶

131. All financial aid to the country was .... after our ambassador was dismissed.

    (A)   taken off
    (B)   closed off
    (C)   sealed off
    (D)   cut off

132. The midnight shift .... by the other shifts starting January first.

    (A)   will be absorbed
    (B)   absorbed
    (C)   will absorb
    (D)   absorbing

133. New sources of energy are constantly being looked for .... fossil fuels continue to dwindle.

    (A)   when
    (B)   as
    (C)   besides
    (D)   however

134. Our analysts are encouraging the .... of more sophisticated water treatment facilities.

    (A)   constructive
    (B)   constructs
    (C)   construction
    (D)   constructed

135. We were asked to read the instructions .... using any of the equipment.

    (A)   before
    (B)   since
    (C)   in front of
    (D)   near to

136. Mrs. Davis expressed some .... over the sudden increase in Paul Roger's travel expenses.

    (A)   compliance
    (B)   consent
    (C)   concern
    (D)   control

137. Being fluent in German, he realized that he might be called upon to act as a translator for the group .... the need arise.

    (A)   could
    (B)   would
    (C)   if
    (D)   should

138. The product was .... by the manufacturer because of a faulty closing mechanism.

    (A)   rehired
    (B)   released
    (C)   resent
    (D)   recalled

139. The other members of the committee were not able to .... his point of view.

    (A)   see
    (B)   reckon
    (C)   think
    (D)   figure

140. No .... than three banks were forced to close their doors this last year.

    (A)   fewer
    (B)   lesser
    (C)   less
    (D)   lower

PART VI

Directions: In **Questions 141–160**, each sentence has four words or phrases underlined. The four underlined parts of the sentence are marked (A), (B), (C), (D). You are to identify the **one** underlined word or phrase that should be corrected or rewritten. Then, on your answer sheet, find the number of the question and mark your answer.

Example:

All employee are required to wear their
    A   B

identification badges while at work.
    C   D

Sample Answer
● Ⓑ Ⓒ Ⓓ

The underlined word "employee" is not correct in this sentence. This sentence should read, "All employees are required to wear their identification badges while at work." Therefore, you should choose answer (A).

Now begin work on the questions.

---

141. When the new laptop hit the market,
    A   B
hundred consumers flocked to the computer
        C   D
stores.

142. My secretary will book you an afternoon flight
           A
and has you picked up at the airport
  B   C
when you arrive.
    D

143. The packages were tied altogether so that they
           A   B
would be easier to carry.
    C   D

144. He would lost his license if he didn't take a
      A   B
refresher course, according to my broker.
  C   D

145. Even today, the transmission of telephone calls
    A   B
and billing of rooms – both of which take time
            C
and energy – is handling by the operators.
          D

146. Analysts reported the economy it is moving
      A   B
in a steady, upward direction.
  C   D

147. The basic that you'll need to start your own
    A   B   C
business are provided in the seminar.
        D

148. When he retired, he was told that his trade
    A   B
journal subscription will not be canceled.
        C   D

GO ON TO THE NEXT PAGE ➤

149. Did you know that we lease the top floor of the
    A   B
    87-years-old Brigham building and the adjacent
    C   D
    storage area?

150. Mr. Rossini, who already heads several
                  A
    committees, have accepted yet another
                B   C
    position in the Foreign Affairs Commission.
            D

151. We chose to take a trip to the Far East because
    A   B
    it was advertised as adventurous and intrigued.
                        C   D

152. Initially, your completing loan application will be
                  A   B
    sent to the loan officer, who must check your
                            C
    credit standing before making any preliminary
                    D
    decision.

153. The first global pollution convention was held in
        A   B
    Hong Kong and it was attended by scientists
                        C
    from over the world.
        D

154. The Prime Minister has flew back to his country
                        A
    after successfully negotiating the long-awaited
                    B   C
    trade agreement with China.
                    D

155. The manager told the newly arrived hotel
                        A
    guests that there were a piano in the lobby
            B
    with live jazz on Friday and Saturday starting at
        C   D
    eight o'clock.

156. We spent the afternoon playing with the
        A   B
    childrens down at the beach.
    C   D

157. I am familiar with the difficult situation
            A
    she was on but I can't condone her
        B   C
    negligent behavior.
        D

158. The consultant, who is employed by several
                    A
    firms, is very knowledgeable on mutual funds
        B   C
    and junk bonds.
        D

159. Dozens of applicants showed up for the
    A   B
    position, but when it came time to interview
                    C
    them, we could talk to only handful.
                        D

160. While on our tour of the refinery, we saw that
        A   B
    both propane also gasoline are
                C
    by-products of crude oil.
            D

PART VII

Directions: Questions 161–200 are based on a selection of reading materials, such as notices, letters, forms, newspaper and magazine articles, and advertisements. You are to choose the **one** best answer (A), (B), (C), or (D) to each question. Then, on your answer sheet, find the number of the question and mark your answer. Answer all questions following each reading selection on the basis of what is **stated** or **implied** in that selection.

Read the following example.

> The Museum of Technology is a "hands-on" museum, designed for people to experience science at work. Visitors are encouraged to use, test, and handle the objects on display. Special demonstrations are scheduled for the first and second Wednesdays of each month at 13:30. Open Tuesday–Friday 12:00–16:30, Saturday 10:00–17:30, and Sunday 11:00–16:30.

> When during the month can visitors see
> special demonstrations?

Sample Answer
(A) ● (C) (D)

> (A)   Every weekend
> (B)   The first two Wednesdays
> (C)   One afternoon a week
> (D)   Every other Wednesday

The reading selection says that the demonstrations are scheduled for the first and second Wednesdays of the month. Therefore, you should choose answer (B).

Now begin work on the questions.

GO ON TO THE NEXT PAGE

Questions 161–162 refer to the following article.

An exhibition of contemporary Filipino art will be held in Madrid in late August with a portion of the proceeds going to the orphanage of Katrina Speidel in Madrid. The Philippine embassies in Madrid, Paris and Lisbon are contributing to the exhibition, as are an array of international business people who support Filipino art.

161. Where will the exhibition take place?

(A) London
(B) Madrid
(C) Paris
(D) Lisbon

162. Who will benefit from the show?

(A) Private investors
(B) The contributing embassies
(C) A home for children without parents
(D) The Filipino Art Gallery

Questions 163–164 refer to the following classified advertisement.

Turkish male, 36 years old with fifteen years' managerial experience with a main bank in Istanbul. Bachelor's and master's degrees from Turkish university. Also knowledgeable in marketing and research. Turkish native speaker. Good command of spoken and written English. Proficient in Russian and French. Seeking similar managerial position in Moscow.

163. What field does the person prefer to work in?

(A) Banking
(B) Marketing
(C) Linguistics
(D) Education

164. In which language is this person most fluent?

(A) English
(B) Turkish
(C) Russian
(D) French

YES! I want to save. Please start my subscription to *Homeowners*.

I want to learn about money-saving ideas for decorating and redesigning my home as well as tips on house and property maintenance. I understand I will also receive a free guide to home security systems and their distributors.

Check one: __ **36** issues for **$30.75** (Save 70%)
__ **24** issues for **$23.95** (Save 65%)
__ **12** issues for **$17.00** (Save 50%)

Name _____

Address _____

City _____State _____Zip _____

Applicable sales tax will be added. Allow 4-6 weeks for delivery.
Savings based on newsstand price of $34.20.
Canadian orders add $5.00 per year.
Foreign orders add $10.00 for postage and applicable taxes.

165. What is this form designed to sell?

(A) Homes
(B) Alarm systems
(C) Financial securities
(D) Magazines

166. What price would the person pay to save half on the newsstand price?

(A) $10.00
(B) $17.00
(C) $23.95
(D) $34.20

167. What information is asked for?

(A) Where one lives
(B) Country of origin
(C) Age
(D) How long one has been a homeowner

GO ON TO THE NEXT PAGE ▶

Robert Barr
65 Chamberlain Street
E. Grinstead
West Sussex RH19 2DZ
England

THE MUTUAL FUNDS MONITOR
Attn: Mr. Marvin Malloy
Velliveien 21
N-1344 JAR, Norway

Dear Mr. Malloy,

I would like to extend my personal thanks for maintaining a superior level of excellence and high standards at MFM. I have been a long-time member because I trust your economic sense, respect your judgment, and appreciate your conservative, well-rounded approach.

I appreciate the fact that you always "tell it like it is." It was your tip on an up-and-coming growth fund that made me £6,800 in just seven months!

Perhaps the greatest value, though, is having time to myself again. Hiring you to do my reading and advising has given me back precious time for myself and my family.

Sincerely yours,

Rob Barr

Rob Barr

168. What was the purpose of this letter?

(A) To ask for more investment advice
(B) To inquire about a position at MFM
(C) To acknowledge and thank Mr. Malloy
(D) To renew a membership

169. What does Mr. Barr consider most valuable?

(A) Mr. Malloy's assessment ability
(B) His freed-up time
(C) The investment in a growth fund
(D) Reading about investment possibilities

170. How would Mr. Malloy be best described?

(A) Considerate
(B) Appreciative
(C) Persistent
(D) Well-informed

Saturday, June 12 (1-4 PM): The Friends of Jeffrey Logan, known as the "Local Guardians," and the Lenour Heights young persons' neighborhood group, sponsored by Daniella Bard, will be doing their end-of-summer PARK CLEAN-UP in Jeffrey Logan Park in Lenour Heights. They are urging our readers to join in on what promises to be a lovely summer afternoon. Bring your brooms, shovels and gloves. Neighbors and area residents are also invited to a meeting afterwards in the main library downtown to discuss a two-year plan for the recreational development of the park. Refreshments and food will be provided. For those of you new to the area, the park is just north of the historic district.

Please call Daniella Bard for more information at 387-9888.

171. What will the people initially be gathering to do?

(A) To go purchase cleaning equipment
(B) To plan the future of the park
(C) To clean up the park
(D) To offer assistance to local residents

172. Where is the park?

(A) In Lenour Heights
(B) At the beach
(C) In the historic district
(D) In the downtown area

173. Who makes up the "Local Guardians"?

(A) The subscribers to the newspaper
(B) Residents of the Historic District
(C) Young people in Lenour Heights
(D) The Friends of Jeffrey Logan Park

174. Why will they meet in the library?

(A) To eat after the clean-up work
(B) To go over plans for the park's development
(C) To listen to a lecture by Daniella Bard
(D) To meet other area residents

GO ON TO THE NEXT PAGE

At a stockholders meeting in Montreal, Canada, today, the Julliard Ribbons Corporation announced that sales for the first six months of this year surpassed all previous six-month periods. An aggressive and innovative advertising campaign was credited for the upswing. The vice president, Mr. Charles Tundy, speaking at the yearly meeting, reported quarterly earnings of $112,000, an 18% jump over the same time last year. Mr. Tundy predicted that the $125,000 mark would be reached by year's end. He concluded his speech with praise for the management and the loyal support of the stockholders, but stressed that the marketing team deserved most of the credit.

175. Where did Tundy make his announcement?

(A) At a stockholders meeting
(B) At an advertising rally
(C) At a news conference
(D) At a management seminar

176. What was considered the main source of the rise in profits?

(A) The stockholders' tenacity
(B) The effectiveness of the ad campaign
(C) The company leadership
(D) The efforts of the sales teams

177. Who did Mr. Tundy single out for special praise?

(A) The shareholders
(B) The marketing group
(C) The managers
(D) The vice president

AUGUST 1 - 14:
TWO-WEEK SALES AND USE TAX EXEMPTION ON GARMENTS

The tax law has been changed to allow for another two-week exemption from North Carolina State's 3% sales and use taxes for certain garments. However, the latest amendment differs considerably from the same type of sales exemption that took place at the beginning of the year. This exemption does NOT apply to footwear. The new two-week exemption only applies to purchases of garments. Additionally, this latest exemption is limited to purchases with a cost of less than $100 per item, whereas the previous exemption had a cost limitation of $500. Although a suit could sell for $200, it could be broken down into $100 for the jacket and $100 for the pants, thus enabling the buyer to meet the $100 requirement. This will be the last exemption of this kind this year. The exemption applies to most clothing, assuming it is to be worn by human beings. Fabric, yarn, buttons, zippers, etc., are also covered, provided that these notions are actually part of the clothing itself. Although jewelry, watches, hats, etc., are worn on the body, they will remain taxable as under the previous exemption rules.

178. What is this exemption compared to?

(A) North Carolina's taxes
(B) Sales exemptions
(C) A previous exemption
(D) Longer exemptions

179. How many weeks have been exempt this year?

(A) Two
(B) Four
(C) Six
(D) Eight

180. What is the difference in cost limitation since the beginning of the year?

(A) $100
(B) $200
(C) $400
(D) $500

181. What could be bought under exemption at the beginning of the year but no longer?

(A) Jewelry
(B) Watches
(C) Hats
(D) Shoes

182. Which garment items would not be covered by the exemption?

(A) Yarn to repair a shawl
(B) Buttons for a winter coat
(C) A head scarf
(D) Dress-making fabric

GO ON TO THE NEXT PAGE

Year end Dec. 31 (in millions)	Year 1	Year 2	Percent change
Total Revenue	$5,256	$7,890	31%
Operating Cash Flow	$1,862	$2,232	7%
Net Earnings (Loss)	(134)	(765)	(440%)
Total Assets	$23,034	$27,124	18%
Total Debt	$12,880	$14,913	15%
Stockholder Equity	$2,845	$1,863	(35%)

183. What figure includes property, plant and equipment for Year 2?

(A) $2,232
(B) $7,890
(C) $14,913
(D) $27,124

184. How much money did the company have at their ready disposal in Year 1?

(A) $134
(B) $1,862
(C) $2,845
(D) $5,256

185. What figure represents the total liabilities in Year 2?

(A) $1,863
(B) $7,890
(C) $14,913
(D) $27,124

186. What percentage did profits on sales drop over the two years?

(A) 15%
(B) 18%
(C) 35%
(D) 440%

The field of engineering can be broken down into various specialties. Civil engineering is the branch that deals with the construction of roads, bridges, railroads and waterways. Mechanical engineering deals with the models, designs and materials which are used in the construction of the various types of machinery. Electrical engineering deals with the creation and distribution of electrical energy. Other areas of engineering include chemical, aeronautical and military.

187. What type of engineer would the highway department of a town most likely hire?

(A) A mechanical engineer
(B) A civil engineer
(C) A chemical engineer
(D) An electrical engineer

188. A manufacturer of labor-saving devices and equipment would most likely hire which kind of engineer?

(A) A mechanical engineer
(B) A military engineer
(C) A chemical engineer
(D) A civil engineer

189. What would an electrical engineer be familiar with?

(A) Rock drilling equipment
(B) The nature of various building materials
(C) Power lines
(D) Surveying techniques

GO ON TO THE NEXT PAGE

It is noteworthy that the International Monetary Fund (IMF) appears to be developing two forms of credit for the economies of Third World countries. Money is flowing very freely from the IMF – much more so than ever before, which has bankers worried that the creditworthiness that used to be associated with a loan from the IMF no longer carries the same import. It is feared that the credit standards of the IMF have been lowered.

Commercial banks, who will be funding most of the projected $220 billion deficit of the developing countries, must be able to maintain their confidence in the IMF programs. The managing director of the IMF insists that the nations which are recipients of these loans have exhibited successful economic reform, a prerequisite for becoming eligible for the loans.

Forty-nine percent of the IMF debt was shouldered by industrial nations. It is now down to 9%, while the share carried by oil-poor developing countries has risen from 51% to 91%. Also, 45% of the Fund's outstanding loans are to nations with gross national products of less than $700 per capita.

190. What is the concern of the commercial banks?

(A) The IMF is running out of money.
(B) Eligibility for IMF loans is too lax.
(C) The IMF is exercising too much influence.
(D) Third World economies are changing too slowly.

191. What percentage of the debt did developing countries used to carry?

(A) 9%
(B) 45%
(C) 49%
(D) 51%

192. What percentage of the IMF loans do industrial nations carry today?

(A) 9%
(B) 49%
(C) 51%
(D) 91%

The warming of the Pacific Ocean creates weather patterns that affect the world. When the waters warm, the amount of rainfall in Indonesia and the surrounding region decreases. Australia could even experience a drought. On the other hand, Chile, which borders the Pacific Ocean, is preparing for severe rainstorms. In Pakistan and northwestern India, the weather pattern makes the monsoon season weaker and makes the area much drier.

This phenomenon is called *El Niño* and is used by weather forecasters to make long-range weather predictions. Forecasters know that *El Niño* will bring unusually heavy rains to the southwestern part of the United States and make the central part of the country drier.

El Niño itself used to be predictable. It would occur every two to seven years. But now, the weather pattern is becoming more constant. Scientists are unsure of the reason for this change.

193. What would characterize the effects of *El Niño*?

(A) They're widespread.
(B) They're benign.
(C) They're short-lived.
(D) They're decreasing.

194. What phenomenon defines *El Niño*?

(A) The rainstorms in Australia
(B) The drought in Chile
(C) The warming of the Pacific Ocean
(D) The dryness of southwestern U.S.

195. Which region will be abnormally wet?

(A) Pakistan
(B) Australia
(C) Southwestern U.S.
(D) Central U.S.

196. Which is not an effect of *El Niño*?

(A) Droughts
(B) Heavy rainfalls
(C) Weak monsoons
(D) Global warming

GO ON TO THE NEXT PAGE

Feel out of touch? Just because you're in a taxi, on a plane, or in a line, doesn't mean that you are cut off from the world. As a business executive, you know how important it is to maintain communication with your office and with your clients. You know that if you aren't talking to your customers, your competition will be.

We have the solution. The portable **SE-543** mini-phone fits easily into a pocket. It's all digital, so your communication is secure. And you can plug it into any phone jack to pick up your e-mail. It has a 56.6 Kbps built-in modem and 1 MB memory for storing both voice mail and e-mail messages.

Stay ahead of the pack. Stay in touch with our SE-543.

197. Who is the advertisement aimed at?

(A) People who are lonely
(B) People who communicate a lot by phone
(C) People who work short hours
(D) People who dress well

198. According to the advertisement, why is it important to be in touch?

(A) To maintain good client relations
(B) To use a fast modem
(C) To learn about your competitors
(D) To work out a solution

199. What is the advantage of a digital phone?

(A) It's cheaper.
(B) Communication is protected.
(C) The modem is faster.
(D) It stores e-mail messages.

200. What is required to access e-mail?

(A) An executive order
(B) A battery pack
(C) A password
(D) A phone jack

Stop! This is the end of the test. If you finish before one hour and fifteen minutes have passed, you may go back to Parts V, VI, and VII and check your work.

Tapescripts

Practice Test One - Listening Comprehension

PART I

Sample question:

(A) They're looking out the window.
(B) They're having a meeting.
(C) They're eating in a restaurant.
(D) They're moving the furniture.

1. (A) The customers have a standing order.
   (B) The chef displays her wares.
   (C) The exhibit hall is open.
   (D) The stock trade's low.

2. (A) He's greeting the dinner guests.
   (B) He's carrying a tray of food.
   (C) He's cooking in the kitchen.
   (D) He's shopping for lunch.

3. (A) The shoes are on the steps.
   (B) The cowboys are wearing boots.
   (C) They are taking off their shoes.
   (D) The floor is fourteen feet long.

4. (A) The flowers are lining the walk.
   (B) The clerk is taking a break.
   (C) The tailor is altering the tuxedo.
   (D) The guest is registering at the hotel.

5. (A) The man is using a microphone.
   (B) The man is talking on a cell phone.
   (C) The man is buying new sunglasses.
   (D) The man is putting his hands in his pockets.

6. (A) They're giving the woman a haircut.
   (B) They're launching a spacecraft.
   (C) They're examining something.
   (D) They're wrapping a gift.

7. (A) Most of the chairs are occupied.
   (B) The jungle leaves are thick.
   (C) There are lamps on every table.
   (D) Few people are in the room.

8. (A) The trays are stacked against the wall.
   (B) The workers are wearing protective caps.
   (C) The conveyor belt is carrying goods from the trucks.
   (D) The glasses are washed by machine.

9. (A) She's choosing produce.
   (B) She's polishing her silver.
   (C) She's growing her own vegetables.
   (D) She's weighing herself.

10. (A) The man is giving a presentation.
    (B) The movie theater is dark.
    (C) The lecture room is empty.
    (D) The students are standing on their chairs.

11. (A) All of the signs are for parking.
    (B) Parking is forbidden in this area.
    (C) The largest sign points to the left.
    (D) The advertisement is in large letters.

12. (A) They're commuting to work.
    (B) They're working at their computers.
    (C) They're standing in line.
    (D) They're sharing a meal.

13. (A) The women are changing uniforms.
    (B) The women are eating their lunch.
    (C) The women are cleaning the chairs.
    (D) The women are chopping some sticks.

14. (A) He's taking a bow.
    (B) He's crossing his fingers.
    (C) He's resting on the stairs.
    (D) He's reading the paper.

15. (A) The man is scrubbing the sink.
    (B) The man is taking a bath.
    (C) The man is washing his hands.
    (D) The man is holding a plate.

16. (A) The passenger is looking out the window.
    (B) The spectator is watching the game.
    (C) The witness is describing the accident.
    (D) The bystander is walking behind.

17. (A) The tourists are hanging out the laundry.
    (B) The tour guide is pointing out a feature.
    (C) The inspector is filling out a report.
    (D) The citizens are waiting to vote.

18. (A) The meeting is over.
    (B) They are all wearing glasses.
    (C) The windows are shut.
    (D) One woman is standing.

19. (A) The scientists are adjusting the instruments.
    (B) The technicians are putting away their lab coats.
    (C) The attendants are putting gas in the car.
    (D) The researchers are opening the blinds.

20. (A) The tankers are at sea.
    (B) The ships are sailing in open waters.
    (C) The boats are in the harbor.
    (D) The freighters are leaving the port.

PART II

Sample question:

Good morning, John. How are you?
(A) I am fine, thank you.
(B) I am in the living room.
(C) My name is John.

21. Your office is still open, isn't it?
(A) It should be.
(B) Yes, I am.
(C) The officer is outside.

22. How can I access these files?
(A) The accessories are expensive.
(B) I can give you the code.
(C) The files are inside the house.

23. Your package arrived on time, didn't it?
(A) I'm afraid I'll be late again.
(B) I lost my luggage.
(C) Right when I needed it.

24. Do you think she'll finish the proposal before noon?
(A) He proposed to her last night.
(B) She promised she would.
(C) She finished second.

25. Where's the opera house?
(A) I think it starts at nine.
(B) It's the building on your left.
(C) I'll meet you at your house.

26. Would you consider moving to Hawaii?
(A) I would if it weren't so hot there.
(B) Hawaiian produce is shipped overnight.
(C) Let's move it later.

27. Does that electronic equipment work?
(A) I'm at work right now.
(B) Let's hope so.
(C) We will equip the workers.

28. You were supposed to hand-deliver that bill, weren't you?
(A) That's not what I was told.
(B) They billed us for an express delivery.
(C) He always supposes the worst.

29. What kind of position are you applying for?
(A) Lying down.
(B) Four of them.
(C) A clerical one.

30. Haven't we already notified the highway department?
(A) I told the department head myself.
(B) I'll be ready shortly.
(C) I know which way to go.

31. Do you inspect every single device?
(A) They inspected every room.
(B) He'll devise a way.
(C) On certain products I do.

32. When did the ambassador leave the office?
(A) The embassy is closed.
(B) He dashed out minutes ago.
(C) He lives near the office.

33. Don't you advertise in the weekly newspaper?
(A) We haven't yet.
(B) I only read it on Sundays.
(C) Sales are weak this year.

34. What did you think of the downtown area?
(A) Let's drive down to the shore.
(B) It's very well laid out.
(C) They'll take aerial photographs.

35. Have the transcripts been reviewed yet?
(A) The movie got bad reviews.
(B) Every conscript has been informed.
(C) They only checked for typing errors.

36. Would you mind helping out in the other store?
(A) Will I get overtime?
(B) I shouldn't have had another helping.
(C) I'll help myself.

37. What rate does the credit union charge?
(A) We won't charge you for that.
(B) It's definitely less than the competition.
(C) They'll credit your account.

38. Do you also sell commercial properties?
(A) This is private property.
(B) Only in the central part of the city.
(C) I sell wholesale.

39. Do you use your e-mail often?
(A) They always open my mail.
(B) I don't know how to use it.
(C) You'll use a lot of nails on that job.

40. Where will we display the new model?
(A) Let's put it in front of the store.
(B) He can play his flute anywhere.
(C) I don't think he knew about this place.

41. Do you know where I can find a stationery store?
(A) I'm looking for a stationary bike.
(B) I know where we can store it.
(C) There's one across town.

42. Are you familiar with the company policy on this?
(A) My family owns most of the land.
(B) The police knew all about it.
(C) I didn't know there was one.

43. Can you repair this for under one hundred dollars?
(A) That's an expensive pair of socks.
(B) That should be possible.
(C) We fixed four hundred of them.

44. When are the dividends usually disbursed?
(A) You should receive yours any day now.
(B) We do a few hours of work each day.
(C) This will help them concentrate.

45. When can we expect to see you again?
   (A) At next week's meeting, I hope.
   (B) She's expecting any day now.
   (C) We'll inspect them again later.

46. Why has the election been called off?
   (A) Please call out your names.
   (B) It hasn't; it's just been delayed.
   (C) He appreciated your selection.

47. The ferry left on time, didn't it?
   (A) I never left the boat.
   (B) I ran out of time.
   (C) It always does.

48. Could we have the banquet in the lower dining room?
   (A) The meal was delicious.
   (B) It wasn't very expensive.
   (C) I don't see why not.

49. When does the supply truck arrive?
   (A) Usually right after the lunch break.
   (B) The ducks arrived early this year.
   (C) The truck drivers are paid on Wednesday.

50. When did the new management take over?
   (A) Early tomorrow morning.
   (B) Late last month.
   (C) Later tonight.

PART III

51.
Woman   I thought the bus leaves on the hour.
Man   It usually does, but this is the holiday schedule.
Woman   I completely forgot. I hope we won't be late for the game.

52.
Woman   May I help you?
Man   Please. I'm looking for foreign magazines.
Woman   They're in aisle two, at the back, next to the greeting cards.

53.
Woman A   Is that sound coming from the engine?
Woman B   I'm not sure. It could be the air-conditioner.
Woman A   Let's pull over and take a look.

54.
Woman   Paul, where did you learn how to read blueprints?
Man   I grew up with them. My parents had an architectural company, and they would always explain things to me.
Woman   I'll be building a house next year. Maybe we can do some business together.

55.
Man   I think that new assistant manager is going to work out, don't you?
Woman   Yes, I've heard that he helps the staff out and hardly anyone calls in sick anymore.
Man   He'll probably be the manager before you know it.

56.
Man   Hello, room service? I ordered breakfast over half an hour ago.
Woman   I'm sorry, sir, but the kitchen has been very busy this morning. We'll have your breakfast up to your room immediately.
Man   Please hurry. We have to check out soon if we're going to catch our plane.

57.
Woman A   Maria, could we go over these blueprints for the supermarket after lunch?
Woman B   Yes, I just have to fax these specifications to the draftsmen.
Woman A   I hope it won't take long. We need to make some minor changes.

58.
Woman   That's a pretty good sunburn you got there, Sam.
Man   I know. We were just about to leave the beach when we ran into some old friends.
Woman   Here, try this cream. It should help.

59.
Woman   Do you know where the key to the closet is?
Man   I believe Nancy left it on top of the filing cabinet next to the water cooler.
Woman   Would you remind her to return it to the key holder?

60.
Man   How should I price these calculators?
Woman   They were $39.95, Anthony, but let me check the current price list.
Man   Yes, I think the sales representative mentioned a price increase.

61.
Woman A   Let's see if we can make it to the island.
Woman B   I don't know Jane, that's pretty far away and I'm a little tired now.
Woman A   Just float for a while or do the backstroke if you get tired. Come on, you can do it.

62.
Woman   I'll never take my car downtown again.
Man   Did you get another ticket, Sue, or couldn't you find a parking space?
Woman   I wish it were just that. My car was broken into.

63.
Man   Emily, we're going to have lunch down by the shore. Why don't you join us?
Woman   I'd love to Stan, but Jack needs the inventory report by two.
Man   Well, maybe next time. You'd like the way they prepare their swordfish.

64.

Man · The marketing department needs more labels for this week's marketing campaign.

Woman · There should be plenty in the supply office.

Man · Actually, they used them up in last week's big mailing.

65.

Man · Did you know that Shundoor's stocks have been rising steadily?

Woman · No, but I'm not surprised. The company's new director was hired because of her very successful track record with Morely and Sons.

Man · Interesting. I think I'll give my broker a call.

66.

Woman · Will we have time to go out for lunch?

Man · I think we should have it delivered to the office.

Woman · You're right, we can't afford to be late for that conference call.

67.

Man A · Ms. Wang in the relocation department found you a house just outside Manila, Mr. Bendor.

Man B · Good. I was afraid we'd have to live downtown.

Man A · If you were in the center of the city, you wouldn't have to commute.

68.

Woman · That looks like a pretty bad cut, Raul. How did you do that?

Man · I was using the paper cutter, but I was in too much of a rush.

Woman · I think there's a first aid pack in the kitchen.

69.

Man · The noise level in this office is too high.

Woman · Maybe we should put down wall-to-wall carpeting. That would reduce the sound.

Man · It'd also be expensive to install and maintain.

70.

Man · Have you seen the commercials of the Society of Engineers promoting their profession?

Woman · The ones about the city's sewer system and the underground cable network?

Man · Yes, but the best one was about maintaining bridges and tunnels.

71.

Man · Sebastian faxed me that he called the repairman two days ago.

Woman · But did he come? It's still hot and humid in here.

Man · I'll e-mail him right now and find out.

72.

Man · Excuse me, how far back is the dining car?

Woman · Two cars, sir.

Man · Thank you. I hope they're still serving breakfast.

73.

Man · Is it possible to get a guided tour of the islands?

Woman · Yes, just sign up in the same office where you rented the boats.

Man · I wonder if we can get a discount since there are six of us.

74.

Woman · Have you seen the new design for the warehouse?

Man · No, but I'd like to. I want to see where they're putting the conveyor belt.

Woman · Here, take a look. The conveyor belt is here and the service elevator is right next to it.

75.

Woman · Is this the express train to Paris?

Man · No, ma'am, the express doesn't run until four o'clock.

Woman · That's a shame. I wanted to get there before noon.

76.

Woman · Would it be possible to have these copies stapled and collated by this afternoon?

Man · Yes, if Jerry can fix the machine this morning.

Woman · Oh, I hope so. We're putting together two hundred course packs for the sales seminar tonight.

77.

Woman · How is the report going, Bart?

Man · The chairman of the board wants it by five and I don't think I can do it.

Woman · Bart, Judith and I can help you.

78.

Man · I think I'll take the train to Paris.

Woman · Flights are not much more expensive, and you'd be there much faster.

Man · That's fine, but I'm not really in a rush and besides, I have so much I have to read.

79.

Man · I heard that we won the bid for the construction job for those two restaurants.

Woman · We did, but I had to adjust our prices three times before we won.

Man · Well, the market is down, so competition is at its peak.

80.

Man · What is your minimum order for delivery purposes?

Woman · One hundred dollars. And deliveries are made on Monday, Wednesday and Friday.

Man · Then could you add two rolls of fax paper and some stationery with a floral design?

PART IV

Questions 81 through 83 refer to the following announcement.

We learn how to work for money at school and on the job but we don't really learn how to make our money work for us. This workshop teaches how to make your money work for you. Whether you want to work independently, plan for early retirement or pay for college, you will discover how you can earn money from the stock market with this simple and proven approach. Find out how much capital is needed for your desired lifestyle, and spot wise investments. Make your money work harder, so you don't have to.

Questions 84 through 86 refer to the following report.

After reviewing all the data, I have determined that the purchase of a Sharp Penny postage meter would result in time savings and increased office efficiency. Our volume of mail, at least 10,000 pieces a month, justifies the expense. The initial expense would be $350 for the meter and a monthly rental charge of $15. Servicing and maintenance and the replacement of any parts would be free of charge by Sharp Penny. Office workers could be taught how to use the machine inside of a half hour.

Questions 87 and 88 refer to the following introduction.

Ladies and gentlemen, I would like to introduce our first speaker tonight: Stanley Lake. Stan has been a private jet pilot for over fifteen years and is also the vice president of marketing at the Follenworth Company. Stan will, I hope, share some exciting excerpts with us tonight from his new book, *Piloting the Rich and Famous*, before we get down to the business of airport safety management.

Questions 89 through 91 refer to the following notice.

All local buses labelled with a blue "B" have been fitted with special racks to allow for bike transport. Always mount your bike from the curbside. Let the operator know you plan to use the rack. Remove water bottles, air pumps, or other items that could slip from your bike and potentially create a hazard. For safety reasons, the operator may not leave his seat to assist you, but he or she can answer your questions. This program is part of our effort to improve air quality and keep you healthy.

Questions 92 through 94 refer to the following news story.

Despite the opposition of the U.S., the European Union, and the opponents of the SLORC party, Myanmar has finally been admitted to the Association of Southeast Asian Nations (ASEAN). Myanmar Shipyards has just won a three million dollar contract to build two freight vessels for Singapore's Jaya Marine Lines International. This will be the third contract Myanmar Shipyards has won, bidding for foreign shipping lines. Indonesia's PT Container Company and Singapore's Casey Marine Limited were the first two contractors.

Questions 95 through 97 refer to the following talk.

I would like to thank everyone who participated in the development of the Brazilian market. Our position there is looking very good. The four-door sedan sales have gone up 9 percent and the mini-vans 6.5 percent. While on tour last month, I visited our factories and dealerships there as well as in Venezuela and was very pleased with the reorganization and the new safety measures that have been implemented. I would like to take this opportunity to acknowledge Mr. Carreras, the general manager. He has been running the operations in Brazil for just six months, and efficiency and morale there have improved considerably.

Questions 98 through 100 refer to the following advertisement.

How would you like to build your own home and pay only $5,000 for the building materials? You can, you know. Just call 1-800-652-8000. We're Dome Home Builders. Using our pre-cut, color-coded kits, you can easily assemble your own dome for as little as $5,000. These homes are attractive and energy-efficient. For just $15, we'll send you a variety of floor plans and a 100-page catalog. To learn more, call now for a Home Dome color video for just $10.

Practice Test Two - Listening Comprehension

PART I

Sample question:

(A) They're looking out the window.
(B) They're having a meeting.
(C) They're eating in a restaurant.
(D) They're moving the furniture.

1. (A) The waiter is clearing the table.
   (B) The diner is finishing his meal.
   (C) The cook is having some coffee.
   (D) The innkeeper is taking a reservation.

2. (A) The work stations are empty.
   (B) The train is leaving the station.
   (C) The trainer is explaining a computer function.
   (D) The monitors are attached to the wall.

3. (A) She's writing on the wall.
   (B) She's resting an elbow on the table.
   (C) She's smelling the flowers.
   (D) She's filling her cup.

4. (A) The vendor is selling art outdoors.
   (B) The painter is painting a picture.
   (C) The curator is installing a show.
   (D) The artist is sketching a customer.

5. (A) The bus door is open.
   (B) The floor of the bus is wide.
   (C) The train station is empty.
   (D) The riders pay their fares.

6. (A) He's looking through some files.
   (B) He's holding the ball in place.
   (C) He's adjusting the height of the apparatus.
   (D) He's staring out the window.

7. (A) The parking lot is full.
   (B) The square is lined with trees.
   (C) The patrol car is being waxed.
   (D) The police officers are by their car.

8. (A) The man is crossing the street.
   (B) The man is getting a paper.
   (C) The man is broadcasting the news.
   (D) The man is writing in his journal.

9. (A) She's looking at a road map.
   (B) She's asking directions.
   (C) She's signing a check.
   (D) She's holding a sign.

10. (A) He's getting a check up.
    (B) He's checking the wiring.
    (C) He's tightening the wires.
    (D) He's sending a wire.

11. (A) The road winds through the mountains.
    (B) The lane is straight and narrow.
    (C) The path passes by the stream.
    (D) The highway ends at the shore.

12. (A) The women are on a break.
    (B) One woman is putting on her coat.
    (C) The women are wearing jackets.
    (D) The women are in front of the shelves.

13. (A) The coffee beans are in bags.
    (B) The patrons are sitting in the sun.
    (C) The chairs are stacked against the wall.
    (D) The customers are feeding the birds.

14. (A) He's painting the wall.
    (B) He's mixing the paint.
    (C) He's removing the furniture.
    (D) He's coloring the floor.

15. (A) A tree grows out of the steps.
    (B) Palm trees border the walk.
    (C) The ferns are in the pot.
    (D) Water runs down the hill.

16. (A) The baker puts the pastry in the oven.
    (B) The shopkeeper is behind the counter.
    (C) The driver pays the toll.
    (D) The florist cuts a flower.

17. (A) He's taking off his glasses.
    (B) He's shutting the pen.
    (C) He's handing her a pencil.
    (D) He's signing his name.

18. (A) They're striking one another.
    (B) They're exchanging cards.
    (C) They're shaking hands.
    (D) They're waving good-bye.

19. (A) The magazines are on display.
    (B) The journalist gave an interview.
    (C) The books are off the shelves.
    (D) The sea shells are on the floor.

20. (A) They're having a discussion.
    (B) They're choosing a tie.
    (C) They're rolling up their sleeves.
    (D) They're stacking bricks on the table.

PART II

Sample question:

Good morning, John. How are you?
(A) I am fine, thank you.
(B) I am in the living room.
(C) My name is John.

21. How did this stock perform last year?
(A) They were out of stock.
(B) The show wasn't the best.
(C) It did very well.

22. You checked the fuse box, didn't you?
(A) Yes, the mail box is empty.
(B) I'll get you the check now.
(C) I did that this morning.

23. How high could the interest rates go?
(A) Up to twenty percent, I'm told.
(B) I wouldn't go any higher.
(C) This new subscription rate is very low.

24. Did everyone in the office see this memo?
(A) I saw them all yesterday.
(B) I believe so.
(C) They've been to our other offices.

25. Your sales are doing well, aren't they?
(A) We're selling the house this year.
(B) They're sailing to Wales.
(C) No, in fact, they're dropping.

26. Do you offer senior citizen discounts?
(A) Yes, he has seniority here.
(B) No, this counter is closed, ma'am.
(C) Yes, I'll just need to see your ID.

27. How much cement will be needed for the foundation?
(A) We found what we needed.
(B) Several tons, I would say.
(C) Rubber cement would work.

28. Does this plane stop in Dublin?
(A) It does, but only briefly.
(B) Be sure to stop and see the islands.
(C) The stop sign is in this lane.

29. You were at your sister's house, weren't you?
(A) No, he sold his house yesterday.
(B) I was there last night.
(C) My sister works at home.

30. What kind of museum would you like to visit?
(A) One with dinosaurs would be nice.
(B) I can't stay very long.
(C) I haven't seen that kind before.

31. Have you ordered the microphone yet?
(A) Yes, but the microscope was expensive.
(B) I'll order a new phone right away.
(C) Not yet, I need a part number.

32. Do you work day or night shift?
(A) No, only in the winter.
(B) I work nine to five.
(C) Yes, it's alright.

33. Is the printer plugged in?
(A) I'll check.
(B) No, it's working fine.
(C) The print is much too light.

34. What role did he play in the negotiations?
(A) He was the chief negotiator.
(B) These rolls are stale.
(C) He plays every Saturday.

35. Has your manager been given some time off?
(A) Yes, she always came on time.
(B) Yes, she's in Hawaii now.
(C) Yes, she was the first to get back on.

36. Why should the media be invited?
(A) We need the exposure.
(B) All middle management was invited.
(C) Let's go together.

37. Don't you think this ad will attract attention?
(A) They're an attractive couple.
(B) It will only add to the tension.
(C) It most definitely will.

38. Would the contract include the shipping department?
(A) I was told it would.
(B) The ships are departing immediately.
(C) We weren't able to contact the boat.

39. Do you remember which gate we leave from?
(A) He told me the rate before he left.
(B) We shouldn't leave the gate open.
(C) I think it's gate five on concourse B.

40. Have you spoken with the chief engineer about the leak?
(A) The spokes are weak.
(B) I haven't been able to reach her yet.
(C) The engine has a leak now.

41. Where did I leave my credit card?
(A) At the house, I think.
(B) I'm sorry it's overdrawn.
(C) I think it was this afternoon.

42. Do you mean he was fired?
(A) He was all fired up.
(B) That's what Miriam told me.
(C) He can be mean when he's tired.

43. Are the ambassadors still in the building?
(A) They left an hour ago.
(B) The embassy is just down the street.
(C) Please be still while you are in here.

44. Can flight reservations be made this late?
(A) There are a few tickets for the fight left.
(B) Normally not, but I'll try.
(C) This table is reserved.

45. Why should she take all the blame?
    (A) She laid claim to the inheritance.
    (B) She took what she could carry.
    (C) Well, she was responsible.

46. How do I get this fax to start?
    (A) It would help to verify the facts.
    (B) You have to type in your codeword.
    (C) Fax machines start at about forty dollars.

47. George is showing up late again, isn't he?
    (A) He thinks no one notices.
    (B) They don't bloom until late in the season.
    (C) I watched the late show last night.

48. Who's answering the phone at the front desk?
    (A) She only answers to Mrs. Walton.
    (B) She's very polite on the phone.
    (C) The receptionist should be there.

49. How often has that mechanic repaired this car?
    (A) The mechanic has ordered a pair.
    (B) More than once.
    (C) There's at least two of them.

50. You're Roberto's supervisor, aren't you?
    (A) I'm actually one of his colleagues.
    (B) I'll talk with the superintendent.
    (C) He's got a great visor.

PART III

51.
Woman A Natalie, has Manuel said if he can make the meeting next Monday?
Woman B Not really. He said he prefers Wednesday, but he wants to check with his secretary first.
Woman A Wednesday's fine, but please tell him he'll need to get back to us by Friday.

52.
Man Oh no, I don't remember where I left my mobile phone.
Woman You brought it from the car when we went into the restaurant.
Man Maybe I left it at the cash register when I paid the bill.

53.
Woman Why don't we just rent a car for this trip? Tokyo is only three hours away.
Man That would be more interesting than flying or taking the bus.
Woman The train would be faster, but driving is more fun.

54.
Woman Could you help me? I bought this yesterday, and I'm trying to find a tie that would go well with this design.
Man Does this wavy pattern interest you?
Woman Yes, but do you have it in a shade similar to the suit?

55.
Man I'm looking for a street map of Hamburg.
Woman Would you like a plain one for $8 or a laminated one for $15?
Man A plain one is fine. We'll just be passing through.

56.
Man I'm sorry ma'am, but all passengers are limited to only one carry-on item.
Woman These are extremely fragile.
Man Oh, in that case we'll ask that you put both of them in the overhead compartment above your seat.

57.
Man We'd like all the new employees to attend the orientation lecture first.
Woman What time will that be? I'd like to squeeze in a brief tour of the plant before noon.
Man The orientation doesn't start until eleven. You'll never fit in a tour before lunch.

58.
Woman This new printer is the most sophisticated piece of office equipment I've seen.
Man It's sure not the most user-friendly.
Woman Maybe we should test it for a few days before we decide to buy it.

59.
Man There are so many people in this lobby, I wonder if we'll see him.
Woman He told me that he would be wearing a green and blue cap and carrying lots of luggage.
Man Well, that definitely narrows it down.

60.
Man How long does it take to get to the airport?
Woman If there's no traffic, it's about a twenty minute drive.
Man The roads are probably crowded. We should leave soon.

61.
Man Did you attend the seminar on the new international banking regulations?
Woman Yes. It's remarkable what's happening. The investment field is now wide open to the banks.
Man Well, with competition up, brokerage fees should be going down.

62.
Man Is that teleconference scheduled for this afternoon, Mary?
Woman Yes, I think they want to have it at three o'clock sharp.
Man I'll send a memo around reminding everyone.

63.
Man Bita, is the audio-visual room available this afternoon?
Woman I believe it is, but let me check the scheduling board.
Man Thanks. I have some very important clients coming.

64.
Man We're going to Rudy's Restaurant after the meeting. Why don't you join us?
Woman I'd love to, but my office is expecting me to take part in a demonstration for the bank managers this afternoon.
Man Well, maybe you can come later if it doesn't take too long.

65.
Man Do you have batteries for this particular make?
Woman No, not in stock, but I can order them. They'll be here tomorrow.
Man That's fine. For now I'll get about a dozen rolls of film. I'll be going on vacation next week.

66.
Man Joan, I was told that the electrician would need to access the panel behind your desk. Would you like to work in my office today?
Woman That would be very nice, George. I hope I won't be in your way.
Man No, not at all. In fact, it might be a good time to go over the budget plans.

67.
Woman The morale in the factory seems to be down lately.
Man Do you think the new foreman has anything to do with it?
Woman Possibly. He's experienced, but not particularly friendly.

68.
Man Could you tell me how many people are employed here? I'm doing a survey.
Woman At least three hundred. What is the survey for?
Man To determine how heavily the nearby roads are being used.

69.
Man Could you run this package over to the post office for me?
Woman I'll be going over at four o'clock. Can't it wait until then?
Man Yes, as long as it's mailed today.

70.
Man I don't like it but I think we'll have to cut back the research budget.
Woman That could be very costly. We could lose our hard-earned competitive edge.
Man Well, it hasn't been decided yet, but we are looking at it.

71.
Woman We're moving corporate headquarters and we need more space. How much are rentals in this part of town?
Man One hundred and twenty-five dollars per square foot and that's a very good deal for this area.
Woman Do you have a card? I'd like to get back to you.

72.
Man The ferry is out of commission again which means that the service to the island will be cut for about a month.
Woman That's going to be devastating for the commuters.
Man I know. Bill lost a good amount of pay when that happened last year.

73.
Man Rosa, do you know if there's enough petty cash to buy a few boxes of copier paper?
Woman I don't really know Hans, but Karla would.
Man Thanks. I'll call Karla.

74.
Man They promised to start the meetings on time from now on.
Woman I know. I raced over here from across town so I wouldn't be late.
Man Well, from now on, we'll start at six sharp, no matter who's late.

75.
Man What type of clothing should I take when I go to Sweden?
Woman Some friends of mine were there last year and they said it can get pretty cool at night, even in the middle of summer.
Man Maybe I'll pack a few sweaters then.

76.
Man Won't you be coming to the celebrations? You know how your staff appreciate your being there.
Woman I know, but the deadline for this project is next week and I have to report to the committee in the morning.
Man I understand. But we could all do some overtime, and you could go to the party. You have to.

77.
Man The coffee maker is broken again.
Woman Ask the driver to run out and pick one up. The president is going to want some when he meets with Mr. Sikarda.
Man Good idea. I'll speak to the driver right away.

78.
Man Excuse me, miss, but photographs aren't allowed here.
Woman But it's so pretty.
Man We've found that the flashes disturb people who are praying. We ask that you don't take photographs.

79.
Man I wonder why everyone is so late today.
Woman They're not late. They're not coming.
Man Oh my gosh. The office is closed today, isn't it?

80.
Man We can't wait all day.
Woman It's only been a half-hour. Let's just wait for another half-hour.
Man I'll wait a few more minutes, but then I'm leaving. This is absurd.

PART IV

Questions 81 and 82 refer to the following report.

Today will be partly sunny and very hot and humid. The high will be 100 with a southwesterly wind at 6-12 miles per hour. Tonight will be warm with possible thunderstorms. The low will be 72. Tomorrow and Tuesday will be cloudy and breezy with possible thunderstorms and a high of 82. After that, though, we should have pleasant weather right up through to the weekend.

Questions 83 and 84 refer to the following study.

Nearly 80% of over 2,000 employees polled by Brigham Consulting Incorporated recommend their company as an employer, but 45% would leave for a mere 10% increase in pay.

Questions 85 and 86 refer to the following news story.

Philippine researchers, while studying Asian flu, have found a gene that causes colon cancer. They also found that this gene is particularly common in people of Nordic ancestry. Researchers say that the gene may be responsible for about 10% of the 100,000 new cases of colon cancer that will be diagnosed this year alone. Fortunately, a blood test has been devised which can detect the gene.

Questions 87 through 89 refer to the following announcement.

All managers are requested to report to the VIP Lounge for a meeting at one o'clock. We're going to coordinate our activities for the move to the top floors of the new building. Please bring a list of all your files, books and belongings, so that we can give it to the movers. All boxes need to have the old as well as the new office room numbers clearly marked on them.

Questions 90 through 92 refer to the following introduction.

Ladies and gentlemen, we should all be crazy rich by now, right? We read any investment and financial magazine we can get our hands on. We listen to every financial guru who steps up to the podium, subscribe to any newsletter that promises the gold. And yet the money, the big money, still eludes us. Is tonight's speaker just one more link in the chain? His statistics clearly indicate otherwise. And so does my experience working with him. May I introduce Mr. Michael Faulkenberry, author of *Money Is Everything*.

Questions 93 through 95 refer to the following report.

Help-wanted advertising has been holding steady throughout June and July because of continued consumer confidence and demand for labor. "The labor market shows no signs of slowing down," says economist Joe Bloomberg. The unemployment rate is 4.8% with 250,000 new jobs opening up. "There's never been a better time to look for a job," Mr. Bloomberg added.

Questions 96 and 97 refer to the following talk.

I'd like to pass on to you the advice a very successful executive once gave to me. Float from job to job for a while with this purpose; to learn one phase of business at one place and another phase of the same business at another place. Once you become to some degree qualified in these areas, once you are able to coordinate the practice of business with what you are learning, you can then entertain the idea of starting your own business. You can even reach for the executive position.

Questions 98 through 100 refer to the following news story.

Even though for shorter distances, it's faster and more economical to travel by train, many travelers still prefer to fly. A one-way flight from Yamagata to Sendai costs between $45 and $185 and it takes three hours, including the 60 minute check-in time and transportation to and from the airport. The same journey can be done on the train for $19 in half the time. Why do people do it? One commuter said "Force of habit". Another less obvious reason is that the train companies are not actively advertising for the short-haul commuters. Yet this is a marketer's dream; to offer a superior service at a better price.

Practice Test Three - Listening Comprehension

PART I

Sample question:

(A) They're looking out the window.
(B) They're having a meeting.
(C) They're eating in a restaurant.
(D) They're moving the furniture.

1. (A) He's cleaning the spoons.
   (B) He's putting away the cutlery.
   (C) He's weighing the cutlet.
   (D) He's eating soon.

2. (A) Two chairs are in front of the bed.
   (B) The flowers are beside the bed.
   (C) The window is over the sofa.
   (D) The vase is on the desk.

3. (A) The botanist is growing trees.
   (B) The delivery man is holding a rose.
   (C) The gardener is watering the plants.
   (D) The firefighter is hosing down the building.

4. (A) They're at a computer fair.
   (B) They're at a movie screening.
   (C) They're in an office.
   (D) They're in a board meeting.

5. (A) They're selling hats.
   (B) They're standing on mats.
   (C) They're covering the door.
   (D) They're wearing protective clothes.

6. (A) He's entertaining the children.
   (B) He's playing music.
   (C) He's putting away his trumpet.
   (D) He's blowing on the hot food.

7. (A) The newspaper is on the bench.
   (B) He's reading the information.
   (C) The board is covered with graffiti.
   (D) He's writing the news.

8. (A) The stars are in the sky.
   (B) They're drinking an espresso.
   (C) They're preparing coffee.
   (D) The machines are outside.

9. (A) The cat is catching its prey.
   (B) The animal is wearing him out.
   (C) The boy is standing by the door.
   (D) The athlete is buying cigarettes.

10. (A) The professor is handing out the exam.
    (B) The barber is testing his arm.
    (C) The doctor is performing a test.
    (D) The optician is checking her eyes.

11. (A) The women are posting a notice.
    (B) The photo service takes a long time.
    (C) The postcards are joined together.
    (D) The tourists are taking pictures.

12. (A) They're shaking the bottle.
    (B) They're greeting each other.
    (C) They're painting a frame.
    (D) They're hanging a picture on the wall.

13. (A) The chef is working in the kitchen.
    (B) The technician is finishing his work.
    (C) The owner is opening the restaurant.
    (D) The apprentice is looking at the soil.

14. (A) He's returning his pass.
    (B) He's riding his bicycle.
    (C) He's purchasing a ticket.
    (D) He's entering for free.

15. (A) The car is leaving the refinery.
    (B) The instruments are stored in the drums.
    (C) The oil is flowing through the street.
    (D) The winery is divided by a road.

16. (A) The group is welcoming the band.
    (B) The tourists are packing their bags.
    (C) The visitors are arriving by land.
    (D) The passengers are boarding the van.

17. (A) The car is stopping for them.
    (B) The man and the women are crossing the street.
    (C) They are standing on the curb.
    (D) The bus is coming around the corner.

18. (A) There is a key in the lock of the cabinet.
    (B) The keyboard is under the counter.
    (C) The keys are in the door.
    (D) There is a screen on the door.

19. (A) He's painting the seats.
    (B) He's adding a coat of paint to the pipes.
    (C) He's sitting while he eats.
    (D) He's choosing a seat on the floor.

20. (A) The plates are piled in the sink.
    (B) The bowls are almost empty.
    (C) The food is displayed in serving dishes.
    (D) The produce is in boxes.

PART II

Sample question:

Good morning, John. How are you?
(A) I am fine, thank you.
(B) I am in the living room.
(C) My name is John.

21. Where is the phone?
    (A) I'm applying for a loan.
    (B) It's on the desk.
    (C) We can run there.

22. May I help you?
    (A) May is always pleasant here.
    (B) I can't help it.
    (C) Yes, I'd appreciate that.

23. Where is the embassy?
    (A) It's behind the parking lot.
    (B) The ambassador is upstairs.
    (C) I've been there myself.

24. Have you spoken with the travel agent yet?
    (A) No, I prefer to travel by jet.
    (B) She spoke of you often.
    (C) Yes, and she's made the reservation.

25. Should we take the train or the bus?
    (A) The train is more convenient.
    (B) You really should.
    (C) I waited for you at the bus stop.

26. Why not form a partnership with them?
    (A) I don't know them well enough.
    (B) They're already married.
    (C) My partner is out of town.

27. When is your client coming?
    (A) He'll stay overnight.
    (B) He's coming for a whole week.
    (C) We're expecting her any minute.

28. Do you have any small change?
    (A) We only have medium and large sizes.
    (B) Yes, here are some coins.
    (C) No, there were quite a few changes.

29. How is Mr. Bennet doing?
    (A) Much better, I'm told.
    (B) We've been so busy.
    (C) He's been doing the payroll.

30. Was our committee chosen for the award?
    (A) Unfortunately, it wasn't.
    (B) We chose not to attend.
    (C) He won the vote.

31. How do I find Twentieth Street?
    (A) The sooner the better.
    (B) Yours is the twenty-first seat.
    (C) Take a right at the corner.

32. Who closes the office on Wednesdays?
    (A) The night manager does.
    (B) Jeff is always close by.
    (C) I try to leave my work at the office.

33. May I leave a message for Ms. Gallo?
    (A) She's leaving a message now.
    (B) No, the messenger didn't pick it up.
    (C) Yes, I'll make sure she gets it.

34. What task will he be assigned?
    (A) I'll ask for help.
    (B) An easy one, I'm sure.
    (C) He'll be assigned his own room.

35. What did she say about the seminar?
    (A) She enjoyed seminary school.
    (B) She's getting a new car.
    (C) It was informative.

36. When will the awards be given?
    (A) They'll be presented during dinner.
    (B) The ceremony is at the town hall.
    (C) We were given very little notice.

37. Did you know the conference will be in Hong Kong?
    (A) No, I was never there.
    (B) I referred her to Mr. Chang.
    (C) Yes, I received an e-mail about it.

38. Don't you have these sweaters in stock?
    (A) Normally we do.
    (B) These socks make my feet sweat.
    (C) Those are goose feathers.

39. Where are the refreshments?
    (A) The air is fresher by the window.
    (B) You'll find them on the balcony.
    (C) A shower is refreshing.

40. When does the library open?
    (A) The public may enter at ten.
    (B) The book shop is closed today.
    (C) The library is open to everyone.

41. How does this machine work?
    (A) By listening carefully.
    (B) By turning on this switch.
    (C) By being on time.

42. How simple are these tests?
    (A) I tested almost all of them.
    (B) They're easy to get along with.
    (C) I don't find them at all difficult.

43. Where is there a hotel with an indoor pool?
    (A) We have pool tables inside.
    (B) There are several in the downtown area.
    (C) Let's stay outside for a while.

44. Will they accept personal checks?
    (A) If they know you.
    (B) The clerk is a personal friend of mine.
    (C) He took it personally.

45. When did you receive the promotion?
(A) We were given suntan lotion.
(B) The commotion lasted all night.
(C) The week we finished the project.

46. Were the representatives satisfied with the meeting?
(A) They met in the boardroom.
(B) All of them were pleased.
(C) Yes, the present was acceptable.

47. Could you show Ms. Tashiko our new office?
(A) She liked her new office.
(B) We can make the last show.
(C) It'd be a pleasure.

48. This fax machine has a warranty, doesn't it?
(A) I can't guarantee the results.
(B) The fact is, he doesn't have it.
(C) I was told it has a lifetime one.

49. Where are my plane tickets?
(A) In the envelope.
(B) I made the reservations.
(C) Up in the sky.

50. What do you think of the lamp shades?
(A) I like lamb.
(B) They're in the shade.
(C) The color seems a bit off.

PART III

51.
Man   Can I get you anything else?
Woman   Just some ice water and the check, please.
Man   I hope you enjoyed the meal.

52.
Woman A   Welcome to the Park Hotel. Your room is on the second floor.
Woman B   Thank you. Could you tell me where the dining room is?
Woman A   Yes, it's just down this hall on your left.

53.
Man A   My hotel room doesn't have a fax machine.
Man B   We'll give the fax to the concierge at the front desk to send.
Man A   They always charge more per page there, but I need to get these notes to my secretary.

54.
Woman   My brother is looking for work. Do you have any openings in your construction company?
Man   Possibly. Does he know anything about carpentry?
Woman   Yes, he's been building homes for the last two summers.

55.
Woman A   Do you know when it's supposed to stop raining?
Woman B   Yes, I think it's going to be sunny tomorrow.
Woman A   Good. Maybe we can have a picnic if it's nice out.

56.
Woman   We've run out of paper for the printer.
Man   That's my fault, actually. I let the Accounting Department have two packs.
Woman   Please order more next time — enough for both departments.

57.
Woman   How long have you received the *New York Times*?
Man   My mother gave me a subscription last summer.
Woman   I buy it every day at the newsstand.

58.
Man   Shall we take a taxi or drive ourselves?
Woman   Let's leave our cars here and take the train into the city.
Man   Good idea. We won't have to worry about parking and it'll be cheaper.

59.
Woman   Do you know when the field staff will get the updated price lists?
Man   I was told they're at the printers. Should be a matter of days.
Woman   Great, because right now we always have to check with the main office when we make a sale.

60.
Man   Tickets. Tickets, please.
Woman   Excuse me, sir. Is there a dining car on this train?
Man   Yes, ma'am. It's the second car down.

61.
Man   I wonder if these proposals will be approved by the president?
Woman   They will be, if there isn't any data missing.
Man   Well then, we shouldn't have any problem.

62.
Man A   You could have the display model for $3,000 less, Mr. Samo.
Man B   Really? How many miles does it have on it?
Man A   I'd have to look, but I do know it was only used for test drives.

63.
Man   I'm thinking of expanding our computer furniture line and cutting back on the bedroom furniture in the showroom.
Woman   I looked at the analysis, too. Eighty-percent of the sales were from the computer area.
Man   Let's try it out for a few months.

64.
Man — I'd send your package by courier, but they're all on strike right now.
Woman — I think I'll take it over there myself then.
Man — Use my car, it's right out front.

65.
Man — Mrs. Laburi, what time would you prefer to leave Hong Kong?
Woman — Early morning would be ideal.
Man — Then I'll make your reservations for the 7:00 a.m. flight.

66.
Man — When I'm at the library I like to sit at the long tables in the reference section.
Woman — I prefer to read in the cushioned chairs in the mystery area.
Man — I know, but it can get pretty noisy over there.

67.
Man — The two of us try to make all local deliveries before noon.
Woman — How early do you start?
Man — 6:00 a.m. on weekdays. After 12 o'clock I do the out-of-town deliveries.

68.
Man — We'll definitely need more chairs for our meeting this afternoon.
Woman — But these are rental chairs, and I don't know if the rental company can accommodate us that quickly.
Man — We're good customers of theirs. They'll come through for us.

69.
Man — Sixty-five desks and tables are arriving before lunch.
Woman — I'll ask Sam and David if they'll help us unload the truck.
Man — Good idea. They can bring in the furniture and we'll unpack it.

70.
Man — What seems to be the problem, Mrs. Garcia?
Woman — When I look at fine print, doctor, I can barely read it.
Man — Well, you might need a new prescription. Let's examine your vision.

71.
Man — Roberta mentioned that the company may be filing for bankruptcy.
Woman — Unfortunately, she's right. We're having a hard time paying all the new staff.
Man — I had no idea the situation was that serious.

72.
Man — I have to get my car worked on this afternoon and then I'm going shopping.
Woman — Let's go together. I need to get some steaks for our barbecue tonight.
Man — I'll pick you up in front of your house around three.

73.
Man — In the phone book there are several one-page ads for snow removal.
Woman — Those companies probably all need part-time help. Let's call and see if they're hiring.
Man — OK, but we won't get rich doing seasonal labor.

74.
Man — The power company called to say that the electricity would be off from three to five.
Woman — Then our incoming fax orders will have to be re-routed.
Man — I'll call the telephone company to have them sent to the Cairo office.

75.
Man — I'm sorry, but tonight's concert is sold out.
Woman — Isn't there any standing room?
Man — No, but you can wait in line in case someone returns a ticket.

76.
Man — The magazine reporters are already here.
Woman — Have they come in yet?
Man — No, they're waiting outside until the ceremony is over.

77.
Man — That was really a magnificent spread — filet mignon, roast turkey and even duck.
Woman — And did you see the dessert table?
Man — Yes, the caterer really went all out for this event.

78.
Man — I would add a screened-in porch to this entrance.
Woman — And maybe a sliding door?
Man — Yes, that's a good idea. I'll change the blueprints.

79.
Man — The patients were wondering what happens in the operating room in the event of a blackout.
Woman — We have generators that switch on automatically.
Man — That's good to know for patients who are on life-support systems.

80.
Man — I don't see Tom anymore. Was he transferred?
Woman — Didn't you hear? He's the vice-president at corporate headquarters now.
Man — It makes sense. He's worked very hard all these years.

PART IV

Questions 81 and 82 refer to the following introduction.

My dear friends, I would like to turn the podium over to Mr. Makowitz, who will tell you about the reason for this fund-raiser. You all know him as the Personnel Director, but you may not be aware of the role he plays in our community. Through his dedicated efforts, over five hundred underprivileged children have been able to participate in the Literacy Crusade which he helped found and of which he is also a board member. Please help me give Mr. Makowitz a warm welcome.

Questions 83 through 85 refer to the following announcement.

As the hotel will be closed from November through March for renovations, the entire housekeeping staff will be on leave with pay during this time. The same will hold true for the kitchen, banquet and dining room staff. Only management must report to work during this period. Arrangements for direct deposit of your paychecks can be made with Mrs. Tuttle in accounting. The grand re-opening will take place on the eighth of April. New uniforms will be issued to all personnel at that time.

Questions 86 through 88 refer to the following announcement.

Ladies and gentlemen, the fire marshal is with us today to supervise the evacuation of the entire building. The front offices are to use the north stairwell. Rear offices should exit through the south stairwell. Everyone else is to use the east wing stairs. No one may use the elevators. When you hear the alarm, please proceed quickly and in silence to your respective stairwells and then gather outside in the parking lot. Once everyone is accounted for, the fire marshal will tell us about the new fire detection equipment which has been installed to ensure our safety. Thank you for your cooperation.

Questions 89 through 91 refer to the following recorded announcement.

You have reached the office of Doctor Malcolm. Our office hours are Monday through Friday from 8:00 a.m. until 5:00 p.m. The office is located at the intersection of Highway 55 and Route 1. Parking is in the rear of the building. If this is a dental emergency, please press 9 for immediate attention. If you would like to make an appointment to have your teeth cleaned, press 1. For any other message, wait for the beep.

Questions 92 and 93 refer to the following radio advertisement.

If you want to succeed in this fast-paced financial world, you can't ignore the advice given in *Investor's Choice*. Our columnists give investment strategies to help you keep pace with a rapidly changing global economy. The opportunities will be breathtaking for those able to interpret the new dynamics, but not so for those stuck in the past and worried about inflation. Today's persistent inflation may very well not be some temporary aberration. Don't be fooled. Stay abreast. Read *Investor's Choice*.

Questions 94 through 96 refer to the following announcement.

Please follow company policy regarding compensation for your expenses. Turn in all expense reports before Thursday at two if you want to be reimbursed on the following payday. All receipts must accompany the report. This policy has been in effect for some time now and yet accounting still complains of last minute attempts to push reimbursement requests through without the required paperwork. The accounting department already has its hands full with all the new computers we have just installed. Let's not burden them unnecessarily.

Questions 97 and 98 refer to the following bulletin.

After five years of testing, the St. Petersburg Transportation Bureau has finalized its plans for the implementation of their first magnetic train. Conventional trains ride directly on a steel rail. This revolutionary and economical design will literally float the train inches above the track by means of powerful magnetic forces. Needless to say, the greatly diminished friction will allow the train to whisk along at unprecedented speeds.

Questions 99 and 100 refer to the following announcement.

Your attention please. When boarding the train, please hold small children by the hand. We would like to point out that special seats are reserved for the elderly and the disabled. The sound of the bell indicates that the train doors are about to close. We ask that you refrain from smoking, eating or drinking while in the subway system. You will find elevators to the street at each end of the platform. If you need assistance, please press the red button to the right of the elevator door.

Practice Test Four - Listening Comprehension

PART I

Sample question:

(A) They're looking out the window.
(B) They're having a meeting.
(C) They're eating in a restaurant.
(D) They're moving the furniture.

1. (A) The tracks are in front of them.
   (B) The conductor is at the window of the train.
   (C) The racks are nearby.
   (D) The rain is heavy.

2. (A) The menu is in his hand.
   (B) The beverages are under the counter.
   (C) The food is behind glass.
   (D) The coffee is in the cup.

3. (A) He's holding his keys.
   (B) He's taking a nap in the chair.
   (C) He's taping his notes.
   (D) He's resting the computer in his lap.

4. (A) The cars are passing under the arch.
   (B) All the buildings have one story.
   (C) Stoplights are lining the streets.
   (D) A few trees are between the lights.

5. (A) They're putting on overalls.
   (B) The boat is ready to sail.
   (C) They're building a yacht.
   (D) The lumber is for the ship.

6. (A) The tourist is leading the group.
   (B) The guide is speaking into the mike.
   (C) The traveler is showing her slides.
   (D) The guard is leading the hike.

7. (A) She's tipping the waitress.
   (B) She's standing at the check-out.
   (C) She's paying by credit card.
   (D) She's bagging her own groceries.

8. (A) The plane is landing on the runway.
   (B) The people are getting off the plane.
   (C) The plane is taking off.
   (D) The passengers are boarding.

9. (A) The chemist is mixing a solution.
   (B) The dentist is looking into her mouth.
   (C) The scientist is peering at something.
   (D) The designer is focusing on the shapes.

10. (A) The escalator is very steep.
    (B) They are coming down the steps.
    (C) The man is climbing the ladder.
    (D) The stairs are made of wood.

11. (A) The conference room is occupied.
    (B) The office doors are closed.
    (C) The work space has no dividing walls.
    (D) The warehouse is full of computers.

12. (A) The patrons are being seated.
    (B) The tables are arranged in rows.
    (C) The lamp light is very bright.
    (D) Several seats are empty.

13. (A) He's selling socks.
    (B) He's waiting for a part.
    (C) He's talking in a phone booth.
    (D) He's using a moblie phone.

14. (A) The palm trees are in the park.
    (B) The traffic is at the stop sign.
    (C) The driver is turning a corner.
    (D) The pedestrian is standing by a car.

15. (A) They're operating on the patient.
    (B) They're cutting the meat.
    (C) They're removing the tubes.
    (D) They're massaging the muscles.

16. (A) She's cleaning the glass.
    (B) She's filling the glass.
    (C) She's making coffee.
    (D) She's drinking the beverage.

17. (A) The waiter is taking down the umbrella.
    (B) The couples are swimming in the lake.
    (C) The diners are eating by the water.
    (D) The customer is serving a drink.

18. (A) The bellboy is assisting guests with their bags.
    (B) The presenter is waiting for the attendees.
    (C) The elevator operator is pressing a button.
    (D) The officer is buttoning his jacket.

19. (A) The plants grow against the wall.
    (B) The bicycle is on top of the car.
    (C) The highway runs in front of the house.
    (D) The wall surrounds the home.

20. (A) The cash is in a bag.
    (B) The register has change.
    (C) He is putting the currency in a safe.
    (D) He is handing the customer the bill.

PART II

Sample question:

Good morning, John. How are you?
(A) I am fine, thank you.
(B) I am in the living room.
(C) My name is John.

21. Has the ship arrived yet?
    (A) All shipments undergo inspection.
    (B) It's entering the harbor now.
    (C) I'll get it.

22. Don't you remember the name of the song?
    (A) I know it was an unusual one.
    (B) I can't remember his name.
    (C) I'm a member of the songwriter's club.

23. How fast can this new plane travel?
    (A) He once flew a supersonic plane.
    (B) Pack plain and simple clothes for traveling.
    (C) It's top speed is five hundred miles an hour.

24. Who's in charge of the office while you're away?
    (A) My secretary will be away all week.
    (B) We're closing until I return.
    (C) You weren't charged for the first visit.

25. Can I use these batteries in this flashlight?
    (A) There are very few gas lights left.
    (B) I'd rather use the fluorescent light.
    (C) Yes, but you'll need four of them.

26. Can you establish how many potential readers we'll have?
    (A) Yes, we'll be doing marketing surveys.
    (B) I only read magazines.
    (C) They set up twenty-five book stores.

27. How many cars do you think are on that train?
    (A) I think trains are faster.
    (B) There must be twenty of them.
    (C) We have two cars.

28. You'll call when you get there, won't you?
    (A) They don't know what to call the new perfume.
    (B) As soon as I walk in the door.
    (C) Yes, it's all for your hair.

29. When will we open our office in Seoul?
    (A) By the end of the month, I hope.
    (B) We'll have a few openings next week.
    (C) She'll be the sole proprietor.

30. What did you think of the opera?
    (A) I couldn't find the operating room.
    (B) I liked the set and the costumes.
    (C) If only she would cooperate.

31. Why did you change your mind?
    (A) They didn't mind at all.
    (B) These changes aren't mine.
    (C) I haven't.

32. This is the summary report, isn't it?
    (A) Let's ask Mary, she'll know.
    (B) It should have been reported.
    (C) We enjoyed the summer breeze.

33. Is this auction open to the general public?
    (A) These are your functions.
    (B) On the weekends it is.
    (C) The public's welfare comes first.

34. Haven't you put an ad in the paper yet?
    (A) I will, first thing in the morning.
    (B) I can add these numbers for you.
    (C) I'll put a pad of paper on your desk.

35. Why did you choose to sell real estate?
    (A) I'm selling the estate.
    (B) It's more lucrative.
    (C) You're so choosy.

36. She mailed it express, didn't she?
    (A) I would like to express my sympathy.
    (B) She said she would press them.
    (C) Let me call and ask her.

37. Can't you call ahead to warn them?
    (A) I don't have their number with me.
    (B) It's warmer up there.
    (C) We're almost ahead of them.

38. Have you put a bid in on the project?
    (A) I put a bib on him.
    (B) Mine was the first one they received.
    (C) I never objected to their plan.

39. You'll come to the anniversary celebration, won't you?
    (A) They came late again.
    (B) It was no later than 2:15.
    (C) Of course I will.

40. Do you sell laboratory equipment?
    (A) We used to, but only wholesale.
    (B) The lab is in the cellar.
    (C) There's a lavatory downstairs.

41. What accounts for this high electric bill?
    (A) I can't jump that high.
    (B) These accounts need to be updated.
    (C) It was probably the air-conditioners.

42. You were nearly at a standstill, weren't you?
    (A) Yes, and then Bill came up with a solution.
    (B) No, we didn't have to stand still.
    (C) I almost did a handstand.

43. How will I explain this to my boss?
    (A) Her boss explained it well.
    (B) The plain design is better.
    (C) Just tell him the truth.

44. How did they figure it out so quickly?
    (A) I learned how to figure skate.
    (B) They had the answer sheet.
    (C) He figured it would sell quickly.

45. Would you like to tour the plant with us?
    (A) Yes, and thank you for asking.
    (B) There are so many plants.
    (C) No, I'll pour it myself.

46. Why not ask the company's lawyer about this?
    (A) I'll do that this afternoon.
    (B) I don't like to do laundry.
    (C) I enjoyed your company.

47. Your boss hasn't arrived yet, has he?
    (A) My boss prefers to drive himself.
    (B) His plane doesn't land for another hour.
    (C) I'll get it at five o'clock.

48. Would a tax break be incentive enough?
    (A) If it was substantial, it would be.
    (B) He can be pretty insensitive.
    (C) I couldn't even break it with an ax.

49. How much notice will she need?
    (A) They put the notice up right away.
    (B) She never notices me.
    (C) A few hours will be enough.

50. What do you suggest we do with the extra income?
    (A) I'll let the guests come in.
    (B) I'd like to save it for a house.
    (C) I bought the extra soft tissues.

PART III

51.
Woman Could I have the bill, please?
Man   No, no. My meal was much bigger and you paid last time.
Woman Well, thank you. Then I'll get the tip.

52.
Woman A The new accountant wants to see last year's financial records.
Woman B And we boxed them up for storage just last week.
Woman A That's OK. He's only interested in a sample.

53.
Woman A Did you hear that Stefan was reprimanded by the boss today?
Woman B Yes, he's been calling in sick when he's actually down at the beach.
Woman A He should be careful or he'll find himself looking for a new job.

54.
Woman I'd like to have all the offices and the cafeteria recarpeted. How long would that take?
Man   We'll be able to do it over the weekend if we can start by Friday at one.
Woman Excellent. I can manage that for you and I'll also have the rooms cleared out.

55.
Woman I don't like wearing all this safety equipment.
Man   I don't either, but it does protect our lungs from the poisonous vapors.
Woman You're right. I just wish it were more comfortable.

56.
Woman Are there any other requirements for this position?
Man   Yes, you have to be bilingual.
Woman Well, I can speak Spanish and a little bit of French.

57.
Man   I'll have two weeks vacation next winter. Do you have any special package tours?
Woman Do you prefer relaxing in the sun or being active?
Man   I'd like a resort where I can go swimming.

58.
Man   Good morning, Mrs. Bailey. Did you enjoy yourself last night?
Woman Yes, but could you help me? Would you call the police? My car has been stolen.
Man   Of course, right away! How terrible!

59.
Man   I'm afraid we've run out of time for the next demonstration.
Woman We still don't have a final decision on which computers to buy.
Man   We can discuss it further when we meet again.

60.
Man   I have some extra funds that I would like to put into a savings account.
Woman Just a minute then and I'll give you a passbook.
Man   Thank you. I'll just look over this investment brochure.

61.
Man   My partner and I are looking for advice on foreign markets.
Woman Which ones, in particular, are you looking at?
Man   The Indonesian computer market. We need information on taxes, zoning laws, economic conditions ... things like that.

62.
Woman What time does the concert start, George?
Man   At seven. Why don't we call a taxi?
Woman Good idea. We won't have to find parking.

63.
Man   The red light on the fax machine is blinking again.
Woman Check the paper supply and the printer connection.
Man   The paper is fine, but the tray is in crooked.

64.

Man   I'm sorry but I can't check the inventory until the computer is back on line.

Woman   Could you call one of your branches and find out?

Man   Yes, I could. You wanted one of the black swivel chairs, right?

65.

Woman A   Have you seen the remodeling they did on the ladies rooms?

Woman B   Not yet. Are they modern or old-fashioned?

Woman A   Very modern. They have lots of glass and mirrors and recessed lighting.

66.

Man   Sonya, have you decided which projector is best for our office?

Woman   I've spoken with several sales people and I'm waiting for the last one to call me back.

Man   Maybe you can try him again. We've got an important presentation in two weeks.

67.

Man   Maria, would you mind picking me up one of those new dictaphones while you're in Hong Kong?

Woman   Just give me the model number and make you want.

Man   I really appreciate it. Those devices save me a lot of time when I travel.

68.

Man   Let's discuss this further at next week's Friday meeting.

Woman   Unfortunately, I'll be leaving for London Thursday afternoon.

Man   Well, maybe we can talk that morning over breakfast.

69.

Man   Could you tell me where the lightweight suits are, please?

Woman   Yes, down the middle aisle. Casuals are on your left and formals on your right.

Man   Thank you. I'll need something for the office.

70.

Man   Do you think you could check the toner and the collator on the upstairs machine, too, Ms. Carreras?

Woman   Let me see what I can do.

Man   Thanks, we're having a marketing seminar and everyone needs copies of the course booklet.

71.

Woman   Would you know where I can buy Japanese newspapers?

Man   Yes, as you leave the baggage claim area you will see an international newsstand on your left.

Woman   Thank you. Maybe I can also get a copy of the Korean Sun.

72.

Man   Rita, our office is forming a bowling league. Are you interested?

Woman   I am, but I'm not a good bowler.

Man   That's not a problem. We just want to have fun, not win a trophy.

73.

Man   How did you know how to fix the program?

Woman   I have the same software on my computer at home.

Man   That's impressive. No one has been able to figure it out all day.

74.

Man   I read yesterday that Lubricants, Incorporated, donated $50,000 to the state's Environmental Clean-Up Fund.

Woman   They also have a state-of-the-art waste disposal system.

Man   It's good to see such a commitment to safeguarding the public.

75.

Woman   I'd like to take the five o'clock shuttle. Are there any seats left?

Man   That's our busiest flight, ma'am. Let me see what I can do.

Woman   I appreciate your help. I missed the last flight and now I'm late for a meeting.

76.

Man   Could we take an alternate route? It's rush hour and I have to be at the airport by ten.

Woman   I do this every day, sir. We're better off staying right where we are, the traffic gets lighter after this junction.

Man   I knew I should have set the alarm clock earlier.

77.

Man   Did you get a copy of the notice that the company is downsizing?

Woman   Yes, I sure hope our area won't be affected.

Man   My boss told me that only marketing and finance will be affected.

78.

Man   This is the perfect sofa for our living room, but it won't fit in the car.

Woman   We can deliver it by the end of next week.

Man   Oh, actually we need it right away. We're having a large family reunion in a few days.

79.

Man   I need a new ink cartridge for my printer. Do you stock them?

Woman   Yes. Do you know what make you have?

Man   It's a Pentor 500 printer with a color option.

80.

Man   We're going to lose customers if this strike keeps up.

Woman   I know. Several have already canceled their orders.

Man   I'm meeting with a representative from Express Deliveries this afternoon.

PART IV

Questions 81 and 82 refer to the following report.

This is WPLA with today's weather. This afternoon will be partly cloudy with severe thunderstorms later tonight. Residents of Blair and Gorham Counties are being advised to keep travel to a minimum. Local residents have called in with reports of street flooding and baseball-size hail. We will keep you posted on any changes. Stay tuned to 98.5 for the latest reports.

Questions 83 and 84 refer to the following message.

Mr. Stokes, I'm sending a substitute driver to take you and the company president to the airport this morning. John's wife was rushed to the delivery room over the weekend. All is well, though, and he should be back to work by the end of the week.

Questions 85 and 86 refer to the following recorded announcement.

This is a recorded message from Crown Movies located next to Bernstein and Company in the North Star Shopping Center. Our feature today in Theater 1 and Theater 2 is *Left and Right. Gemstones for Sale* is playing in Theater 3. Playing times are 4:30, 7:30 and 10:30. Adult tickets are $8.00 and children under 12 are $3.00. Thank you for calling Crown Movies.

Questions 87 through 89 refer to the following speech.

Today we are going to re-affirm the importance of safeguarding our national treasures by dedicating our country to restoring our river heritage. Our lawmakers are reviewing a proposal which will provide financial assistance for cleaning up our entire river system. It will help local people apply for protection for their rivers. I am told that some western lawmakers are against this idea, fearing it will give the government greater say on the use of private land. They will see, however, when they study the proposed law carefully, that this very point has received considerable attention.

Questions 90 through 92 refer to the following study.

The ability to have children in the fifth decade may be a marker for slow aging and the subsequent ability to achieve extreme longevity. Researchers at the Mongolian Medical School in Beijing studied records of two groups of women born in 1896. Many women in one group were still alive at the age of 100 while most women in the other group died in their seventies. Women who lived to be at least 100 were four times more likely to have had children in their forties than women who survived only to the age of 73.

Questions 93 through 95 refer to the following news report.

A survey released yesterday by *Investor's Choice* magazine found that despite the healthiest economy in decades, Europeans are extremely worried about their money, especially since their wages have not been keeping pace with inflation. Jules Brandsen, Senior Vice President of Munich Publishing, which conducted the survey for the June issue of *Investor's Choice*, said this: "Although people are confident about how the economy is doing and how they are doing personally, their optimism is guarded." Why? Rising stress, unhappiness with corporate downsizing, concerns about financial privacy, and a growing feeling that taxes are not being put to good use.

Questions 96 and 97 refer to the following announcement.

For many years, drinking has been allowed on the premises of the fairgrounds. However, because of several very unfortunate incidents in the last two years, the park management, in cooperation with local authorities, has decided to serve only non-alcoholic beverages in the restaurant and at beverage stands throughout the park this year. It will also be unlawful to bring any alcohol into the fairgrounds. The Restaurant Association of Blooming County would like to remind you of the many fine dining and entertainment establishments outside the park.

Questions 98 through 100 refer to the following announcement.

Good morning and welcome to Margroves. Although you all know which department to go to, I'd like to go over our scheduling before you meet your department heads. We have flextime here. That means that you decide when you start and finish your work day. However, everyone must be here during the ten to three o'clock period. Your minimum work time should be thirty-seven hours a week with a maximum of forty-one. At the end of any month, your overtime can't be more than ten hours. If you have any questions, please see your department head. Thank you.

Answer Key

Answer Key

Practice Test One

In the following Answer Key, the first explanation provided for each question is the correct option.

PART I

1. (C) The picture shows the *exhibit hall* of a trade show *open* for business. (A) *Customers* and *order* are associated with a trade show; *standing* could be confused with the noun *stand* which means booth, or stall. (B) *Displays* and *wares* are associated with a trade show, but there is no *chef* in the picture. (D) This option confuses the sounds of *trade's low* with *trade show*.

2. (B) The chef is *carrying a tray of food* with his left hand. (A) The man is smiling as if he is *greeting* someone, but the dinner guests are *already* seated at their tables. (C) *Cooking* and *kitchen* are associated with a chef, but he is in the *dining room*, not the *kitchen*. (D) *Lunch* is associated with food, but this is a *restaurant*, not a *shop*.

3. (A) People have removed their *shoes* and left them *on the steps*. (B) *Boots* are a type of footwear, but there are no *cowboys* in the picture. (C) People have *already* taken off their shoes, the picture does not show them doing this. (D) The word *feet* is associated with shoes, but not in this context, where it is a measurement.

4. (D) A man is writing something at the desk of a hotel while the front desk clerk watches. He could be a *guest* who is *registering at the hotel*. (A) The *flowers* are on the reception desk, they are not *lining a walk*. (B) The clerk is *attending to a guest*, not *taking a break*. (C) The clerk is *wearing* a tuxedo, nobody is *altering* it.

5. (A) The man, probably a tour guide, is *using a microphone* to address his audience. (B) The man is *talking*, but not on a *cell phone*. (C) The man is *wearing* sunglasses; they may or may not be *new*. He is not *buying* them. (D) The man is gesturing with his right hand and holding the microphone with his other hand, so he is not putting them *in his pockets*.

6. (C) The three people are *examining*, or looking closely at what the man is holding in his hand. (A) The woman's hair is long, but they are not *cutting* it. (B) The poster indicates space travel, but they are not *launching a spacecraft*. (D) Nobody is wrapping anything.

7. (D) There are not many, or *few people* sitting *in the room*. (A) There are a lot of *chairs*, but *most* are not *occupied*. (B) The plants in the room could be tropical, but this room is not a *jungle*. (C) There are lamps on *some*, but not *every* table.

8. (B) The food service employees wear *protective caps* to keep their hair from falling in the food. (A) *Lids* are stacked in the picture, but *trays* are not. (C) There is a *conveyor belt* that carries the food trays from one part of the kitchen to another, but there isn't one that carries *goods from the trucks*. (D) The glasses *may* be *washed by machine*, but that is not evident in this picture.

9. (A) The woman is shopping and is *choosing*, or selecting, items of *produce*. (B) The woman is not *polishing* anything. (C) There are *vegetables* in the picture, but the woman is not *growing* them. (D) *Weighing* is associated with shopping; the clerk will weigh the woman's produce before she buys it, but the woman is not *weighing herself*.

10. (A) The man is directing the listeners' attention to the projected material on the screen. He does seem to be *giving a presentation*. (B) A screen would suggest a *movie theatre*, but the room is not *dark*. (C) The *lecture room* is not *empty*, there are at least two listeners in the room that we can see. (D) The people are *sitting* in their chairs, not *standing* on them. They are probably not *students*, they are just listening to a lecture.

11. (C) The *largest* road sign, in the foreground, has an arrow pointing *to the left*. (A) One of the *signs* in the picture is not *for parking*, it directs traffic flow, so this option is incorrect. (B) The international symbol for available *parking* is on two signs, which means parking is *permitted*, not *forbidden*. (D) The words on the sign in the foreground are in *large letters*, but the sign is a traffic information sign, not an *advertisement*.

12. (B) Two people are sitting side-by-side *working at their computers*. (A) This option confuses the sound of *commuting* with *computing*. *Work* is an associated word. (C) They are working side-by-side, in a *line*, but they are *sitting*, not *standing*. (D) They are sharing space at a long desk, but they are not *sharing a meal*.

13. (B) The two uniformed women are *eating their lunch* from trays. (A) They are *wearing* uniforms, but they are not *changing* them. (C) They are *sitting* on the chairs, not *cleaning* them. (D) One woman is using *chopsticks* to pick food off the other's plate, but they are not *chopping sticks*.

14. (D) The man is *reading the paper* in the sun. (A) His head is *bowed* because he is reading, but he is not *taking a bow*, as a singer would at the end of a performance. (B) His *legs* are *crossed*, we cannot see both hands to talk about his *fingers*. (C) He's sitting or *resting*, on an *iron rail*, not *stairs*.

15. (C) The man is *washing his hands* under running water from the tap. (A) The words *scrubbing* and *sink* are both appropriate for the picture, but they do not describe the correct action. (B) The man is only washing his hands, not *taking a bath*. (D) There is no *plate* in the picture.

16. (A) The person in the back seat of the car is a *passenger*. He is *looking out the window*. (B) The person is in a car, he is not a *spectator* at a sporting event. (C) The person could be a *witness* to an event, but he is not *describing* anything. (D) A *bystander* is someone who watches an event, and the person in the car may be watching something. However, he is not walking. *Behind* is used to suggest the back of the car.

17. (B) One man, probably a *tour guide*, is *pointing* to something in the distance, a *feature* perhaps, and talking about it to those around him. (A) The people may be *tourists* and there is *laundry* hanging from some windows, but the tourists are not *hanging it out*. (C) There is no indication that this man is an *inspector*, nor is he *filling out* anything. (D) The people listening may or may not be *citizens* of the area, but there is no indication that they are *waiting to vote*.

18. (D) One woman in the picture is *standing* between her two seated colleagues. (A) The meeting is *in progress*, it is not *over*. (B) This option is incorrect because only two of them are *wearing glasses*. (C) We cannot see any *windows* in the room at all, so we do not know if they are *shut*.

19. (A) The two men are surrounded by scientific *instruments*, we can assume they are *scientists* who are *adjusting* them. (B) They could be *technicians,* but they are not *putting away* their lab coats, they are *wearing* them. (C) They could be *attendants,* but they are not *putting gas* in a *car*. (D) They could be *researchers*, but they are not opening the *window blinds*. These remain closed behind them.

20. (C) The *boats* are docked in the *harbor*. (A) They could be *tankers*, but they are not *at sea*. (B) They are *ships,* but they are not in *open waters*. (D) They could be *freighters,* but they are not *leaving the port*.

PART II

21. (A) According to what the speaker knows, the office *should* be open. (B) *Yes* may sound like a good answer to the question, but *I am* cannot refer to the office. (C) *Officer* sounds like *office*, but the question is not asking about a person.

22. (B) Computer *files* are often accessed with a given *code.* (A) *Accessories* sounds like *access*, but the meaning is different. (C) *Files* is repeated in both the question and the option. However, this option answers *where* not *how*.

23. (C) The package arrived at the exact time that it was needed. Remember, tag questions are not always answered with a direct *yes* or *no.* (A) *On time* contrasts with *late*, but the question does not ask about the *speaker's* timeliness. (B) *Package* and *luggage* have similar meanings, and *arrived* and *lost* sometimes have opposite meanings. However, this option does not answer the question.

24. (B) The answer indicates that the proposal *will* be finished because someone made such a promise. (A) In this option, *proposed* relates to a proposal of marriage. Therefore it does not answer the question. (C) *Finish* is repeated, but this response does not answer the question.

25. (B) This option correctly answers *where* the opera house is located. (A) This option answers *when* the opera begins. (C) *House* is repeated in both the question and the answer, but the question is referring to an *opera house*, not a personal residence.

26. (A) The respondent answers that they *would* think about *moving to Hawaii*, if the weather were different. (B) *Hawaiian* is used in the answer, and *moving* and *shipped* both describe transportation. However, this option does not answer the question. (C) *Move* is repeated, but the question asks about a person. *It* relates to an object.

27. (B) The person *hopes* that the *equipment works*. (A) *Work* is repeated, but this option answers *Where are you?* (C) *Equip* and *equipment*, and *work* and *workers* are related, but this option does not answer the question.

28. (A) The answer indicates that the person did not *know* they were supposed to hand-deliver the bill because they were not informed, or *told* to. (B) *Billed* is used in this option. Also, *deliver* and *delivery* are related. However, the answer is incorrect. (C) This option confuses *supposed to* and *supposes*, and *weren't* and *worst*.

29. (C) *Clerical* is an adjective referring to a position of *employment*. (A) *Lying down* is a physical position, but in this question *position* means *job*. (B) The question does not ask *how many* positions are being applied for.

30. (A) The highway department was notified by the respondent. (B) *Already* and *ready* sound similar, but the meaning and the context is different. (C) When you are on the highway, which way to go is an important thing to know, but the question does not ask about direction.

31. (C) On particular, or *certain* products, *every single device* is *inspected* by the respondent. (A) *Inspect* and *every* are used in both the question and the answer. However, the question is about *devices*, not *rooms*. (B) This option confuses the sounds of *device* and *devise*.

32. (B) *Minutes ago* answers *when* the ambassador left. (A) *Ambassadors* often work at *embassies*, and an *office* can be *closed*, but this is not an answer to the question. (C) *Office* is used in both the question and the answer, but the question asks *when* not *where*.

33. (A) They have not advertised in the newspaper *yet*, but they may in the future. (B) This option answers *when* the weekly newspaper is read. (C) *Weak* and *weekly* sound similar, and *advertise* and *sales* are often related. However, this option does not answer the question.

34. (B) The respondent gives his opinion of the *downtown area*. (A) The word *down* is in *downtown*, and a person can *drive* downtown. However, this option suggests a leisure activity and does not answer the question. (C) *Aerial* and *area* sound similar but their meanings different.

35. (C) The transcripts have been reviewed, or *checked*, but only for *typing errors*. (A) *Review* is used in both the question and the answer, but the question is not about a movie. (B) *Transcript* and *conscript* have the same root but different meanings.

36. (A) Whether or not there is *overtime* will influence the person's decision to help in the *other store*. Though you might expect a *yes / no* answer, the response is a question instead. (B) and (C) *Help* is used in both the question and the answers, but neither option is correct.

37. (B) The rate at the *credit union* is *less* than the rate of the *competition*. (A) *Charge* is repeated in the answer, but *we* does not relate to the question. (C) *Credit* is used in both the question and the answer, and you might associate *credit unions* with *accounts*. However, the context is incorrect.

38. (B) Commercial properties *are* sold, but only in certain areas. Watch for qualified answers like this on the TOEIC. They are common and they make the correct response harder to see than a simple, black-and-white answer. (A) *Private* is the opposite of *commercial*, and *property* is repeated, but this option does not answer the question. (C) *Sell* is repeated, but *selling wholesale* does not answer the question.

39. (B) A person who does not know *how* to use e-mail surely does not use it *often*. (A) *Mail* is used in both the question and the answer, but the answer relates to *other people*, not to the respondent. (C) This option confuses the rhyming sounds of *mail* and *nails*.

40. (A) The *front of the store* is suggested as a place to display the model. (B) *Display* and *play* sound similar, and *anywhere* is often an answer to *where?* However, this option does not answer the question. (C) This option confuses the sounds of *new* and *knew*. Also *place* might answer a question about location.

41. (C) *Across town* is the location of the stationery store. (A) *Stationery* and *stationary* sound alike but have different meanings. (B) *Store* is repeated in both the question and the answer, but in different contexts.

42. (C) *I didn't know* means no, the person was not familiar with the policy. (A) *Family* and *familiar* sound similar but have different meanings. (B) *Policy* and *police* sound similar but have different meanings.

43. (B) It *should be possible*, or doable, for the speaker to repair the item for *under $100*. (A) A *pair of socks* for one hundred dollars *would* be *expensive*, but the question is not about socks. (C) *Repair* and *fix* have the same meaning, and *hundred* is repeated. However, the question is not about quantity.

44. (A) *Any day* is an answer to *when* dividends are disbursed. (B) *Each day* is a possible answer to *when*, but this option does not answer the question. (C) Test takers who do not know the words *dividends* or *disbursed* may be attracted by yet another long word, *concentrate*.

45. (A) *At next week's meeting* answers *when* they expect to see each other. (B) In this option, *expecting* relates to having a baby. (C) *Later* could answer *when*, but this option confuses the sounds of *expect* and *inspect*.

46. (B) The election is still taking place, just at a later date. The question assumes inaccurate information; that the election has been *called off*. The response both corrects the question and answers it. (A) *Call* is used in both the question and the answer, but with different prepositions and therefore different meanings. (C) This option confuses the sounds of *election* and *selection*.

47. (C) The ferry *always* leaves at the right time. (A) A *ferry* is a type of boat, and *left* is used in both the question and the answer. However, this option does not answer the question. (B) *Time* is used in both the question and the answer, but the contexts are different.

48. (C) There is no reason *not* to hold the event in the *dining room*. (A) *Banquet* and *dining room* relate to *meals*, but this option does not answer the question. (B) The question does not ask the *cost* of the banquet.

49. (A) *Right*, or *just after* lunch is *when* the truck arrives. (B) *Arrive* is used in both the question and answer, but this option confuses the sounds of *truck* and *duck*. (C) *Truck* is used in both the question and the answer and *Wednesday* is an answer to *when*. However, the question does not relate to pay.

50. (B) The question implies that the new management has *already* taken over, so the answer must be in the past tense. (A) and (C) *Tomorrow morning* and *Later tonight* would answer the question *When will the new management take over?* If the new management had not *yet* taken over, we would expect the answer to clarify, for example *They haven't yet. They start tomorrow.*

PART III

51. (A) Because the woman is asking about the bus departure time, they must be at a *bus stop*. (B) There is no mention of a *train*, although trains also have *schedules*. (C) Because the conversation is about transportation and timeliness, you might think *car* is a good response. However, this answer is not correct. (D) The woman mentions their destination; a *game*, but they are not there yet.

52. (A) The man is looking for *foreign magazines*, which are *imported*. (B) *Two* and *back* are repeated in the dialog and the option, but in different contexts. (C) The magazines are *next to* the greeting cards, but the man does not *want* a greeting card. (D) *Foreign* is repeated in both the dialog and the option, and *car* sounds like *card*. However, the man is not buying a car.

53. (C) *Pull over* is the key to understanding that they're in a *car*. (A), (B) and (D) All of these options would be possible, in that each could logically have an *engine* and an *air conditioner*. However, only a car can be *pulled over*.

54. (D) The woman is surprised by Paul's ability to read *blueprints*. (A) The woman is *building a house* next year, but we do not know if Paul can do that. (B) Paul's parents had an *architectural company*, but Paul is probably not an *architect*, otherwise he would not explain his parents' business as the reason for his reading blueprints. (C) *Explain* is similar in meaning to *teach*, but there is no mention of Paul teaching.

55. (B) He is an *asset* because he *helps the staff* and the level of sick leave has gone down. (A) *Sick* is used in the dialog, but not in relation to the new employee. (C) The possibility of the employer *becoming* manager is mentioned, but we are not told if he knows the existing *manager*. (D) *Calls* are mentioned in the dialog, but it is not said that the employee does not return phone calls.

56. (B) *Room Service*, *up to your room* and *check out* are indicators of a *hotel*. (A) *Check out* could be confused with *check in* which, with *catch our plane*, are words associated with an airport. (C) *Room* could refer to an *office*, but not in this context. (D) *Breakfast* and *kitchen* are associated with food and could therefore suggest they are in a restaurant. However, this is not the correct answer.

57. (B) *Blueprints* are tools of an *architect*, or designer. (A), (C) and (D) There are words in the dialog which might suggest one of these options is the right answer. However, none of them is correct. (A) *Client* and *fax* are often associated with an *office*. (C) *Lunch* is associated with *caterers*. (D) *Blueprint* and *printer* have the same stem.

58. (A) Sam stayed at the beach, and therefore in the sun, longer than he expected to because he *ran into*, or met, *friends*. (B) *Friends* is repeated in both the dialog and question. However, the dialog says nothing about *playing sports*. (C) The *beach* is mentioned in both the question and the answer, but the information that Sam *tripped*, or fell, is not given. (D) *Ran into* is used in both the question and the answer, but with different meanings.

59. (D) The man thinks that Nancy left the *key* on the *filing cabinet*. (A) The key is *to* the *closet*, but it is not in the closet now. (B) The woman would like it *returned* to the *key rack*, or holder, but it is not there now. (C) *Next to* and *beside* have the same meaning. However, a *water cooler* is not the same as a *water fountain*.

60. (C) The woman will *check* the *price list* to find out the price. (A) There is no mention of making any calls. (B) There is no mention of speaking to the *sales representative* directly. (D) The woman will *check* the *price list*, not the *invoice*.

61. (A) *Float* and *backstroke* are both associated with *swimming*. The activities in Options (B), (C), and (D) do not involve floating or backstroke.

62. (A) The woman's car was *broken into* while she was downtown. (B) *Parking* is asked about in the dialog, but it is not what upset Sue. (C) The woman was *downtown* at the time, but there is no mention of an *accident*. (D) *Parking tickets* are mentioned in the dialog, not *concert tickets*.

63. (D) Jack needs the *inventory report* and that is why Emily is unable to go to lunch. (A) *Swordfish* is a kind of *fish*, but the context is a *restaurant*, not a *club*. (B) *Stan* may be going to *eat in a restaurant*, but *Emily* is not. (C) *Swordfish* is repeated in both the dialog and the option, but Emily is not going to *cook*.

64. (D) Last week's *mailing* used all the available labels. (A) There is no mention of this mistake being made. (B) A *supply office* and a *cabinet* serve similar functions, but are not the same. (C) *Marketing* is repeated, but no mention of a *clerk* is made in the dialog.

65. (B) The man is impressed by *Shundoor's rising stocks* and says he will call his *broker*. He implies that he may *invest* in Shundoor. (A) A new director was hired for Shundoor, but the man is not considering hiring anyone himself. (C) *Track record* is repeated in the option, but in the dialog it refers only to Shundoor's new director. (D) The man is going to *call* his *broker*, he is not thinking of *becoming a broker* himself.

66. (B) The two speakers are trying to decide if they should *go out for lunch* or *stay in*. (A) The speakers are not discussing this topic. (C) Both *time* and *delivery* are repeated in the dialog and the option, but the discussion is about what they *will* do. The answer cannot be in the past tense. (D) *Afford* is associated with *cost*, but in the dialog it refers to time.

67. (C) *Outside Manila* means the house could be located anywhere outside the city, even in a *distant province*. However, the adjective *just* limits the location to a *suburb*, a community located close to the city. When the TOEIC tests a detail, such as a location, a name, or a date, you will commonly hear that detail discussed at least twice. Here the location is discussed three times. (A) Living in the *city center* is mentioned as a hypothetical situation.
(B) *Downtown* is mentioned as the place Mr. Bendor does *not* want to have a house. (C) *Distant* is similar to *outside* a city, but the distance is qualified by *just*.

68. (C) Raul was using the *paper cutter*, when he cut and hurt himself. (A) *Kitchen* is used in both the dialog and the option, and a *knife* can be associated with a *cut*. However, this is not the correct answer. (B) There is no mention of Raul needing *help*. (D) *In too much of a rush* means *hurrying*, but there is no mention of Raul falling.

69. (D) A *high noise level* indicates a *noisy office*. (A) There is no reference to the state of the walls. *Wall-to-wall* refers to the carpeting that completely covers a floor. *Maintain* is repeated in the option, but in the dialog, it refers to the carpets. (B) The carpeting might be *installed* not *replaced*. (C) *Volume* is a word associated with sound level but it is incorrect in this context.

70. (A) The commercials *promote* the profession represented by the Society of Engineers, in other words, they seek to *increase interest in engineering*. (B) The sewer system is *discussed* in the commercials, but not, as far as we know, with the intention of exposing its condition. (C) *Municipal* is associated with *city*, but *bonds* are not mentioned. (D) *Bridges* and *tunnels* are mentioned in both the dialog and the option, but there is no mention of building new ones.

71. (B) A broken *air conditioner* would explain why it is *hot and humid*. (A) *Fax* and *e-mail* are both associated with *computers*, but there is no suggestion a computer is broken. (C) Sebastian *called the repairman* and *calling* is associated with *telephones*, but a telephone is not broken. (D) *Fax* is repeated in the dialog and the option, but there is no reason to believe the *fax machine* is no longer working.

72. (D) Only in a *train* can you find a *dining car two cars back*. (A), (B) and (C) There are words in the dialog which might suggest one of these options is the correct answer. However, none of them is correct. (A) *Dining* and *breakfast* are associated with *restaurants*. (B) *Car* has the same meaning as *automobile*. (C) Addressing someone as *sir* has the formality of a *hotel*.

73. (A) The man would like a *tour of the islands*. (B) The man wants a *guided tour*, not a *guide book*. (C) *Boat* is repeated in the dialog and the option, but the man wants a *tour* not just a *ride*. (D) *Six* is mentioned in the dialog in reference to the number of people in the man's group. The man is told to *sign up*. There is no reference to any *signs*.

74. (B) The man wants to see *where* the conveyor belt is. (A) The design is of a *warehouse*, and *size* is often associated with *design*. However, the man does not express interest in size. (C) A *service elevator* is mentioned, but only in relation to the location of the conveyor belt. (D) An *inventory* is associated with a warehouse, but one is not mentioned in the dialog.

75. (D) The *express train* is the *fast train,* and the woman is concerned with time. (A) The man tells her the time of the express train, but she does not request a *timetable*. (B) *Earlier* relates to time. The sound of *train* is repeated with *training*. However, the topic is different. (C) The woman wants the express *train*. There is no mention of an express *postal service*.

76. (A) Jerry is trying to fix the *copy machine*, so we know that he's a *copier technician*. (B) *Sales* is repeated in both the question and the option, but this is not Jerry's job. (C) There is no mention of moving. (D) *Seminars* are often associated with *lectures*, but Jerry is not a *lecturer*.

77. (A) Bart needs to have the report *completed* by five o'clock. (B) The chairman requires the *report*, not an *inspection*. (C) It is Judith who will help *Bart*. (D) In the dialog, five refers to time.

78. (C) The woman thinks that flying is faster and not much more expensive. Therefore, she is implying it is *better* than going by train. (A) *Reading* is mentioned by the man. It is not suggested by the woman. (B) *Faster* and *rush* both refer to time, but *take his time* means *not* rushing and the woman does not suggest this. (D) The reference to cost in the dialog only concerns the price of flights.

79. (C) The prices were adjusted *three times* before winning the bid. *Adjust* means *change*. (A) This option confuses the sounds of *won* and *one*. (B) In the dialog, *two* refers to the number of restaurants on the site. (D) This option confuses the sounds of *for* and *four*.

80. (B) *Fax paper* and *stationery* are found at an *office supply store*. (A) *Rolls* are associated with a *bakery*, but in this dialog the man is referring to *rolls of fax paper*. (C) A *floral design* on the stationery is desired, and *delivery* is often associated with flowers, but the speaker is not a *floral designer*. (D) *Bookstores* often sell stationery, but it is unlikely that such large orders would be placed with one.

PART IV

81. (D) The announcement is for people who want to *earn money from the stock market*, that is, *potential investors*. (A) *College* is only mentioned as a major expense. Students are not specified as the targeted audience. (B) *Factory workers* are people who work for a living. However, they are not mentioned in particular as the targeted audience. (C) *Unemployed* people are not mentioned in the passage.

82. (B) *Workshop* and *course* are synonymous. (A) *College* is mentioned, and the intention of the workshop is to *give advice*. However, the advice is not on colleges. (C) *Capital* is mentioned in the announcement, but none is being offered. (D) Some of the terms could relate to *real estate*, such as *money* and *capital*. However, real estate is not being offered.

83. (D) The announcement claims that you can *earn money from the stock market*. (A) *Early retirement* is mentioned as a life expense, but not as a guarantee of the workshop. (B) *Work independently* is similar in meaning to *become an independent contractor*, but this is not what is being claimed. (C) Again, *independent* is repeated in this option, but there is no claim of *financial independence*.

84. (C) A *postage meter* automates mailings. (A) *Sharp Penny* makes the postage meter, but there is no complaint being made in this report. (B) *Mail* can relate to *stationery*, but a *stationery order* is not the topic. (D) *Volume, expense* and *rental* are all words that could be associated with *reserve*, and some mail machines do have *reserve accounts*. However, this is not the topic.

85. (A) An *office manager* would normally have access to costs and mail volume, make purchasing decisions, and consider training time. (B) A *mail clerk* does not generally make decisions and would not be concerned with training the office workers to use the machine. (C) A *Sharp Penny salesperson* should not need to defend the price of acquiring a *Sharp Penny postage meter*. (D) *Office clerks*, or workers, are mentioned as the ones who need to be taught how to use the machines.

86. (B) Maintenance is included in the list of what is *free of charge*. (A) The report does not say that *training* is free. (C) *Month* and *rental* are repeated in both the report and the options, but there is no mention of any free rental costs. (D) *Month* is repeated in the report and option, but there is no mention of *stationery supply*.

87. (D) The speaker refers to Stanley's new book, *Piloting the Rich and Famous*. (A) Stanley is the *vice president of marketing* at the *Follenworth Company*. We do not know if he is a *shareholder*. (B) Stanley's personality traits are not discussed. (C) There is no mention of anything associated with *door-to-door sales*.

88. (C) At the end of the introduction, the speaker announces that later they will be discussing *airport safety management*. (A) A book is mentioned in the dialog, but this introduction is not a sales pitch for potential buyers. (B) Although Stanley himself is a *vice president*, he is addressing airport staff. (D) Stanley is the vice president of *marketing*, but there is no indication that he is addressing the *marketing staff*.

89. (C) The notice informs *bicyclists* how to use buses to transport their bikes, so bicyclists are the audience for the notice. (A) *Bike* is repeated in both the notice and the option, however there is no mention of manufacturers. (B) *Buses* and *bikes* relate to *transportation*. However, it is more likely that transportation authorities *wrote* this letter, than that they would *read* it. (D) This notice is aimed at *bike riders*, not *bus drivers*.

90. (B) The notice is announcing the new system that allows bus riders to transport their bikes on board the bus. (A) While the new program does *promote healthier lifestyles*, promoting healthy lifestyles is not the purpose of the notice. (C) The notice makes no effort to *sell* bikes. (D) Buses have *schedules*, but this notice does not mention a *new* schedule.

91. (D) The notice specifically says that for safety reasons, the operator's help is mostly limited to *answering questions*. Options (A), (B) and (C) would be helpful, but the driver cannot do anything that would require *leaving his seat*.

92. (D) The story says that Myanmar has been admitted to the *ASEAN*. (A) The European Union, (B) the *U.S.*, and (C) the *opponents of the SLORC party*, are all groups that *opposed* the admission.

93. (D) The U.S. and the European Union were in *opposition* to the admittance. (A) The tone of the story is somewhat *enthusiastic*, but the U.S. and the European Union were *not* enthusiastic. (B) Being admitted to ASEAN implies *approval* from some source, but that source was specifically *not* the U.S. or the European Union. (C) There is no suggestion the admittance was accepted with *resignation*.

94. (B) Myanmar Shipyards will *build two freight vessels*. *Freight vessel* and *cargo ship* are synonymous. (A) *Singapore* is mentioned in both the story and the option, but there is no mention of Myanmar Shipyards being an administrator. (C) Jaya Marine Lines International is repeated in both the story and the option, but there is no mention of *inspecting* them. (D) While Myanmar Shipyards *has* successfully negotiated contracts, nobody has hired them to do this.

95. (A) A *car manufacturer* would be in the best position to praise growth and management of an overseas manufacturer. (B) A *construction foreman* may work at a car factory or dealership, but would be unlikely to quote sales statistics or judge management. (C) The speaker went *on tour*, but the speaker is not a *tour guide*. (D) A *safety inspector* may work at a car factory or dealership, but would be unlikely to make the points made.

96. (C) The talk focuses on *business in Brazil*. First, the speaker thanks all who participated in that market. Then, he quotes sales statistics from Brazil. Finally, he praises the general manager in Brazil. (A) *Venezuela* is mentioned, but the speaker does not say it needs more attention. (B) *Four-doors* and *mini-vans* are mentioned in the talk, but they are not the focus of the message. (D) Brazil and Venezuela are both in *South America*, and they both appear to have excellent markets. However, information focuses on Brazil.

97. (C) The speaker acknowledges Mr. Carreras's contribution in general. (A) *Personnel changes* are not specifically mentioned. (B) *New safety measures* are mentioned, but they are not described as *stricter*. (D) While Mr. Carreras is fairly new in Brazil, he is being acknowledged for his successful management. He is not simply being *introduced*.

98. (B) The advertisement offers *kits* for building a home. The kit includes *building materials* and, we can assume, as all kits do, *plans*. (A) A home is built on *real estate*, but real estate is not being advertised. (C) Many home owners *buy* insurance, but this advertisement is not *selling* insurance. (D) *Energy* is repeated in both the ad and the option, but *free conservation audits* are not being offered.

99. (B) The opening line of the advertisement touts the low-cost, or *affordability*, of the kit. The low price is then repeated later. (A) *Attractive* relates to *aesthetic value*, but this is not the focus. (C) The advertisement says that assembly is *easy*, but this point is not emphasized. (D) The kits are *color-coded*, but we do not know if there are really any *color options*.

100. (B) *Learn more* and *find out more* are synonymous. For this, the reader can order a *color video*. (A) There is no mention of *visiting Home Dome Builders*. (C) There is no mention of *viewing*, or visiting, other homes. (D) *Catalog* and *brochure* have similar meanings, but this advertisement does not mention a *free* brochure.

PART V

101. (D) The present perfect is needed after *would* in this conditional sentence. (A) *Stock up* is the simple form following *would*. (B) *Would* is needed to complete the sentence. (C) *Had stocked up* is the past perfect form.

102. (B) The participle form is needed after *spent*. (A) *To visit* is the infinitive form. (C) The *going* in *going visiting* is incorrect. (D) *Go to visit* is the base form plus the infinitive and is incorrect.

103. (B) The gerund form or a noun is used after *before*. (A) *Invested* is the past tense of the verb. (C) *Investment* is the wrong noun form of the word. (D) *I will invest* uses the future tense.

104. (B) *It goes without saying* is the correct idiom. (A) *Tell* is a synonym of *say*, but is not correct in this sentence. (C) *Repeating* is the wrong word choice. (D) *Regarding* has the wrong meaning for this context.

105. (A) *Anything* is the correct pronoun referring to a thing. (B) *Anyone* is a pronoun referring to a person, and a person cannot be signed. (C) *Another* refers to a different contract, but there is only one contract. (D) *Anyway* is an adverb.

106. (B) *For a long time* is the correct prepositional phrase. (A) *At a fast pace* is illogical if the inflation rate is low. (C) The sentence says that the rate continues, and *in a decline* indicates a change. (D) *Throughout* needs to be followed by a noun.

107. (B) *By the doctor* indicates the passive voice, in the singular to agree with the subject *the patient*. (A) *Were* is the past plural form. (C) *Has* is missing the verb form *been*. (D) *Have been* is the plural form of the present perfect.

108. (C) *Them* is the correct pronoun for the plural noun *Argentineans*. (A) *They* is the subject not the object pronoun. (B) *Ourselves* is the first person plural reflexive pronoun. (D) *We* is the plural subject pronoun.

109. (C) *Booking* means reserving tickets. (A) *Buying* would need to be followed by the object, *tickets*. (B) *Postponing* means *putting off* or *delaying*, which is illogical. (D) *Canceling* means *stopping* or *calling off*, which is illogical.

110. (B) *Devastating* is the participle form used as an adjective. (A) *Devastate* is the base form of the verb. (C) *Devastated* is the past tense form. (D) *Devastation* is the noun form.

111. (A) *Expanding* is used as an adjective. (B) *Expend* is the base verb form and it means *to use up*. (C) *Expanse* is a noun. (D) *Expended* could be used as an adjective; however the meaning is incorrect.

112. (D) A phrase following *about to* will be in the simple past tense. (A) *Was winning* is the past progressive form. (B) *Will win* uses the future tense. (C) *Had won* is the past perfect.

113. (C) *Supplement* means *to add to*. (A) *Implement* means *to start*. (B) *Compliment* means *to say something nice to someone*. (D) *Compartment* is a noun.

114. (D) A relative pronoun introduces a clause. (A) and (C) *Of* and *for* are used to introduce prepositional phrases. (B) If *what* was used as the relative pronoun it would replace *the effect*.

115. (B) The sentence needs a conjunction which indicates a period of time. (A) *During* is a preposition. (C) *Only* is an adverb. (D) *Meanwhile* is an adverb.

116. (D) *Or* follows *either*. (A) *And* is a conjunction used for similar clauses. (B) *But* is a conjunction showing contradiction. (C) *Nor* follows *neither*.

117. (A) The past participle form is used in the passive voice. (D) *Demolishing* is the participle form. (C) *Demolish* is the base form of the verb. (B) *Demolishes* is the simple present, third person singular form.

118. (C) *More or less* is the correct idiomatic phrase. (A) *Much or little* is not a correct expression. (B) *Here or there* refers to place and not time. (D) *To or from* indicates movement.

119. (B) The future tense is required here. (A) and (D) *Have been transferred* and *will be transferred* are in the passive voice. (C) The auxiliary verb *to be* is missing.

120. (B) The clause indicates some future action. (A) The future perfect needs to have another action: *will have shipped it by the time ...* . (C) *Shipped* is the past tense. (D) *Shipping* is the progressive form.

121. (C) The candidate with the most votes wins. (A) *Preferences* means *choices*. (B) *Wishes* means *desires*. (D) *Choices* means *options*.

122. (D) *Than* indicates that a comparative, *wealthier*, is needed. (A) *Wealth* is the ordinary noun form. (B) *Wealthy* is an adjective. (C) *Wealthily* is an adverb.

123. (D) *Of* is the correct preposition to complete the expression. (A), (B) and (C) *To, for* and *by* are incorrect prepositions.

124. (C) *Good management* is singular and takes the simple present, third person singular form. (A) *Will be listened* is the passive form and would require the phrase *by the employees*. (B) *Are listening* is the plural, progressive form. (D) *Listens* is the plural, simple present form.

125. (B) *By means of* means *with the help of*. (A) *Mean* is the verb form, or a noun form with a different meaning (= *average*). (C) *Meant* is the past tense form of the verb. (D) *Meanings* is a plural noun, referring to significance.

126. (D) *Formidable* means *large and difficult to accomplish*. (A) A *precise task* wouldn't necessarily require more staff. (B) and (C) *Superfluous* or *short tasks* definitely would not require additional help.

127. (C) *Per* is the preposition used for units of measurements. (A), (B) and (D) *For, in* and *at* are incorrect prepositions.

128. (D) An adjective is needed after the verb *to be*. (A) *Respondent* is a noun. (B) *Responsive* is an adjective, but means *reacting quickly*. (C) *Responding* is the participle form.

129. (A) *By the time you arrive* indicates that some past time must be shown. (B), (C) and (D) *Shall run, will be running* and *will run* indicate future time.

130. (A) An adjective follows *we were; reluctant* collocates with the preposition *to*. (B) *Doubtful* is an adjective, but is usually followed by the preposition *about* or *of*. (C) *Refusing* is the progressive form of the verb. (D) *Hesitant* is possible, but implies fear of something.

131. (A) *Find out* means *to discover*. (B), (C) and (D) *Up, about* and *on* do not form phrasal verbs with *find*.

132. (D) *Front* is the noun which indicates location. (A) *Prominence* is a noun but cannot be used with the preposition *of*. (B) and (C) *Forward* and *ahead* are adverbs.

133. (B) *Than* indicates a comparison. (A) *Big* is the simple adjective form. (C) *More* is not preceded by the indefinite article. (D) *Most* is a superlative and is used with non-count or plural nouns.

134. (D) *Arrange* means *to set up*. (A) *Transact* means *to conduct*. (B) Nothing is being connected or *installed*. (C) A teleconference is not *performed*.

135. (A) *At* is used to indicate position when a precise point in time is referred to. (B) *About* is used to indicate an approximate position. (C) *Throughout* is used to indicate a period of time. (D) *Inside* is used to indicate a physical position, e.g. *inside the building*.

136. (B) *Inception* means *beginning*. (A) *Incentive* means *a type of reward*. (C) *Incision* means *a cut*. (D) *Incitement* means *being stirred up or excited*. None of these indicate a time.

137. (D) *Files* and *documents* are arranged by *category*. (A) *Covering* means *something that covers or hides*. (B) *Level* refers to positions. (C) *Rank* refers to people.

138. (C) *Pulled down* means *lowered*. (A) *Pulled* does not combine with *below*. (B) *Pulled off* means *removed*. (D) *Pulled up* is not logical.

139. (D) The correct gerund *pinpointing* means *to specify*. (A) *Sighting* is a noun meaning *the instance of somebody or something being seen*. (B) The gerund *focusing* needs the preposition *on*. (C) *Predicting* is not logical because the verb *fine-tune* indicates they knew exactly what the public liked.

140. (A) The plural, present progressive is used for a firm arrangement. (B) and (C) *Have been met* and *were met* indicate past time in the passive, yet the sentence indicates the future and is active. (D) *Will be met* is in the passive voice and would need the preposition *by*.

PART VI

141. (A) *Like* and not *as* is used in the comparison. (B) and (C) *Can* and *staple* are the correct forms of the verb. (D) *In half the time* is a prepositional phrase.

142. (C) *Pollution* is a non-count noun and does not form the plural with an *-s*. (A) *Taking measures* is the progressive form of the verb plus a plural noun. (B) *From* is the correct preposition. (D) *With each passing year* is a prepositional phrase indicating time.

143. (C) *Decided* is followed by *to* plus infinitive. (A) *After reviewing* is a correct adverbial phrase. (B) *We decided* is the correct subject and past tense verb. (D) *Except marketing* is a prepositional phrase.

144. (A) Barret is the lawyer for the defendant, who is a male. She is *his* attorney. (B) *Defended* is the past tense form. (C) *In* is the preposition describing how Mr. Stevenson was defended. (D) *Determined* is an adjective which collocates with *fashion*.

145. (A) *Make out* is the incorrect phrasal verb; it should be *make up*. (B) *Booked* is the simple past tense. (C) *Direct flight* is the correct form of the adjective and noun. (D) *To* is used as a preposition to show direction.

146. (D) The correct form of the adjective is *dramatic*. (A) *One evening* shows the correct time reference. (B) *Were entertained* is the plural, passive voice indicating past time. (C) *By* is the preposition used in the passive to show who performed the action.

147. (B) Two prepositions with similar meanings are used, while only one is necessary. (A) *Had to* is the simple past tense. (C) *For an hour* indicates the time period. (D) *Getting* is the correct gerund form used after *before*.

148. (C) The gerund *freezing* is needed to parallel *reversing*. (A) *Investors* is the noun form. (B) *Reversing* is the gerund which follows the preposition *by*. (D) While *money* is often used as a non-count noun, *monies* is the correct plural form in this sentence.

149. (A) *Any* can be used to mean *an unspecified number of*, but it is followed by a noun. In this case *any* could be replaced by *a lot* or *suddenly*. (B) *Going to continue* is the correct progressive form followed by an infinitive. (C) *We've been using* is the present perfect progressive. (D) *The very start* indicates the time frame.

150. (B) *They* has been omitted from this relative clause. (A) *After* is the correct preposition. (C) *Than* follows *much more*. (D) *Needed* is the correct simple past tense form.

151. (B) *Prefer* must be followed by a gerund or *to* plus infinitive, not by the bare infinitive. (A) *On* is the correct preposition to use with *vacation*. (C) *And* is a conjunction combining *sightseeing*, *lying*. (D) *On the beach* indicates location.

152. (C) *Any* and not *some* is the correct determiner to use with a negative verb. (A) *Shareholders* is the plural noun form. (B) *That* is the relative pronoun used to introduce a clause. (D) *Paid out* is the correct phrasal verb meaning *distributed*.

153. (A) The gerund *going* follows *before*. (B) *Always* is the correct adverb. (C) *To hire* is the correct infinitive form following *try*. (D) *In house* means *within the company or business*.

154. (C) The singular form *year* is used as an adjective. (A) *Structurally unsafe* describes the building. (B) *Too* is the correct quantifying adverb. (D) *Demolished* is the past participle used in the passive voice.

155. (A) The singular form of the verb *is advising* refers to the singular subject: *agency*. (B) *Carefully* is the correct adverb modifying the verb *read*. (C) *Using* is the correct gerund form following *before*. (D) *Outdoor* and *cooking* describe equipment.

156. (D) *Marriage* is a noun; in this case, the adjective *married* is necessary. (A) *Looked at* is the correct phrasal verb. (B) *File* is a synonym for *records*. (C) The adverb *still* is correctly positioned.

157. (C) The noun *sightings* is needed in this context. (A) *Feared* is the simple past tense. (B) *Might be* indicates possibility. (D) *In the last decade* is the correct prepositional phrase indicating time.

158. (A) *Standard Tires* in this case is the name of one company and therefore the verb should be the singular *has*. (B) *To fund* is the correct infinitive form. (C) and (D) *Research into* and *manufacture of* are noun forms plus prepositions.

159. (B) An *if*-clause in the past tense calls for *would*. (A) *If the zoning* is the beginning of a conditional sentence which refers to something unreal or unlikely. (C) *Down the street* indicates location. (D) *Redesign* is the infinitive form which parallels *to purchase* earlier in the sentence.

160. (B) The preposition *of* is needed to indicate possession: *many of its employees*. (A) *Factory* is the singular form of the subject. (C) *It* refers back to the singular noun *factory*; *had automated* is the past perfect tense. (D) *Many* is the determiner quantifying *operations*.

PART VII

161. (A) The purpose is to encourage *energy conservation*. (B) The offer is not *to help local contractors*, but the contractors might do the work. (C) *To help businesses with cash flow problems* is not mentioned. (D) *Low income home owners* might be eligible for the program, but there are many other eligible people.

162. (C) *Garage construction* is not mentioned and the announcement refers to *repair and remodel*, not new construction. (A) and (B) *Kitchen* and *windows* are both mentioned. (D) *Ceiling* is similar to *roofing* and could be included in *room conversions*.

163. (A) The company will send an invoice which indicates *the itemized account of goods*. (B) No *discounts* are mentioned. (C) There is no mention of *advertising*. (D) The $4.00 is a charge for shipping and handling, not a *rebate*.

164. (D) The agreement mentions *installments*. (A), (B) and (C) *Before getting the merchandise*, *upon delivery*, and *within one month* are not mentioned.

165. (D) *Pines* and *firs* are types of trees. (A) *Furs* refer to the skin or pelt of an animal. (B) *Inflation* is not mentioned. (C) The *prices* are for the trees, not for *gifts*.

166. (D) The report mentions *five to six foot range*, which is a measure of height. (A) *Thickness* is not mentioned. (B) Some of the trees' names include a *color*, but that does not affect the price. (C) *Proximity to market* is not mentioned.

167. (C) The report informs readers about *transplanted trees*. (A) *To encourage nature conservation* is not mentioned. (B) The increase mentioned concerns size and not *sales*. (D) *Prices* are mentioned, but not challenged.

168. (B) The notice says: *of Southampton, England*. (A) and (C) *Trinidad* and *Guyana* were mentioned as places where sales were made. (D) *Texas* is the location of a branch office.

169. (C) There is a branch office in Mexico *which provides service to customers in South America*. (A) There is a *joint venture* in Canada, not in Latin America. (B) *Where the pagers are produced* is not mentioned. (D) *Trains marketing personnel* is not mentioned.

170. (D) *Distributors*, mentioned in the notice, have the same function as *sales representatives*. (A) *Technicians* are not mentioned. (B) A contract was won from the Broadcasting Committee in China. (C) *Clerical personnel* is not mentioned.

171. (A) The last sentence mentions *light or heavy manufacturing*. (B) The airport is mentioned for transportation, but not *airline companies*. (C) and (D) *Water purification facilities* and *management consultants* are not mentioned.

172. (B) The advertisement states that expert assistance with *permits* is available. (A) The *airport* is only ten minutes away, but *transportation* is not provided. (C) *Drivers licenses* are not mentioned. (D) *Helping the staff to relocate to the area* is not mentioned.

173. (D) *Adequate water and power* are assured. (A) and (B) Neither *a skilled work force* nor *extensive market research* is mentioned. (C) *The port of Gizan* is mentioned, but not that *docking permits* are assured.

174. (C) *Our location is hard to beat: just ten minutes from* [the] ... *airport.* (A) *Warehousing* is not mentioned. (B) *Shipping and docking facilities* are not mentioned. (D) *Traffic* is not mentioned.

175. (A) People are bused to the Fairfield County Government Center. (B) and (D) Residents live in *Huntsville* and *Lawton*, but that is not where they are being bused to. (C) *The City Center Station* is the starting point.

176. (B) *Four* in the middle of the day are the extra trips made. (A) There are *two* additional trips at night. (C) *Six* additional round trips are being made per day. (D) There are now *eight* trips in total.

177. (D) *Rush hours* are peak hours. (A), (B) and (C) *In the late morning, in the afternoon* and *late at night* are not mentioned.

178. (B) $20,000 is closest to the down payment category of $19,000 which is for a home of *$145,000.* (A) A home of *$85,000* requires a down payment of $8,500. (C) A home of *$245,000* requires a down payment of $44,000. (D) A home of *$400,000* requires a down payment of $85,000.

179. (B) The chart shows monthly payments with the *variables* of different interest rates, down payments, and home costs. (A) *To sell homes* is not mentioned. (C) The chart doesn't indicate whether the *rates* are *low* or not. (D) *To encourage customers to switch banks* is not mentioned.

180. (C) *Home buyers* would be interested in the information. (A) There is no mention of *apartments*. (B) The information is for people buying, not selling homes. (D) *The International Revenue Service* is not mentioned.

181. (D) A *profit sharing plan* allows employees to share in company growth. (A) *Crystal* is not mentioned. (B) The wages that are offered are *competitive*, not *above-average*. (C) The equipment used is *the highest quality*, but there is no mention of it being *custom-made*.

182. (B) *Computer skills* are not mentioned. (A) *Office management* is listed under job duties. (C) *Interpersonal skills* are mentioned in the last line. (D) *Bookkeeping skills* are the same as *accounts payable* and *accounts receivable* which are mentioned under job duties.

183. (D) The text is a classified ad, therefore *an unemployed office worker* would be interested. (A) The *hotel chain that rents dining ware* might be interested in the company, but not in the ad. (B) *A senior advertising specialist* would not be interested in an ad for an office job. (C) A consumer magazine is mentioned, but the ad would not interest *critical consumers*.

184. (C) The first line in the second paragraph states that *EMFs could be dangerous to your health.* (A), (B) and (C) EMFs are found near radio stations, computer terminals and power lines, but they do not *interrupt radio transmissions, disrupt computer operations,* or *damage power lines*.

185. (A) Individuals should *identify the EMF problem clearly*, which is the same as *determine exactly what is occurring.* (B) *Power stations* are not mentioned. (C) *Blood pressure* is mentioned in reference to effects on Soviet workers. (D) *Turn off any computer equipment in the area* is not mentioned.

186. (B) The article says to make your demands known *to the Public Utilities Commission.* (A) *Atlantic Gas & Electric* is a company that detected EMFs. (C) Workers were found with health problems near the *Omsk Power Station.* (D) *Oakville Power Authority* is a company who were the focus of a campaign by concerned citizens.

187. (B) The article says that companies that plan to erect new lines should *prove there is a strong need.* (A) *Have the lines put up in isolated areas* is not mentioned. (C) Citizen groups have tried to attract the attention of the media. (D) *Have health surveys done of nearby residents* is not mentioned.

188. (B) The memo is directed to *the various sales people* who are mentioned at the top. (A) The sales people will notify *the office manager* about their car choice. (C) *Sales assistants* are mentioned, but the memo is not addressed to them. (D) *Automobile manufacturers* are not mentioned.

189. (A) The territories are to be turned over to the *sales assistants.* (B) and (D) Either *the office manager* or *the receptionist* will gather information about the cars. (C) *The accountant* is not mentioned.

190. (D) Sales meetings will be held *every other Monday.* (A) *Every day* is not mentioned. (B) *Every other Friday* is not mentioned. (C) Meetings used to be held *every Tuesday.*

191. The foot traffic is the greatest at the *enclosed mall* (D), followed by the *strip mall* (C), the *downtown location* (B) and finally the *hotel complex* (A).

192. (B) The foot traffic at the enclosed mall is *35%* more than the strip mall. (A) *5%* is not mentioned. (C) The foot traffic at the enclosed mall is *55%* more than the downtown location. (D) The foot traffic at the enclosed mall is *75%* more than the hotel complex.

193. (D) With more foot traffic, the enclosed mall store *should get more customers.* (A) *Parking* is not mentioned. (B) The *length* of the strip mall is not mentioned. (C) The *rent* at the enclosed mall is actually 30% higher than at the strip mall.

194. (A) *252,000 square feet of adjacent space is under lease.* (B) and (C) The property can be divided into two pieces: one of *300,000* square feet and the other of *450,000* square feet. (D) *750,000* square feet is the total site.

195. (D) The facility ... *is ideally suited for ... distribution.* (A) and (B) The tenants in the adjacent property are doing *research* and *development.* (C) *Heavy manufacturing* is mentioned, but not *light manufacturing.*

196. (A) The advertisement states that *subdivision ... is possible*; therefore the owner is willing to *sell a portion of it.* (B) and (C) Help can be provided but the owner will not *issue building permits* or *grant distribution licenses.* (D) The word *meet* appears; however there is no mention of *meeting with company representatives.*

197. (B) The first shopping center opened on the *outskirts,* or *at the edge of town.* (A) Faneuil Hall Market is *in the downtown area.* (C) and (D) *On a subway line* and *far from the city* are not mentioned.

198. (A) *Updating* is a synonym for *renovating.* (B) *Outlet malls* were the fastest growing type of mall in 1990. (C) Malls are moving from the suburbs to the city. (D) There has been a 70% decrease in growth, not a *70% loss of business.*

199. (A) Words like *salary* and *application* and a list of qualifications indicate that this announces a job to be filled. (B) The announcement is for an Open Test that is to take place. Results cannot be posted yet. (C) A police officer *finds criminals,* but that is not the purpose of the announcement. (D) There is a test mentioned in the qualifications, but the purpose is not *to announce testing for a job position.*

200. (C) *Illiterate people* are not qualified as there is a written test. (A) *People under 21* can apply if they will be 21 when they start. (B) The announcement mentions height, but *very tall people* are not necessarily disqualified. (D) Candidates must have *graduated* from high school, not *from college.*

Answer Key

Practice Test Two

In the following Answer Key, the first explanation provided for each question is the correct option.

PART I

1. (A) The *waiter* is *clearing away*, or removing, the glasses and dishes from the *table*. (B) A *meal* has been finished, but the man in the picture is not the *diner*, he is a waiter. (C) There is a coffee pot on the table, but the man is not necessarily a *cook* and he is not *drinking coffee*. (D) The man *could* be an *innkeeper*, somebody who manages an inn, but he is not *taking a reservation*.

2. (C) The man talking at the front of the room is presumably a *trainer* who is *explaining* how to use a *computer* application. (A) A computer *work station* consists of a keyboard and monitor. Only *one* of the work stations pictured is *empty*, there are people seated at the other two. (B) *Train* sounds similar to *trainer*, and train station could be confused with *computer work station*. (D) The *monitors* are on the table, they are not *attached to the wall*.

3. (B) The woman is *resting* her head on her hand, and her *elbow* on the *table*. (A) She is writing on a pad of *paper*, not the *wall*. (C) There are *flowers* on the table, but she is not actively *smelling* them. (D) There's a *cup* on the table, but she is not *filling* it.

4. (A) The *vendor* sits in his chair surrounded by the art he is *selling* on the street. (B) The man may be a *painter*, but he is not *painting*. (C) The man may be a *curator* in a museum, but he is not *installing* exhibits, or hanging pictures right now. (D) The man may be an *artist*, but he is not *sketching*, or drawing, a portrait of a *customer*.

5. (A) The door to the rail station shuttle bus is wide open. (B) This option confuses the sound of *floor* with *door*. The door is *wide open*, the floor is not *wide*. (C) The phrase *rail station* is written on the side of the bus. The bus *seems* empty, but we have no idea whether the *train station* is empty or not. (D) *Riders* and *fares* are words associated with bus travel, but nobody is *paying their fare* in this picture.

6. (C) The technician seems to be *adjusting the height* of some kind of scientific equipment, or apparatus. (A) He's *looking at* the apparatus, not *through some files*. (B) He is holding something that is *rectangular*. It is not a *ball*. (D) He's *staring*, or looking at the apparatus, not *out the window*.

7. (D) Two uniformed *police officers* are standing *by*, or beside, *their car*. (A) The police car is *parked*, but this is a public square not a *parking lot*. There is only one car in the square, it is not *full*. (B) This option is incorrect because there are no *trees* visible. There is only a bush in the foreground. (C) The police are *watching*, not *waxing*, their *patrol car*.

8. (B) A man is *getting*, or taking, a newspaper from the stand. (A) He is *standing* at the end of a crosswalk. He is not *crossing the street*. (C) He may be getting a newspaper, but he is not *broadcasting the news*. (D) The awning has the word *journal* on it, but the man is not *writing* in a journal, or diary.

9. (D) The woman is possibly a tour guide who is *holding a sign* for tourists. (A) The word *road* is on the sign, but she is not *looking at a road map*. (B) *Directions* is a word associated with *road*, but she is not *asking* anybody anything. (C) This option is incorrect because the verb *sign* is out of context here.

10. (B) The technician has opened the electrical box and appears to be *checking the wiring*. (A) This option is incorrect because you would get a *check up* from a doctor. (C) The wires *may* be loose, but he is not seen to be *tightening* them. He is looking at them. (D) He's *looking* at the wires, not *sending a wire*, or a cable.

11. (A) The two-lane road *winds*, or twists and turns, *through the mountains*. (B) The road is too large to be a *lane*. It is not *straight* or *narrow*. (C) There may be a *stream* by the road, but the road is too large to be a *path*. (D) There is no indication in the picture that this *highway* ends at the *seashore*.

12. (D) Both women, one standing, one seated, are *in front of the shelves*. (A) The women do not appear to be *on a break*, or resting, they seem to be *working*. (B) One woman is *wearing* a *coat*, or jacket, but nobody is *putting* anything on. (C) This option is incorrect because only *one* woman is *wearing a jacket*.

13. (B) The *patrons*, or customers, of this outdoor café are enjoying the sunshine. (A) *Coffee* is associated with outdoor cafés, but there is no sign of *coffee beans in bags* in the picture. (C) The *chairs* are all occupied, they are not *stacked against the wall*. (D) *Customers* are associated with cafés, and there is a *bird* in the picture, but nobody is *feeding* it.

14. (A) The painter is using a roller to apply *paint* to a *wall*. (B) *Mixing* is associated with painting, but he has *already* mixed the paint. (C) The *furniture* has *already* been removed from the room. (D) *Color* is associated with painting. *Coloring* also sounds like *covering* and the painter did cover the floor with a protective cloth. However, this option is incorrect.

15. (B) *Palm trees* and bushes grow alongside, or *border,* the brick path, or *walk.* (A) There are *steps* and *trees,* but a tree is not growing *out of the steps.* (C) The palm trees, or palm *ferns,* border the walkway, but they are not in a *pot.* (D) There is a *hill,* but *water* does not *run down* it.

16. (B) The woman *behind the counter* in a pastry shop is a *shopkeeper.* (A) The woman may or may not be a *baker,* but she is not putting *pastry in the oven.* (C) This option confuses the sound of *toll* with *roll* which is associated with this kind of shop, and there is no *driver* in the picture. (D) This option confuses the word *flower* with *flour* which is associated with pastry and cakes.

17. (D) The man is standing at the counter *signing* something with a pen; he could be *signing his name.* (A) He's *wearing* glasses, not *taking them off.* (B) This option uses the word *pen* in the context of an enclosure for animals, which is not relevant. (C) *Handing* could be confused with the word *hands* which are evident in the picture. Although he could have a pencil rather than a pen, there is no woman in the picture to hand something to.

18. (C) The man and woman are *shaking hands.* (A) This option is incorrect because *striking* is an aggressive form of physical contact and this is not apparant here. (B) Their hands are clasped together. They might be *exchanging greetings,* but there are no *cards* in sight. (D) They could be saying *good-bye* rather than greeting each other, but they are not *waving.*

19. (A) The *magazines* are *displayed* on the shelves of the shop. (B) *Journalists* write articles in newspapers and magazines after *interviewing* people, but there is no journalist in this picture. (C) There are no *books* in the picture. There are some *magazines,* but they are *on* the shelves, not *off* them. (D) This option confuses the sounds of *shells* and *shelves.*

20. (A) The four men are *discussing* something. (B) One man is *wearing* a tie, but there is no evidence to suggest they are *choosing* one. (C) This option is incorrect because one man has *already* rolled up his sleeves, and nobody else is doing so. (D) The bricks are *already* stacked up on the table, so this option is incorrect.

PART II

21. (C) *Did very well* describes the performance of the stock last year. (A) *Stock* is repeated, but this option does not answer the question. (B) *Perform* and *show* can have similar meanings, but in this case, the contexts are different.

22. (C) This answer affirms that the fuse box *was* checked. It also explains *when* it was checked; *this morning.* (A) *Yes* is often an answer to a tag question, and *box* is repeated, but in the question, they are talking about a *fuse box,* not a *mail box.* (B) *Check* is in the question and the option, but with different meanings.

23. (A) The respondent has been informed that interest rates can go *up to,* or as high as, *twenty percent.* (B) *Higher*

is used, but the option does not answer the question. (C) *Rate* is used in both the question and the option, and *very low* is a plausible answer to *how high?* However, subscription rates are not under discussion.

24. (B) The respondent is not certain, but *believes* that everyone in the office saw the memo. (A) *Saw* is the past tense of *see,* and *them all* could be associated with *everyone.* However, the answer does not relate to the memo. (C) *Offices* is repeated, but the question does not ask about *where* people have been.

25. (C) The sales are *not* doing well at all, they are *dropping,* or declining. (A) *Sales* and *selling* are related, but *houses* are not the topic. (B) This option confuses the sound of *sales* with both *sailing* and *Wales.*

26. (C) They *do* have *senior citizen discounts,* if there is *proof of age.* ID stands for *identification.* (A) *Yes* is a common answer to questions that ask *do you?* Also *senior* and *seniority* have the same root. However, this option does not answer the question. (B) *No* is a common answer to questions that ask *do you?* and *discounts* and *counter* have the same root. However, the context of this option is incorrect.

27. (B) *Several tons* answers *how much* cement is *needed,* or required. (A) *Needed* is used in both the question and the option, but *foundation* and *found* are confused. (C) *Cement* is repeated, but the question is not asking *what kind of* cement is needed.

28. (A) The plane does stop for a short time; *briefly.* (B) *Stop* is repeated, but the option confuses the sounds of *Dublin* and *islands.* (C) Again *stop* is repeated, but the option confuses the sounds of *plane* and *lane.*

29. (B) The speaker was at her sister's house *last night.* Rather than answering directly, the respondent gives additional information which *implies* the answer. (A) *No* is often an answer to a tag question. Also *house* is repeated. However, this option does not answer the question. (C) *Sister* is repeated, and *house* and *home* are similar. However, the question does not ask about the sister's *work.*

30. (A) The respondent would like to go to a museum which has *dinosaurs.* (B) The question is not about *how long* the respondent can stay. (C) *Kind* is repeated, but this option does not answer the question.

31. (C) The microphone could not be ordered because the speaker did not have a *part number.* (A) *Microphone* is confused with *microscope.* (B) *Microphone* and *phone* are confused because they have the same root.

32. (B) The respondent implies the *day shift* by giving the hours *nine to five.* (A) *No* is a common reply to questions that ask *do you?* but this option does not give the correct answer. (C) *Yes* is a common reply to questions that ask *do you?* but this option does not answer the question.

33. (A) The person does not know the answer and must go see, or *check*, if the printer is plugged in. (B) The question does not ask *how* the printer is working. (C) *Print* is repeated, but the question does not ask about *quality*.

34. (A) The role he played was that of *chief negotiator*. (B) This option confuses the words *role* and *roll*. (C) *Play* is repeated, but the question does not ask *how often* somebody does something.

35. (B) On her *time off*, the manager has gone to Hawaii. The speaker answers the question by giving additional information. (A) *Time* is used in both the question and the answer, but in different contexts. (C) *Get back* sounds like a reasonable response to *some time off*. However, this option does not answer the question.

36. (A) The need for *exposure*, or publicity, is why the media should be invited. (B) *Invited* is repeated, but this option confuses the sounds of *media* and *middle*. (C) *Let's go together* can be associated with *invited*. However, the answer does not relate to the media.

37. (C) The ad will *definitely* attract attention. (A) *Attract* is used in both the question and the answer, but what people *look like* is not the topic. (B) This option confuses the sound of *add to the tension* with *attract attention*.

38. (A) According to what the respondent knows, the contract *would* include the shipping department. (B) Words with the roots *ship* and *depart* are repeated. However, this option does not answer the question. (C) *Boat* is associated with *shipping*, but this option confuses the sound of *contact* with *contract*.

39. (C) According to what the respondent believes, they leave from gate five on concourse B. (A) *Leave* and *left* are from the same verb. However, the sounds of *gate* and *rate* are confused. (B) *Leave* and *gate* are both repeated, but the meanings are different.

40. (B) The answer is *no*, because the person has not been able to *reach*, or get in contact with, the chief engineer in order to speak with her. In many countries, it is assumed that the chief engineer will be a man. However, in this dialog, the chief engineer is obviously a woman *(her)*. Do not be misled by an unexpected gender. (A) This option confuses the words *spoken* and *spokes*, and *leak* and *weak. Spokes* can be found on the wheel of a bicycle. (C) *Leak* is repeated, and *engine* and *engineer* have the same root. However, the question is about the *person* not the *object*.

41. (A) The credit card is thought to be *at the house*. (B) *Overdrawn* and *credit card* relate to money. However, the question is about location. (C) The question does not ask *when* the speaker left the credit card.

42. (B) Miriam told the respondent the person was sacked, or *fired*. (A) *Fired* is repeated, but *fired up* means ready to do something. (C) *Mean* is repeated, but with a different meaning. Also this option confuses the sound of *tired* with *fired*.

43. (A) The ambassadors cannot still be in the building, because *they left an hour ago*. (B) *Ambassadors* and *embassies* are associated words that also sound alike. However, the question is not asking about the location of a building. (C) *Still* is used in both the question and the option, but with different meanings.

44. (B) The answer indicates that it is not usual, or *normal*, for reservations to be made so late, but the person will still try to make one. (A) This option confuses the sound of *fight* with *flight*. (C) *Reservations* is often associated with *restaurant tables*, and *reservations* and *reserved* have the same root. However, the topic is about reserving places on a *plane*.

45. (C) This option answers that she should take the blame because she was *responsible*. (A) *Take all* and *inheritance* can be associated. However, this option confuses the sound of *claim* with *blame*. (B) *Took* is the past tense of *take*, but the question is not answered correctly.

46. (B) Office equipment often requires a *code* to work. (A) The sound of *facts* is confused with *fax*. (C) *Fax* and *start* are both repeated, but the *cost* of fax machines is not the question.

47. (A) George thinks that no one *realises*, or *notices*, when he is late. (B) *Late* is repeated, *showing up* might be related to flowers *blooming*. However, gardens are not the topic. (C) *Late* and *show* is repeated, but the words have different meanings.

48. (C) The receptionist *should be* the person who is answering the phone. (A) *Answers* is repeated, but with a different meaning. In this case *answers* means *responds*. (B) *Phone* is repeated, but a person's *manner* is not asked about.

49. (B) *More than once* answers *how often?* (A) *Mechanic* is repeated, but the sounds of *repaired* and *pair* are confused. (C) *Two* might suggest an answer to *how often?* but the context is wrong.

50. (A) The respondent is *not* Roberto's *supervisor*, but rather a co-worker, or *colleague*. (B) *Supervisor* and *superintendent* both have the same root, but the option does not answer the question. (C) *Supervisor* and *visor* also share the same root, but the option does not answer the question.

PART III

51. (D) Manuel must *check with his secretary* to set the date. This implies he is not sure about his *schedule*. (A) Natalie *has* spoken to Manuel about the meeting and he has stated his preference. (B) *Friday* is the day when Manuel will confirm his schedule. (C) There is no reason to think that the secretary is out.

52. (B) The man thinks he may have left his phone in the restaurant. (A) He remembers *paying* the bill, because he thinks he might have left the phone at the *cash register*. (C) Receipts are given after you pay a bill, but the man does not *mention* a receipt. (D) He took the phone from the car, but there is no mention of his not locking the door.

53. (D) Both speakers agree that renting a *car* would be more interesting and fun than any of the other options. (A), (B) and (C) These options are all mentioned as possible ways to get to Tokyo, but the speakers prefer to rent a car.

54. (C) A *salesperson* in a store is commonly asked to help find a specific clothing item. (A) A *tailor* would have been helpful in *making* the suit. (B) *Wavy* can refer to hair, which might suggest she is talking to a *hair stylist*, but in this dialog it refers to the *pattern*. (D) *Design, pattern*, and *shade* can all be associated with *artists*, but this is not the correct option.

55. (D) The man is looking for a *street map* of the city of Hamburg. (A) This option confuses *hamburger* with *Hamburg*. (B) *Laminated* starts with the same letter as *lemonade*, but this is a distraction. (C) *Posters* are also often *laminated*, but in this case a map is being talked about.

56. (D) Although passengers *should* only take on *one* carry-on item, the woman is allowed to take on *both* of her bags if she stores them overhead. (A) *Fragile* is mentioned in the dialog as the reason she wants to carry both bags on, but we have no reason to believe she breaks anything. (B) *Seat* is associated with airplane travel, but we are not told she *changes* hers. (C) The woman does not want to check *either* of her carry-on bags, and the flight attendant allows her to take *both* on board.

57. (A) The orientation starts at eleven. It is inferred that this is *before* lunch because it is stated that there would be no time to fit in a tour between the end of the orientation and lunch. (B) There is no suggestion that eleven is considered *early morning*. (C) *Noon* is mentioned when the woman says she would like to take a tour *before noon*. (D) *After lunch* is not mentioned, but it is inferred that that is the only possible time for a tour.

58. (D) The man says the printer is not *user-friendly*. User-friendly means easy to use, so something that is *not* user friendly would be difficult to use. (A) The office *has* a new printer, so this is not his complaint. (B) *Friendly* does not refer to a *person*. (C) *Office equipment* is used in both the dialog and the option. *Broken down* office equipment is a common complaint in offices, but it is not mentioned in this dialog.

59. (A) They are looking for someone who is carrying a lot of *luggage*, so that person is *probably* a *traveler*. (B) A *lobby* is at the *entrance* of a building, but the speakers are *already* in the lobby as they speak. (C) The man will be *wearing a cap*, which is a type of *hat*, but the speakers are not shopping for anything. (D) *Narrow* is used in both the dialog and the option, but with different meanings.

60. (B) If the roads are *crowded*, it will take longer to get to the airport. The speakers want to leave soon for this reason. (A) When there is no traffic, the trip to the airport takes *twenty minutes*. (C) *Airports* and *planes* are associated, but there is no mention of *their* plane *arriving early*. (D) The woman does not say that she does not like driving.

61. (C) The entry of banks into the investment field is creating *competition* among brokers, so their *fees* can be expected to *drop*. (A) *International* is mentioned in the dialog, but not to explain the drop in brokerage fees. (B) There is no mention of new banks opening. (D) *Investment* is mentioned in the dialog, but not to explain the drop in brokerage fees.

62. (A) The man offers to *send a memo* about the teleconference. Sending a memo will inform everyone. (B) *Schedule* is used in both the dialog and the option, but no *rearranging* is being done. (C) *Three o'clock* is the time of the teleconference. (D) The man will send everyone a memo; he will not *call* them.

63. (B) The man is hoping to *use the audio-visual room* to see his *important clients*. (A) The man mentions clients in the dialog, but he does not discuss *calling* any of them. (C) *Schedule* is repeated in both the dialog and the option, but the man does not want to *change his own*. (D) *Check* is used in both the dialog and the option, but with different meanings.

64. (C) The speakers discuss going to *Rudy's Restaurant* to eat. (A) *Participating in a demonstration* is what the woman is supposed to do for her office. (B) The demonstration is for a *group* of bank managers. The speakers are not going to talk to just *one*. (D) *Rudy's* is the name of the restaurant.

65. (D) *Rolls of film* and *batteries* are associated with a *camera store*. (A) The man *will* be going on vacation, but he does not leave until next week. (B) *Film* is associated with *theater*, but in this dialog the man is referring to *camera film*. (C) *Particular make* might be associated with cars, or an *auto part*, but in this dialog it refers to the man's *camera*.

66. (B) The *electrician* will be working behind Joan's *desk*, so George has offered to share his office. (A) Joan and George will be working in the same room, but that does not mean that Joan is working *for* George. (C) An *office* is the location of this dialog, but there is no mention of *cutting back on office space*. (D) The electrician will be working *at the panel* in Joan's office, but he will not be *paneling the office*.

67. (C) The speakers imply that the new foreman's *personality* may be causing low morale, by saying that he is not very *friendly*. (A) *New boss* and *new foreman* may be referring to the same person, but there is no mention that he is not *productive*. (B) *Factory* is used in both the dialog and the option, but there is no mention of doing any work to it. (D) The foreman is described as *experienced*, not *inexperienced*.

68. (A) The man is trying to determine how much *traffic* there is on the nearby roads. (B) *Employed* is used in the dialog and *employment* in the option, but *employment rates* is not the topic. (C) *Heavily* may relate to *capacity*, and the number of employees may influence *elevator requirements*. However, elevators is not the topic in this dialog. (D) We might associate surveys about employees with *worker satisfaction*, but that is not the purpose of this survey.

69. (D) The woman says she will take the package to the post office when she goes at four. The implication is that she will *mail* it. (A) *Post office* is used in both the dialog and the option, but the woman is not intending to make a telephone call. (B) *Wait* is repeated in the option, but the woman wants to wait until a certain time before she goes, not *wait for the man*. (C) The woman will be *leaving* at four o'clock, not *returning*.

70. (A) By *cutting back on*, or reducing, the research budget, the company may not have new products that will help them keep ahead of the competition. They could lose money in the future which would, in the long run, be *costly*. (B) This option confuses the sound of *use* with *lose*. Their *competitive edge* was hard-earned, not *her money*. (C) At this time, *they* are ahead of *the competition*; they *have an edge* on the competition. (D) They will *lose* their *competitive edge*, not their *employees*.

71. (B) The woman enquires about the cost of *rentals*. She is seeking more space for corporate headquarters. (A) There is no mention of doing any work to the offices. (C) *Card* is repeated in both the dialog and the option, but the woman wants the man's *business card*, she is not *buying* any cards. (D) The woman says she would like to get back to the *man* (be in touch with), not get back to the *office* (return).

72. (A) *Commuters* refers to the people who take the ferry to work. Because the ferry is not working, these workers will not be able to *get to their jobs*. (B) *Commission* is used in both the dialog and the option, and *commissions* can be associated with *sales*. However, there is no mention of *sales agents*. (C) The service will be stopped for a month, but that does not mean it *needs* to be reduced. (D) Bill's amount of pay is mentioned in the dialog, but no *pay raise* is mentioned.

73. (C) Rosa thinks that *Karla* would know about the petty cash. (A) Rosa is *asked* about money, but she recommends asking Karla. (B) This option confuses the sound of *Betty* with *petty*. (D) Hans is *asking* about the money, so he does not know about it.

74. (C) The woman *raced*, or hurried, *across town* in order to be *on time* for the meeting. (A) There is no mention of the woman *finishing her work*. (B) *Race* is repeated in both the dialog and the option, but the meanings are different. (D) *Sharp* is used in the dialog to mean *exactly*. There is no mention of pencils.

75. (C) The woman suggests that it can be cool enough to require *warm clothing*. (A) There is no mention of *cancelling* anything. (B) *Sweden in the summer* is discussed in the dialog, but only to point out that it can still be cool. (D) *Friends* is repeated, but in the dialog, the woman is talking about what her friends *told* her. She is not suggesting the man go with any.

76. (C) The man tells the woman that her staff enjoys having her at the celebration, so she should *join them* at the party. (A) *Staff* is used in both the dialog and the option, but there is no mention of *firing* them. (B) *Finish* is associated with *deadline*, but the woman is talking about a *project* not a *meal*. (D) There is going to be a party, but the woman will not be planning it.

77. (D) The coffee maker is broken, so there is *no coffee*. (A) *Driver* is used in both the dialog and the option, but we are not told he is *absent*. (B) Mr. Sikarda is going to arrive, but his being *picked up* is not an issue. (C) There is no reason to think the president, who is meeting Mr. Sikarda, is late.

78. (B) People who are *praying* would most likely be found in a *religious building*. (A) *Photographs* can be associated with *news*, but the speakers are not in a *news store*. (C) There is no mention of an *immigration office*, although photos are often required to file immigration documents. (D) *Photographs* are associated with *travel*, but there is no indication that this is a *travel agency*.

79. (A) The man had forgotten the office was closed because of the holiday. (B) People might come later than usual because of a change in *schedule*, but that's not the case today. (C) There is no mention of a game. (D) *So late* could refer to time passing, but there is no mention of *how much* time has passed.

80. (B) The woman tells the man they have only been waiting *a half-hour*. (A) The man agrees to wait just *a few more minutes*, but he's *already* waited a half-hour. (C) If they wait for *another* half an hour, it will be *an hour* in total. (D) The man says they cannot wait *all day*, they haven't *been* waiting that long yet.

PART IV

81. (C) The temperature will be 100, which is hot, and the weather is described as *hot and humid. Humid* means *sticky heat.* (A) *Cloudy* is used to describe possible weather for Monday and Tuesday. (B) *Warm* and *breezy* are used in the dialog, but these words do not refer to the weather now. (D) *Wind* is mentioned in the dialog, and rain is part of a thunderstorm, but this is not the correct option.

82. (A) The next days for which weather is reported are Monday and Tuesday, so today must be *Sunday.* (B) *Tomorrow* in the dialog, refers to *Monday.* (C) *Friday* is not mentioned. (D) The *weekend* is mentioned in the dialog, but this is not *Saturday's* report.

83. (D) We can guess that the 80% of employees who would recommend their company, *like* it. 80% is *most of* the employees. (A) Not *all* of the employees would recommend their company as an employer, so we can guess that they do not all like it. (B) 80% is not *very few.* (C) 45% and *less than half* are similar figures, but this is the number of employees that would *leave* the company for an increase.

84. (A) Just a 10% *increase in pay* would entice some workers to leave the company. (B) We can work out that 20% of employees would not recommend their company as an employer, but this figure does not relate to a raise. (C) 45% is the percentage of employees who would be enticed by the 10% increase in pay. (D) 80% of employees would recommend their employer. This figure does not relate to a raise.

85. (C) This story is about a *gene that causes colon cancer.* (A) There is no *new* kind of cancer mentioned. (B) A blood test is mentioned in the dialog as a way to *detect* the gene, but not as a way to *test for cancer.* (D) In the study, Asian refers to the *type of flu,* not a *research center.*

86. (A) The gene is particularly common in people of *Nordic ancestry,* and *Scandinavians* are *Nordic.* (B) Philippine researchers discovered the gene, but they are not most likely to be affected. (C) The gene was discovered while studying *Asian* flu. (D) *Americans* are not mentioned in the study.

87. (D) The managers are requested to report to the *VIP Lounge* for the meeting. (A) The *new building* is mentioned in the announcement, but it is not the location of the meeting. (B) The *old offices* are mentioned in the announcement, but not in reference to the location of the meeting. (C) The move will be to the *top floors* of the new building, but that's not where the meeting is being held.

88. (A) Bringing lists of all the *files, books and belongings* is associated with *organizing* the move. It is also stated that activities are going to be *coordinated.* (B) *Boxes* are mentioned in the announcement, but not as a focus of the meeting. (C) *Room numbers* are also mentioned, but not as a focus of the meeting. (D) The movers will be given the lists, but there is no mention of *meeting* them.

89. (C) The managers are asked to bring a *list* to give to the movers. (A) and (B) The list should indicate their *files* and *books,* but they should not bring these items to the meeting. (D) *Boxes* are referred to in the announcement, but the managers are not required to bring them.

90. (D) The speaker is addressing people interested in making money and receiving *advice* on how to do it. (A) The speaker is discussing ways to learn how to *make* money, not *collect* it. (B) *Newsletters* are referred to in the dialog, but there is no mention of swapping them. (C) *Statistics* is used in both the dialog and the answer, but this is not the focus of the meeting.

91. (B) The speaker refers to his experience *working with* the author. (A) *Newsletters* are mentioned in the dialog, but not one specifically written by the author. (C) *Money* and *statistics* are associated with *consultants.* However, there s no mention of the author being the *speaker's* consultant. (D) The announcer does not say he has listened to the author's speeches before.

92. (A) The announcer addresses the audience as readers of investment magazines and newsletters, and as speech-goers. Obviously, they want more money. (B) and (C) While the announcer says they read *magazines* and *newsletters,* it is impossible to conclude that they are all reading the same ones. (D) *A financial guru* is someone who knows a lot, or is an *advisor,* but there is nothing that says everyone in the audience has one.

93. (A) The steady rate of *help-wanted advertising* is the topic of this report. The report explains why this rate has held steady. (B) *Consumer spending* is related to *consumer confidence,* but this is not the topic. (C) The *labor market* is mentioned in the report, but there is no mention of *strikes.* (D) Joe Bloomberg is an *economist,* but *economics* is not the topic of this report.

94. (C) *Consumer confidence* is one of the reasons why there has been greater *employment opportunities.* (A) *Working conditions* are not mentioned in the report. (B) *Classified ads* have been *holding steady* during this time of low unemployment. (D) There is no mention of the *labor union* in the report.

95. (A) He says that now is an excellent time to *look for*, or *seek*, a job. (B) He says there is *no* indication the labor market is *slowing down*. (C) This is the opposite of what is happening. (D) He makes no reference to *help-wanted advertising*.

96. (A) The speaker advises going through a number of different jobs and learning *on-site*. This suggests the speaker believes *hands-on experience* is most effective. (B) This option is the opposite of what the speaker recommends. (C) *Degree* is used in both the talk and the option, but with different meanings. (D) There is no mention of theory having to *precede* practice.

97. (B) Working at several *different places* is the way to learn different aspects of a business. (A) There is no mention of *taking courses* to learn, although this is a way of learning. (C) There is no mention of *talking with other business people*. (D) *Starting one's own business* is a *goal*, not a way to the goal.

98. (D) This story discusses the benefits of train travel for *shorter distances*, so *long-distance commuters* would not necessarily be interested. (A) *Local travelers* would be very interested in this story as it could save them money and time. (B) *Airline advertisers* would be interested because this story addresses their competition. (C) *Train advertisers* could take advice from this ad, as it is their service being described.

99. (B) The train commute takes *half* the time of the *three hour flight*, so it takes *one and a half hours*. (A) *One hour* is the amount of time it takes to check in and get to and from the airport. (C) *Two hours* is not mentioned in the article. (D) *Three hours* is the total amount of time it takes to fly, including check-in and travel to and from the airport.

100. (A) The *airlines* do not benefit from this news, as the story implies that their service is slower and more expensive. (B) *Commuters* benefit from knowing the cheapest, fastest way to travel. (C) and (D) *Train marketers* and *train stations* can benefit from having their service presented in this favorable way, because it could bring them more business.

PART V

101. (B) The plural form of the noun is needed with the plural verb *have*. (A) *Cost* is the non-count noun form. (C) *Costing* is the present progressive form. (D) *Costly* is an adjective.

102. (A) The infinitive *to ensure* is needed and it answers the question *why?* (B) *Ensured* is the simple past tense form. (C) *For ensuring* is the gerund form and it would be used to answer the question *what?* (D) *Ensure* is the simple present form of the verb.

103. (B) The adverb form is needed: *quickly*. (A) *Quicker* cannot be used with *more*; it means *more quickly*. (C) *Quickest* is the superlative form. (D) *Quick* is the adjective form.

104. (C) *Account for* is the correct phrasal verb. (A) and (B) *Supply* and *create* do not use the preposition *for*. (D) *Look for* means *to search*; people look for jobs, not assembly lines.

105. (B) *Consumer* is a noun form that acts as an adjective modifying *spending*. (A) *Consume* is the base form of the verb. (C) *Consuming* is a participle form, but cannot modify this particular noun. (D) *Consumed* is a past participle and an adjective which does not collocate with *spending*.

106. (D) To *go through* means *to use or work with*. (A) *Go after* means *to pursue or follow*. (B) *Go over* means *to review*. (C) *Go about* means *to proceed with*.

107. (B) *Earlier* is the correct comparative form. (A) *Earliness* is a noun. (C) *Early on* can stand alone, but is not preceded by *in*. (D) *Early to* is not in the comparative form.

108. (A) *But* joins two clauses showing contrast. (B) *Nor* should be preceded by *neither*. (C) *During* indicates when something happened. (D) *When* does not show contrast.

109. (D) *Reflects* means *to show*. (A), (B) and (C) *Realizes*, *inscribes* and *remembers* are verbs that can be used about people, not things, such as *architecture*.

110. (D) The singular form of the verb is needed, referring to *not one*. (A) *Chosen* is the past participle form. (B) and (C) *Were choosing* and *have been chosen* use plural forms.

111. (C) An *if*-clause in the past perfect is followed by *would have* plus past participle. (A) *Called* is the simple past tense form. (B) and (D) *Would call* and *would be calling* indicate unreal situations.

112. (B) *Air conditioner* is singular and requires the singular pronoun *it*. (A) *Them* is a plural pronoun. (C) *Him* refers to *he*. (D) *Your* is the wrong pronoun.

113. (A) *That* is the correct relative pronoun introducing the clause. (B) *Then* is a conjunction used to show a sequence of events. (C) *When* is used to refer to time. (D) *Since* is used for cause and effect.

114. (B) Shares of stock move in a direction: *up* or *down*. (A) *Went out* means *to leave*. (C) *Went away* means *to leave*; *went way* is not possible. (D) *Went to* does not show a direction.

115. (D) *As* introduces the cause clause. (A) and (B) *In spite of* and *despite* indicate a contradiction in the sentence. (C) *Ever since* should be followed by a time reference.

116. (C) A gerund should follow *for*. (A) *Assist* is the base form of the verb. (B) *To assist* is the infinitive, and *to* never follows *for*. (D) *Assisted* is the past participle.

117. (A) Using *even without* is another way to indicate an untrue conditional sentence, i.e. *If the housing boom hadn't happened ...*; *would* plus perfect infinitive is needed in the other clause. (B) *Will have gone* indicates future action. (C) *Were to go* indicates the plural, but *the prime rate* is singular. (D) *Was going* is not a conditional form.

118. (D) *On behalf of* is another way of saying *for*. (A) *In light of* means *because of*. (B) *Because of* is illogical. (C) *On account of* means *due to*.

119. (B) A *cycle* consists of *phases*. (A) You could break a business plan into its various *segments*. (C) You refer to *sectors* of the economy. (D) A large company is made up of *divisions*.

120. (A) *Studies* is plural and needs the plural form: *have shown*. (B) *Shown* is the past participle. (C) *Has shown* is the singular, present perfect. (D) *Are shown* is the passive form.

121. (B) *So* is used to introduce the effect clause. (A) *But* indicates some contradiction. (C) *Because* introduces the cause clause. (D) *Nor* could be used if there were several things that residents should not do.

122. (A) *Than* gives you a clue that the comparative *longer* should be used. (B) In order to use *longest*, you need *the*. (C) *Long* is the adjective. (D) *Longs* is the third person singular form of the verb *to long for*.

123. (C) The present tense is used with a time clause (*before*) in the future. (A) *Will be* is in the future tense. (B) *Would be* indicates conditional. (D) *Were* is the past tense.

124. (B) *Report to* is the correct phrasal verb. (A) *Directly* needs to be followed by *to*. (C) and (D) *Forward* and *aside* are adverbs of place, not prepositions.

125. (C) In a first conditional sentence, the present tense is followed by the future tense: *will have been waiting*. (A) *Has been waiting* is the present perfect progressive. (B) *Has waited* is the present perfect. (D) *Was waiting* is the past progressive.

126. (D) *Entitled to* means *to have power or access to use*. (A) and (B) The sentence would be correct with *authorized to use* or *allowed to use*. (C) A person has *access to* a trust fund.

127. (B) *Improvements* is a plural noun which collocates with *home*. (A) *Impropriety* means *something improper*. (C) *Improvisation* means *something made up on the spot*. (D) *Impulse* means *a sudden determination to act*.

128. (D) The base form of the verb, *accept*, follows *will*. (A) *Acceptable* is the adjective form. (B) *Accepts* is the third person singular form. (C) *Accepting* is the gerund form.

129. (B) Two pieces of land are *connected to* each other. (A) *Fastened* refers to something which is secured or closed. (C) *Put together* is followed by the preposition *with* when two items are joined. (D) Ingredients are *combined with* each other.

130. (D) *Had we ...* is an alternative to the conditional form *If we had ...*, which refers to the (unreal) past. (A) (B) and (C) *Shall, should* and *will* indicate future time.

131. (C) *In deference to* means *out of respect for*. (A) *In charge of* means *in a position of responsibility*. (B) *Because of* is illogical. (D) *In light of* is followed by an impersonal object.

132. (A) The negative *not*, calls for a form of the pronoun *any*. (B) and (C) *Someone* and *somebody* indicate a limited group.(D) The quantifier *many* cannot finish the sentence.

133. (A) *Pollution* is the correct noun. (B) *Environment* does not make sense in this context. (C) *Pollutes* is the simple present form of the verb *pollute*. (D) *Environmental* is an adjective formed from *environment*.

134. (B) *Looking for* in this sentence means *trying to find out*. (A) They *hope to find* a team player. (C) *Inquiring about* is needed in this case. (D)*Seeking* is not used in this context.

135. (C) The simple past tense *helped* is needed. (A) *Helping* needs to be accompanied by an auxiliary verb. (B) *Had been helped* is the passive voice. (D) *Maître d'* is singular and *are being helped* is plural.

136. (D) The gerund form *sightseeing* is needed. (A) *To sightsee* is the infinitive form. (B) The infinitive *to spend* already appears in the sentence. (C) *Going to* is not needed.

137. (C) Stocks can *do badly* or *poorly*. (A) The stocks could *move slowly*, but not *do slowly*. (B) The stocks could *perform weakly*, but you would not use *weakly* with the verb *do*. (D) The stocks could *move up steadily*, but you would not use *steadily* with the verb *do*.

138. (D) The sentence must be completed with a verb indicating past time: *had seen*. (A) *Sees* is the third person singular, present tense. (B) *Was seen* does indicate past time, but it is passive. (C) *Will see* indicates future time.

139. (A) *Might* indicates possibility. (B) There is no obligation in this sentence. (C) and (D) *Can* and *could* are very similar in meaning to *be able to* and therefore would not be used with this verb.

140. (A) *Enticing* means *attractive or tempting*; something is *enticing to* or *attractive to* somebody. (B), (C) and (D) *On, with* and *by* are incorrect prepositions.

PART VI

141. (B)*Looking at over* contains an extra preposition: either *looking at* or *looking over* is correct. (A) *Was charged* is the past tense in the passive voice. (C) *To* is the preposition that introduces the infinitive. (D) *Wrongdoing* is a noun meaning *wrong behavior*.

142. (A) The adverb *initially* and not the adjective *initial* is required. (B) *We found* is the subject pronoun plus the past tense of the verb. (C) *So difficult* is an adjective and intensifier combination. (D) *Eventually* is an adverb modifying the verb *withdrew*.

143. (A) The gerund form of the verb *go, going through*, is needed. (B) *One by one* is an adverbial phrase. (C) *To find* is the infinitive form. (D) *Storage drawer* is a compound noun.

144. (B) *Weather* is a non-count noun. (A) *All things considered* is a correct, reduced clause. (C) *Weather* is considered singular and therefore the correct verb form is *hasn't significantly*. (D) *Of the staff* is a prepositional phrase.

145. (C) The noun *sports* needs to be modified by the adjective *aquatic* not the noun *aquatics*. (A) The gerund *having* introduces the clause. (B) *Told us* combines the correct simple past tense with a suitable pronoun. (D) *Increasingly* quantifies *popular*.

146. (A) *Because* should be replaced by *that* which combines with the verb *repeat* and introduces the noun clause. (B) *She did not want* is the correct past tense negative. (C) *Invested in* is a correct combination of verb + preposition. (D) *High-risk* is an adjective used to describe *companies*.

147. (B) As it is a single sentence, the relative pronoun *who* should be used instead of *they*. (A) *Will be traveling* indicates future time. (C) *Finance* identifies which type of *committee*. (D) *Arts* identifies what type of *center*.

148. (C) The definite article is needed to identify which night: *throughout the night*. (A) *The* is the correct article. `(B) *Worked* is the past tense form of the verb. (D) The apostrophe plus -*s* identifies the possessive.

149. (A) The progressive form of the verb *search* is needed. (B) *Insights into* is the correct noun + preposition combination. (C) *The nature of* means *the type of*. (D) *Cell* is the singular noun.

150. (A) *Nor* follows *neither*. (B) *In his approach* is a prepositional phrase. (C) *Interested* describes the *students*. (D) *Their* refers to *the students*.

151. (A) The gerund form, *remembering*, is needed in this

clause. (B) *The staff decided* is the subject plus the past tense of the verb. (C) *A little* quantifies *overtime*. (D) The infinitive *to avoid* is followed by the object *a recurrence*.

152. (B) *Furniture* is a non-count noun and does not take the final -*s*. (A) The past tense, *went*, of the verb is used, followed by the infinitive, *to pick out*. (C) *Lounge* is a singular noun. (D) *Was opening* is the past progressive form.

153. (C) *Insurance* forms a compound noun with *disability*. (A) The auxiliary in the past tense, *did*, followed by the simple form of the verb, begins the question. (B) *Up to 25 percent* means *not more than 25 percent*. (D) *If you are* introduces the conditional clause in the first conditional.

154. (C) The past participle, *reinstated*, is needed for the passive voice. (A) *Mistakenly* is the correct form of the adverb. (B) *Club membership* is a compound noun and the object of the sentence. (D) *At the latest* describes the time.

155. (A) The simple present, *states*, is used for a general truth. (B) *To have* is the infinitive form following the verb *have*, which means *must*. (C) *Permission of* is followed by someone (*the authors*). (D) The gerund, *copying*, follows *before*.

156. (B) A form of the verb *to be* must accompany *given*, to form the passive voice: *was given*. (A) The pronoun *your*, identifies whose *paycheck*. (C) *The head of* has the same meaning as *boss*. (D) *To pass on to* is the infinitive form of a two-word verb plus the correct preposition.

157. (A) *Interested* is used for people, *interesting* for things. (B) *Were donated* is the correct form of the passive voice. (C) Verbs in the passive voice are followed by the preposition *by* to introduce the agent. (D) *Over twenty years ago* means *more than twenty years*.

158. (C) *Hesitant* is the adjective form; the sentence requires the verb form *hesitate*. (A) *When you show him* is a clause introduced by a relative pronoun. (B) *Letters of recommendation* is a plural noun phrase. (D) The phrase *that you want* defines *the salary*.

159. (A) The sentence is in the past tense, therefore the verb should be *entered*. (B) *We drove* is the subject followed by the past tense of the verb. (C) *Through a tunnel* uses the correct preposition to describe the movement. (D) *Opened into* is the past tense plus a suitable preposition.

160. (D) The correct preposition to follow *along* is *with*. (A) The conditional calls for *would* plus the base form of the verb. (B) The *audience's attention* indicates whose attention with the possessive form. (C) The *if*-clause in the second conditional is in the past tense.

PART VII

161. (C) *Highly energetic* implies the same as *motivated*. (A) *A team player* in this case does not refer to an athlete. (B) and (D) *Diplomatic* and *strong* are not mentioned.

162. (D) *Marketing* involves *product promotion*. (A) The company builds homes, but the person does not need experience in *home construction*. (B) and (C) *Computer programming* and *demographics* are not mentioned.

163. (C) Subscribers are offered *advance ticket purchase*. (A) The subscription to *Forecast* is included in the price. (B) There are no *invitations* included. (D) *Special reserved seats* is not mentioned.

164. (D) The *type of payment* is either check or a request to be billed. (A) *Country* is not requested. (B) The workplace telephone number is requested, but not the *workplace*. (C) The subscriber is asked if it is a renewal, but not for the *renewal code number*.

165. (A) ... *builders of the new international terminal at Singapore Airport* tells the reader that a new terminal will be constructed. (B) A German company is one of the companies, but the article is not about *public relations*. (C) A *training program* is not mentioned. (D) A company from *Great Britain* may invest in Singapore.

166. (D) The decision will be made after a financial analysis. (A) *Completion of preparations* is not mentioned. (B) *Comparing results* is not mentioned. (C) There is no mention of a *meeting* between the two companies.

167. (A) A *feasibility study* means to *find out what can and can't be done*. (B) It is not certain that Dar Handash will win the contract. (C) Dar Handash and Euromill are competitors; they will not *evaluate* each other. (D) *Sending reports* is not mentioned.

168. (B) *Winning cars* suggests *car racing*. (A) *Antique cars* are not mentioned. (C) The book covers car races, not *horse races*. (D) This is not a technical book.

169. (C) The book *gives insight into what's under the hood*, i.e. the *engine*. (A) and (D) *How to build a car* and *locations of car races* are not mentioned. (B) The review mentions the effects on the body of a car but not *body repair techniques*. (D)

170. (B) The author *has taken steps to minimize the use of technical jargon*. (A) There are biographical *sketches*, but not necessarily for the purpose of broadening the book's appeal. (C) The biographical sketches are *entertaining*. (D) *Personal stories* are not mentioned.

171. (B) The factory will be in an industrial park in *Cong Tum*. (A) There is a similar factory in *Malacca*. (C) and (D) Workers will come from *Play Cu* and *Qui Nohn*.

172. (C) The French company has applied for *a license*. (A) Once the building is constructed, the company will hire *up to 450 workers*. (B) A *lease agreement* is not mentioned. (D) The *capital* will be foreign, but they already have it.

173. (D) 75% of the raw materials will be sourced locally; that is *in the Cong Tum region*. (A) The cosmetic giant is from *France*. (B) *Overseas* is incorrect. (C) A similar factory was built in *Malaysia*.

174. (C) $2 million in the 1st year plus an additional million equals *$3 million*. (A) There is an additional *$1 million* expected in the 2nd year. (B) *$2 million* is expected in the first year. (D) *$7.5 million* is the expected construction cost.

175. (A) *An outdated file* means you may not be listed on the voters' list. (B) *Failure to appear* is not mentioned. (C) *Appearing on the voters' list* will allow someone to vote. (D) The *Democratic Party* holds a primary election.

176. (C) *Form VRH 189* is used to register with a particular party. (A) *Form VRR 188* is used to register to vote. (B) You should *call 885-1254* to receive forms. (D) You must sign up before you vote.

177. (D) Voters with no particular party registration *may only vote in special or general elections*. (A) Everyone needs to use their *social security number*. (B) They can only vote in special or general elections. (C) No one is forced to *register as a Liberal*.

178. (A) *Your social security number will only be used for identification purposes ...* . (B) The *Federal Privacy Act* does not allow the number to be used for other purposes. (C) The voter must *update public records*. (D) It cannot be made available for *use in* any *reports*.

179. (B) The letter welcomes the woman to the Executive Board. (A*) To raise contributions* is not mentioned. (C) The letter states when meetings will be held. (D)*Work schedules* are not mentioned.

180. (D) *A schedule for the meeting* is the same as an *agenda*. (A) *A brochure* is enclosed with the letter. (B) The agenda is drawn up for the meeting; it is not a *personal agenda*. (C) *A watch or clock* is not mentioned.

181. (B) *Committee meetings are generally scheduled during the day on the Friday of the board meeting.* (A) Committee meetings appear to be held automatically when board meetings are convened. (C) The Monday meeting was an exception; it was not normal. (D) The Executive Board holds it meetings *on Friday evenings*.

182. (C) Any expenses over £500 must be accompanied by *Form 113*. (A) She would use her *stipend*, but she must also submit a form. (B) The *cashier* is not mentioned. (D) The *finance committee* is not mentioned.

183. (A) Qua Ping is the *first joint-venture foreign trade company*. (B) It is a foreign trade company, but not *foreign-owned*. (C) and (D) The fact that *it is worthwhile* and that *it will trade in both electronics and machinery* does not make it special.

184. (C) *Global Agro Company* has a 21% share. (A) *Eastern Trading Company* has a 52% share. (B) *Fidushi Corporation* has a 27% share. (D) *An Asian-Pacific conglomerate* is not mentioned.

185. (D) Foreign companies will benefit *because of a 3% lowering of tariffs on goods exported to Thailand.* (A) The *business license* has already been issued. (B) *Inclusion in more conferences* is not mentioned. (C) Thailand will learn from *foreign management* styles; however, it doesn't say that they are *superior.*

186. (B) The forum in 1961 was on *economic cooperation*. (A) Presidents of different countries met, not of *joint ventures*. (C) There is no mention that *tariffs were lowered*. (D) *Approval for Qua Ping Trading Corporation* was not given in 1961.

187. (C) The plan is met with *challenges on all sides*, which means that there is *opposition*. (A) Environmentalists are mentioned, but not *environmental effects*. (B) There is no mention of *growth in the California desert*. (D) *Advancements in recycling and compacting technologies* is mentioned, however, it is not the main subject.

188. (B) The *waste sites are not even in full use*. (A) and (C) There is no mention that there are *too many waste sites in California* or that *it will be an economic burden*. (D) There are advances in recycling, however, waste sites are still necessary.

189. (A) Developers *would prefer to have the land developed for homes*. (B) *A theme park* is not mentioned. (C) There is *major resistance* to the idea of the waste site. (D) *Multiple sites* is not mentioned.

190. (C) The *wrong* was Ready Gas claiming that its gasoline cleaned engines. It was *righted* by the new television ad. (A) There was a complaint against Ready Gas, not an *endorsement*. (B) The bulletin criticises the *promotion of high octane fuel*. (D) Reducing *regular auto maintenance* was a claim made by Ready Gas.

191. (B) *Unless the owner's manual for your car calls specifically for high octane fuel ... there's no reason to ...* (A) *To get better mileage* is not mentioned. (C*) Cleaning the engine* was an unfounded claim. (D) *Reducing costs* was an unfounded claim.

192. (A) Ready Gas is placing a television ad to *educate the public*. (B) *Discounts* are not mentioned. (C) Ready Gas is changing its advertisement, not its *advertising agency*. (D) *Issuing new, updated owner's manuals* is not mentioned.

193. (C) The study is about *business people* who travel and those who do not. (A) and (D) *Health insurance agents* and *travel agents* are not mentioned. (B) The study was done by the *University of Tokyo*.

194. (C) There were two studies: one of 4,000 and one of 400, totalling *4,400*. (A) The separate study was of *400* business travelers. (B) The first study mentioned involved the health claims of *4,000* staff. (D) *4,800* is not mentioned.

195. (D) Male travelers make 80% more health complaints, whereas women travelers make only 18% more claims. (A), (B) and (C) *Higher expenses*, *traveling more* and *lower blood pressure* are not mentioned.

196. (B) 85% of women are concerned about *work not getting done at the office*. (A) 60% are concerned about *personal obligations they've left behind*. (C) 58% *feel more pressured to perform ...*. (D) *Stress in the lives of their husbands* is not mentioned.

197. (C) The announcement says to *stay in touch with the IRS*. (A) *Informing yourself of your options* is not mentioned. (B) and (D) *Paying all penalties and interest payments on time* and *being sure to use the form that applies to your situation* is good advice, but not the general policy advised in the announcement.

198. (A) You need to *prove reasonable cause*. (B) You can ask to pay in *monthly installments*, but this is not a minimum requirement. (C) *Form 4868* is used to ask for the extension. (D) *Immediate filing of the tax return* is not mentioned.

199. (D) *Form 9465* is used to ask for payment installments if you have no money. (A) *Form 2688* is used to ask for another extension. (B) *Form 4868* is to request an extension. (C) *Form 8822* is used to change your address.

200. (A) *Form 8822 is available if you need to change your address*. (B) *You will continue to receive tax return packages* automatically if you file form 8822. (C) The IRS may send notices *that require a prompt reply*. (D) Form 8822 is used *if you need to change your address*, not *to request permission to move*.

Answer Key
Practice Test Three

In the following Answer Key, the first explanation provided for each question is the correct option.

PART I

1. (B) The waiter is *putting away* the spoons. Knives, forks and spoons make up *cutlery*. (A) The picture shows *spoons,* but he is not *cleaning* them. (C) *Cutlet,* which is a small cut of meat, sounds like *cutlery.* (D) He is in a restaurant, but he is not about to *eat,* he *works* there.

2. (A) The *two chairs* in the picture are *in front of* the *bed.* (B) The *flowers* are *in front of* the *bed,* not *beside* it. (C) There is a *painting* over the *bed* in this picture, but no *window* over a *sofa.* (D) There is a *vase* with flowers on the *table.* We cannot see a *desk.*

3. (C) The man is a *gardener* who is *watering the plants* with a hose. (A) A *botanist* works with plants and water makes *trees grow,* but there are no trees in the picture. (B) There is a *delivery man* in the background, but he is not holding a *rose. Rose* sounds like *hose,* which the gardener is holding. (D) A *firefighter* uses a hose to put out fires, but in this picture the water is for the plants.

4. (C) The bookshelves, files and computer suggest the two men are in an *office.* (A) The picture shows a *computer.* However, the men are not at a *computer fair.* (B) The computer monitor has a *screen,* but the men are not watching a *movie screening,* or a preview. (D) One man could be typing on the *keyboard,* but this is not a *board meeting.*

5. (D) The men are *wearing protective clothes* including gloves, hard hats, face masks and jackets. (A) The men are *wearing* hats, not *selling* them. (B) The men are *standing,* but the picture does not show what they are standing *on.* Also *mats* may be confused with *hats.* (C) The man is looking at the *floor,* which may be confused with the sound of *door.*

6. (B) The man is playing the trumpet. He is *playing music.* (A) He is *entertaining* someone, but the picture does not show any *children.* (C) He is *playing,* not *putting away,* the trumpet. (D) He is *blowing* into the trumpet to make sound. You may blow on hot food to make it cold, but there is no food in the picture.

7. (B) The man is reading the notices, or *information,* on the board. (A) The *newspaper* is pinned to the board. It is not on a *bench.* (C) The board is covered with *writing,* not *graffiti.* (D) He is *reading,* not *writing,* the news.

8. (C) The picture shows coffee machines and the employees *preparing,* or making, *coffee.* (A) There is a *star* on the woman's uniform and on the milk machine, but we cannot see any in the sky. (B) They may be *making* an *espresso* but not *drinking* one. (D) The machines are *inside* the store, not *outside.*

9. (C) The boy is standing next to, or *by,* the door. (A) There is a picture of a cat, a puma, on the boy's jacket, but it is not *catching* anything. (B) There is an animal on his jacket, and he is *wearing* a jacket. *Wearing him out* means that the animal is making him tired, so this option is incorrect. (D) The boy is *smoking,* but he is not buying any cigarettes. He is wearing trainers, but there is no reason to believe he is an *athlete.*

10. (C) The picture shows a *doctor* doing some type of examination, or *test,* on the woman. (A) *Handing* could be associated with the doctor's physical examination. *Exam* is an associated word, however, its meaning in this instance is different. (B) The *doctor,* not a *barber,* is doing a test on the patient's arm. A barber is a person who cuts men's hair. (D) *Checking* is a word associated with doctors and an *optician* is a type of doctor. However, opticians examine eyes and the picture is of a woman having a test on her arm.

11. (C) The *postcards* are connected, or *joined together.* (A) *Posting* and *postcards* have the same stem and are associated words. However, the women are doing nothing with a *notice* in this picture. (B) The postcards may be photos, but the picture has nothing to do with a *photo service.* (D) The women are probably *tourists,* and one of them has a camera. However, they are not *taking pictures.*

12. (B) The man and woman are shaking hands, or *greeting,* each other. (A) They're *shaking hands,* not *shaking a bottle* in order to mix its contents up. (C) The paintings are *framed,* but they are not *painting* any of the *frames.* (D) There are *pictures* on the *wall,* but they have *already* been hung.

13. (A) The man in the picture could be a *chef* because of his uniform, and he is *working* in a *kitchen.* (B) The chef is *working,* but he is not a *technician,* and there is no indication he is *finishing his work.* (C) The man is in the kitchen, nobody is *opening the restaurant.* (D) The man may be an *apprentice* learning a skill, but he is not *looking at soil.* This option confuses the sounds of *soil* and *foil.*

14. (C) The man is selecting a button to push in order to buy, or *purchase,* a *ticket.* (A) A *pass,* or ticket, can be used for the subway, train or bus, but this man is not *returning* anything. He is *buying* something. (B) The *bicycle* is leaning against the machine, he is not *riding* it. (D) He's buying a ticket, not *entering* something, and if he's buying a ticket, it is not *for free.*

15. (A) The car is driving out of, or *leaving,* the refinery. (B) There are *drums* on the right-hand side of the picture, but there is no indication that there are *instruments* inside. (C) This may be an *oil* refinery, but the picture does not show oil in the street. (D) The sound of *winery* might be confused with *refinery,* and a road does run through the middle of it.

16. (D) The passengers are *boarding,* or getting into, the van. (A) The sound of *band* might be confused with *van.* There is a *group* of people, but they are not *welcoming* anyone, they are about to leave. (B) The picture shows *tourists,* but they have *already* packed their bags. (C) The visitors are *leaving,* not *arriving. Land* might be confused with *van.*

17. (C) They are standing on the edge of the sidewalk, or *curb.* (A) The cars in the picture are all *parked.* There is no *car stopping* for the people. (B) There is a *street,* but the people are not *crossing* it. (D) They are *on* a corner, but there is no *bus* in the picture and we cannot tell if there is one *around the corner.*

18. (B) The *keyboard* for the computer is *under the counter.* (A) The cabinet under the counter has a *lock,* but there is no *key* in it. (C) There is a *door* in the background, but no evidence of any *keys.* (D) There is a *screen* on the monitor of the computer, but there isn't any kind of screen *on the door.*

19. (B) He's *adding,* or putting on, another *coat,* or layer, *of paint to the pipes.* (A) The man is *painting,* but not *seats.* He is *seated* on the floor. (C) He is *sitting,* but he's not *eating.* (D) The man is *sitting on the floor,* not *choosing a seat.*

20. (C) A table is covered with *food* that is *displayed* in *serving dishes.* (A) There is only one *plate* in the picture and it is not in a *sink,* a man is holding it. (B) *Bowl* would not be used to describe these kinds of serving dishes, and the dishes are *full,* not *almost empty.* (D) *Produce* is associated with food, and *boxes* are containers, but *produce* is unprepared vegetables and fruit, and *boxes* would not be used on this type of occasion.

PART II

21. (B) The phone is *on the desk.* (A) This option confuses the sound of *loan* with *phone.* (C) *There* may seem like a good reply to *where?* but the option does not answer the question.

22. (C) The person *would* like help and would *appreciate* it as well. (A) *May* is repeated in the option, but with a different meaning. In this case, it refers to the month. (B) *Help* is repeated, but the meanings are different.

23. (A) *Behind the parking lot* is the location of the embassy. (B) *Ambassador* and *embassy* sound similar and are related words, but the question is asking about the location of a *place,* not a person. (C) *There* is a logical response to *where?* but the answer is incorrect.

24. (C) Not only has the respondent spoken with the *travel agent,* but the reservation has been made. (A) This question could be answered with a *no,* and *travel* is repeated. However, this option confuses the sound of *jet* with *yet.* (B) *Spoke* is repeated, but this option does not answer the question.

25. (A) When deciding between the train and the bus, the respondent points out that the train is *more convenient.* (B) *Should* is repeated, but the answer does not specify whether it is better to take the train or the bus. (C) *Bus* is used in both the question and the option, but again the question is not answered.

26. (A) Not knowing them *well enough* is the reason not to *form a partnership.* (B) *Partnership* and *married* are associated, but marriage is not the topic. (C) *Partner* is used in both the question and the option, but the answer is incorrect.

27. (C) *Any minute,* or very soon, is the answer to *when?* (A) and (B) Both options answer *how long* the client will be staying, not *when* he'll be coming.

28. (B) *Coins,* or metal money, are *small change.* (A) *Medium* and *large* are associated with *small,* but do not relate to *change.* (C) *Change* is repeated in both the question and the option, but with different meanings.

29. (A) *Much better* (than before) is how Mr. Bennet is performing, or *doing.* (B) This option confuses the sound of *been* with *Bennet.* (C) This option answers *what* Mr. Bennet has been doing, not *how* he has been doing.

30. (A) The committee was *not* chosen for the award, and that is *unfortunate.* (B) *Chose* is used in both the question and the option, and *attend* is associated with *committee.* However, this option does not answer the question. (C) *Award* is associated with *won,* and *committee* is associated with *vote,* but *he* is an inappropriate pronoun for *our committee.*

31. (C) Twentieth street is found by going *right at the corner.* (A) This option could answer *when?* but not *how?* (B) This option confuses the words *twentieth* and *twenty-first.*

32. (A) The *night manager* closes the office. (B) A name, such as Jeff, is an attractive answer to the question *who?* However, this option confuses *close,* meaning near, with the verb *close.* (C) *Office* is repeated, but this option does not answer the question.

33. (C) It is alright to leave a message, and the respondent will make certain it is received. (A) *Leave* and *message* are both repeated, but the option does not answer the question. (B) This option confuses *messenger* with *message*.

34. (B) The kind of task that will be assigned will probably be *easy*. (A) This option confuses the sound of *ask* with *task*. (C) *Assigned* is used in the question and the answer, but it is a *task*, not a *room*, which is under discussion.

35. (C) She thought that the seminar was *informative*. (A) *She* is repeated, and the sound of *seminary* which is a place of education, is confused with *seminar*. (B) *She* is repeated, and the sound of *car* is confused with *seminar*.

36. (A) The awards will be *presented*, or *given*, during dinner. (B) *Ceremony* is associated with *awards*, but this option answers the question *where?* not *when?* (C) *Given* is repeated, but the question is not answered.

37. (C) The respondent knew about the conference because of an e-mail. (A) *There* could be associated with a place (Hong Kong), *no* is a logical response to this type of question. However, this option does not answer the question. (B) *Mr. Chang* could be a name for someone from Hong Kong, but this answer does not answer the question.

38. (A) The sweaters are *normally* in stock. (B) This option confuses *sock* with *stock*, and *sweat* with *sweaters*. (C) This option confuses *feathers* with *sweaters*, and *these* with *those*.

39. (B) The drinks, or *refreshments*, are *on the balcony*. (A) *By the window* is a tempting answer to *where? Fresh* is repeated from *refreshments*. However, air is not the topic. (C) *Refreshments* and *refreshing* have the same root, however, taking a shower is irrelevant to the question.

40. (A) The library is open at *ten*. (B) *Closed* is the opposite of *open*, and *book shop* and *library* may be associated, but the question is about the opening hours of the library. (C) This option does not answer *when?*

41. (B) Turning on a switch, activates, or makes the machine *work*. (A) Machines cannot *listen carefully*. (C) *Being on time* is associated with work, but makes no sense in relation to machines.

42. (C) The tests are *not difficult*, so they must be fairly *simple*. (A) *Test* is used in both the question and the option, but there is no mention of *what* the tests are like. (B) *Simple* is synonymous with *easy*, but this option does not answer the question.

43. (B) Several hotels with pools can be found in the *downtown area*. (A) *Pool* is repeated, but the question is about *swimming pools* not *pool tables*. (C) *Indoor* and *outside* are associated, but there is no reference made to swimming pools.

44. (A) They will accept personal checks *only* if they know you. Watch for test questions where you might expect a simple *yes* or *no* answer. Instead, there is often a qualified response. (B) and (C) *Personal* is used in both the question and the options, but neither option is correct.

45. (C) The week the project was finished was *when* the promotion was received. (A) This option confuses the words *lotion* and *promotion* which rhyme and have the same suffix. (B) This option confuses the words *commotion* and *promotion* which rhyme and share the same suffix.

46. (B) *All* of the representatives were *satisfied*, or *pleased*, with the meeting. (A) *Met* and *meeting* are related, and *representatives* is associated with the *boardroom*. However, this option does not answer the question. (C) A simple *yes* answer is attractive for this question, and *satisfied* is associated with *acceptable*. Also *present* can relate to attendance at a meeting. However, in this case the noun *present* refers to a gift.

47. (C) It would be a pleasure for the respondent to show Ms Tashiko the office. (A) *New office* is repeated. However, Ms Tashiko is about to see her new office, so the answer cannot be in the past. (B) *Could* is the past of *can*, but this option confuses the noun *show* with the verb.

48. (C) The respondent was told there was a *lifetime warranty* on the fax machine. (A) *Warranty* and *guarantee* sound alike and are associated, but the meanings here are different. (B) This option confuses the sound of *fact* with *fax*.

49. (A) The plane tickets are *in the envelope*. (B) Plane tickets are associated with *making reservations*, but the question is about location. (C) *Planes* can be *up in the sky*, but not *plane tickets*.

50. (C) The respondent thinks the color of the lamp shades is *a bit off*, or *not quite right*. (A) This option confuses the sound of *lamb* with *lamp*. (B) *Shade* is repeated, but with a different meaning.

PART III

51. (B) *Ice water*, *check* and *meal* are all associated with a *restaurant*. (A) *Can I get you anything else?* is a question that could be asked to a patient in a *hospital*, but a patient would be unlikely to ask for the *check*. (C) *Ice* is repeated in the dialog and option, but the speakers are not in an *ice rink*. (D) *Check* is associated with a *bank*, but the speakers are not in a bank.

52. (D) *Down this hall on your left* has the same meaning as *on the left-hand side of the corridor*. (A) The woman's *room* is on the second floor. (B) *Down* is said in the dialog, but not in relation to *stairs*. (C) There is no mention of the *reading room*.

53. (A) He needs to fax his notes to his secretary. (B) The man *mentions* his secretary, but only because that is who needs to receive the fax. (C) The *hotel* charges more per page, not the *man*. (D) The man just wants to send one fax, not *lease a machine*.

54. (B) The woman is asking on behalf of her *brother*, if there are job openings at the construction company. (A) The man *has* a construction company, but the woman does not want to *start* one. (C) *Carpentry* is repeated in both the dialog and the option, but there is no mention of her wanting to learn any *skills*. (D) *Home* and *summer* are both repeated, but finding a *summer home* is not the topic.

55. (C) The woman asks when the rain is supposed to stop, so we know that it's raining *now*. (A) It may be sunny *tomorrow*. (B) *Foggy* is not mentioned, but *fog* is associated with bad weather. (D) Snow is associated with bad weather, but is not mentioned in the dialog.

56. (B) The man gave the Accounting Department two packs. (A) He gave some away, he did not finish, or *use it up*, himself. (C) *Order* is used in both the dialog and the option, but there is no mention of none being ordered at all. (D) There is no mention of their being unable to *find* paper.

57. (A) She buys it *every day* at the newsstand. (B) There is no mention of *once a month*. (C) There is no mention of *twice a week*. (D) *Never* might be confused with its opposite meaning, *every day*.

58. (A) They decide to take the *train* because it is cheaper and they will not have to worry about parking. (B) *Drive ourselves* means *by car*, but the speakers reject this idea. (C) They do not discuss going *by bus*. (D) Taking a *taxi* is discussed, but they choose the train instead.

59. (B) She wants *updated price lists* so they do not have to check with the main office every time they sell something. (A) The price lists are *at the printers*, but the woman does not want a *new printer*. (C) *A matter of days* is associated with *time*, but the woman does not *want* more time. (D) *Sales* is used in the dialog and the option, but the *sales quota* is not mentioned.

60. (D) The woman asks if there is a *dining car* on the *train*, so she must be talking to a *conductor*. (A) A *waiter* is associated with a *dining car*, but the woman is not in it yet, so is unlikely to be talking to a waiter. (B) *Train* is associated with *travel*, but the woman is clearly on the train already, she is not *booking a ticket*. (C) An *airline attendant* may say *tickets*, but a train is referred to.

61. (A) The man feels there will not be a problem because they have all the *data*, or *information*. (B) *Problem* is repeated in the dialog and the option, but the man thinks there will *not* be any. (C) *President*, *approve* and *proposals* are repeated in the option, but the man is optimistic that the president *will* approve. (D) *Approval* and *prove* might be confused.

62. (B) *Miles* and *test drives* are both associated with *cars*, and offering a lower price is a sign of a *salesperson*. (A) There is no indication the man is a *town clerk*. (C) *Test* is repeated in the dialog and the option, but Mr. Samo is not talking to a *test administrator*. (D) *Miles* and *drives* could be associated with a *chauffeur*, but in this case Mr. Samo is considering *purchasing* a car.

63. (C) They are discussing the high sales of *computer furniture* and the possibility of selling even more. (A) It is computer *furniture* they are selling, not computers themselves. (B) The speakers are obviously involved in furniture sales, and computer furniture may be *large*, but size is not specifically mentioned. (D) *Bedroom* is repeated in the dialog and the option, and *cutting back* may be associated with *smaller*. However, they are talking about furniture not *rooms*.

64. (B) After hearing of the strike, the woman decides to deliver the package *herself*. (A) A *courier* was considered, but they are on strike. (C) *Car* is used in the dialog and the option, but the woman is going to *borrow* one, not *rent* one. (D) *Package* and *courier* can be associated with *shipping*, but this method of delivery is not mentioned.

65. (B) *Travel agents* make *reservations* for flights. (A) *Flight attendants* are associated with *travel*, but a flight attendant does *not* make reservations. (C) There is no suggestion of a *security guard*. (D) There is no suggestion of a *housekeeper*.

66. (C) The woman likes the mystery section because of the *cushioned chairs*, or *padded seats*. (A) In fact the mystery section is described as being *noisier* than the reference section. (B) *Cushioned chairs* are associated with *decoration*, but its being *nicely decorated* is not stated. (D) The *long tables* are in the reference section.

67. (B) The men start the local deliveries at 6:00 a.m. and finish by twelve noon, so they take *six hours*. (A) *Two* refers to the number of people who *make* the deliveries. (C) *Twelve* refers to the time they *finish* the deliveries. (D) *Weekdays* are referred to, but the deliveries do not take a whole week.

68. (A) They need *more chairs* for the meeting. (B) They are *rental chairs*, but there is no mention of *cost*. (C) *Company* and *customers* are associated with a *store*, but there is no mention of anything being *closed*. (D) The meeting has not taken place yet and, there is no mention of it being too long.

69. (C) They have desks and tables that need to be unloaded. (A) *Lunch* is mentioned in the dialog, but only as a time marker. (B) Sam and David will be the *helpers*. The speakers do not need help talking to them. (D) Sixty-five relates to *counting*, but the speakers do not need *help* with counting.

70. (A) The woman is talking to a doctor about being unable to read *fine print*. *Examine* and *vision* are associated with eye doctors, or *opticians*. Options (B), (C) and (D) are all attractive because of the associated words. (B) *Reading* and *fine print* are associated with *libraries*. (C) *Fine print* is associated with *typesetting*. (D) *Prescription* is associated with *pharmacists*. However, none of these options is correct.

71. (D) *Having a hard time paying the staff* means being unable to *meet the payroll*. (A) The situation *is* known; they cannot pay the staff. (B) The company is having trouble *paying* all the new staff. It is unlikely to *need*, or want, more. (C) *Bank* is repeated from *bankruptcy*, and bankruptcy could be associated with *being sued*. However, there is no mention of this.

72. (A) The woman needs *steaks*, which are found at a *supermarket*. (B) The man's car needs some work, but they are not going to a *car wash*. (C) *Steaks* are associated with *restaurants*, but the speakers do not mention *going* to a restaurant. (D) *House* is repeated in the option, but in the dialog, the house referred to is that of one of the speakers.

73. (D) They are calling about *part-time help*, which means a *job*. (A) The jobs are for *snow removal*, but they are not looking for a *shovel*. (B) The *phone book* is a *book*, but there is no mention that they cannot find it. (C) *Phonebook* and *calling* are associated with *telephones*, but there is no indication that they are *looking for* a telephone.

74. (D) The *incoming orders* are being *re-routed* to Cairo while the electricity is off. (A) *Making telephone calls* and the *telephone company* are mentioned, but *telephones* are not being sent anywhere. (B) *Fax orders* are mentioned, but not a *new fax machine*. (C) *Electricity* and *electrical* have the same root, and *fax machines* and *telephones* are types of *equipment*. However, this option is not the correct answer.

75. (B) The woman is willing to wait to see and presumably enjoy, a sold-out show. (A) The woman does not have a ticket to *sell*. She wants to *buy* one. (C) *Wait* is repeated, *standing room* might be associated with a *bus*. However, this is not the answer. (D) *Returning a ticket* is associated with *getting a refund*, but the woman does not have a ticket to return.

76. (A) The people from the media are waiting *outside* until the ceremony is over. *Outside* means *outdoors*. (B) The people from the media are waiting. They are not *on their way* anywhere. (C) The reporters are *magazine reporters*, but they are not at their *headquarters*. (D) *Waiting* is repeated in the dialog and the option, but the dialog does not mention a *waiting room*.

77. (C) *Filet Mignon, turkey, duck*, and *dessert* are all meal items. Also, *caterers* are associated with *food*. (A) This option confuses the sounds of *dessert* and *desert*. (B) *Turkey* and *duck* are types of birds, but in the dialog they are spoken about in the form of food. (D) *Table* is repeated in the option, but in the dialog this refers to the table the food was on.

78. (C) An *architect* would *change blueprints*. (A) *Door* is repeated in the dialog and the option, but the man is not a *doorman*. (B) There is no indication that the woman is talking to a *neighbor*. (D) *Porch* and *entrance* are associated with *houses* and *real estate agents*, but agents do not *change blueprints*.

79. (A) A *blackout* is the result of a *power cut*. (B) *Patients, operating room* and *life-support systems* are all associated with *emergencies* and *operations*, but the event being discussed is a *blackout*. (C) *Automatic* is used in both the dialog and the option, but they are not talking about a *transmission*. (D) *Patients* are mentioned in the dialog, but a *new patient* is not being discussed.

80. (B) Tom was *promoted* to vice-president as the result of his hard work. (A) Someone wanting to work closer to home is a logical reason for a transfer, but there is no mention of this being the case. (C) Tom is described as a *hard worker*. (D) *Didn't you hear?* is a figurative question, but the woman does not really wonder about either the man's, or Tom's, hearing.

PART IV

81. (A) In this introduction, the speaker says that everyone knows Mr. Makowitz as the *Personnel Director*. (B) This introduction is being given at a *fund-raiser*, but *fundraising* is not his job in the company. (C) With his *efforts*, Mr. Makowitz has helped underprivileged children learn to read, but there is no suggestion he was a *tutor*. (D) Mr. Makowitz is a board member at the *Literacy Crusade,* not at the company.

82. (B) A *fund-raiser* is an event intended to *raise money*. (A) The event is to raise money to *help* children read, but *tutoring* them is not going to literally happen at this gathering. (C) Mr. Makowitz is acknowledged, but this is not the *purpose* of the gathering. (D) The *Literacy Crusade* has *already* been formed.

83. (C) During this period, *only management* will report to work. (A) Management is the *only* group who must report. This option *excludes (but)* management. (B) The *entire housekeeping staff* is *on leave*, or on holiday, *with pay*. (D) *All personnel* is repeated in both the announcement and the option, but this is not the correct answer.

84. (D) The re-opening will take place on the *eighth of April*. (A) The hotel closes for renovation *in November*. (B) *February* is not mentioned. (C) The hotel renovations should be complete *in March*.

85. (B) All personnel will be provided with *new uniforms*. *Outfits* can mean *uniforms*. (A) *Paychecks* are given to staff *throughout* the period via direct deposit. (C) In the announcement, *banquet* is used only in reference to the *banquet staff*. (D) The changes taking place *might* be associated with a *revised work schedule*, but this is not mentioned.

86. (A) The announcement is about a *fire marshal* who is there to supervise a *fire drill*. (B) *Front offices, rear offices, the east wing*, could all be associated with *office renovations*, but there is no mention of any renovations being planned. (C) This option confuses *accounted for* and *accounting*. (D) *Stairs* are used repeatedly in the announcement. *New* is also used. However, this is not the right answer.

87. (B) After everyone has evacuated the building, they will *gather* in the *parking lot*. (A) Everyone will *exit* through a stairwell, but they will not *gather* there. (C) No one is allowed to *use* the elevators, there is no mention of *gathering* there. (D) The *front offices* are mentioned in the dialog, but this is not where people will gather.

88. (C) The fire marshal will discuss the *new fire detection equipment*. (A) *Elevators* are mentioned in the dialog, but the fire marshal does not intend to *talk about* them. (B) *Speed* has a similar meaning to *proceed quickly*. (D) *Parking* is mentioned in the announcement, but *parking* is not the topic to be spoken about.

89. (D) The office is located at the intersection of *two main roads*: *Highway 55* and *Route 1*. (A) *University* is not mentioned in this recorded announcement. (B) *Emergency* is associated with *hospital*, but there is no reason to believe the office is *in* a hospital. (C) The office is at an *intersection* of *two main roads*. It is unlikely to be on a *quiet back street*.

90. (B) Because people may be calling with a *dental emergency* or about *teeth cleaning*, we can conclude that this is a *dentist's office*. (A) *Highway* is repeated in the option, but in the announcement it is used to state the location of the office. (C) *Emergency* is repeated, but there is no indication that this is a hospital. (D) *Clean* refers to *teeth* in the announcement. There is nothing about a *cleaning service*.

91. (D) If there is an emergency, *pressing 9* gets *immediate attention*. *Immediate* means *right away*. (A) *Staying on the line* and *waiting for the beep* allows you to *leave a message*. (B) *Regular office hours* are given in the recording, but there is no promise that calling *then* will get you an immediate response. (C) This option confuses the words *beep* and *beeper*.

92. (A) The advertisement is for a *publication* called *Investor's Choice*. (B) *Invest* is repeated in the option. *Fast-paced, rapidly* and *breathtaking* might suggest the idea of investing *quickly*. However, this is not what is being encouraged. (C) *Columnist* is repeated, but listeners will read what the columnists say in the magazine. They are unlikely to *talk* to any of them. (D) Being *conservative* may be a good investing policy, but it is not mentioned in the ad.

93. (D) The columnists are giving advice to deal with a *rapidly changing global economy*, or *worldwide economic change*. (A) *Temporary* is repeated in both the advertisement and the option, but *temporary conditions* are not being discussed. (B) *Stuck in the past* and *worried* are associated with *fear of failure*, but this is not the answer. (C) *Inflation* is not described as *short-term* in the advertisement.

94. (A) This announcement is intended to *reiterate*, or repeat, an old policy which *has been in effect for some time*. (B) *Expense reports* are mentioned in the announcement, but they seem to have *already* been explained. (C) This announcement reminds employees *how* to collect money from expenses, but to collect it *now* is not intended. (D) The policy has been in effect for some time now, so we know that it's not *new*.

95. (C) People are trying to be reimbursed without the required, or *proper*, paperwork. That is, they are *disregarding company policy* about paperwork. (A) The computers referred to in the announcement are *new*, they are not *breaking down*. (B) *Compensation*, *payday* and *accounting* are associated with *paychecks*, but there is no reason to believe that any are missing. (D) *Receipts* is repeated in both the announcement and the option, but there is no mention of any being misplaced.

96. (B) The accounting department *has its hands full*, or is busy with, the *new computers*. (A) *Compensation, payday* and *accounting* are associated with *paychecks*, but *writing paychecks* is not mentioned as part of accounting's current burden. (C) Accounting is *doing* the complaining. They are not *handling complaints*. (D) *Policy* is repeated in both the announcement and the option, but accounting is not revising any policies that we know of.

97. (D) The train will be able to *whisk along at unprecedented speeds*. This means it will be able to travel at very *high* speeds. (A) Trains *require* maintenance, but maintenance is not mentioned in this bulletin. (B) Sleek new trains often have a *streamlined look*, but this is not mentioned in this bulletin. (C) The design is considered *economical*, but *cost-effectiveness* is not mentioned in the bulletin.

98. (C) The train will *float* inches above the track on *magnetic fields*. (A) The train does not *ride* on a rail, rather it floats above it. (B) Because the train is floating, we can assume that it does not use *wheels* to move. (D) The train does not *slide* on anything — it floats.

99. (D) This announcement contains important information for *all* passengers. (A) *Elderly* and *disabled* customers have special seats reserved, but the announcement is not *only* for them. (B) *Small children* are specifically mentioned, but the announcement is not only for them. (C) *Subway personnel* may *make* this announcement, they are not who it is intended for.

100. (A) The bell sounds just as the doors are *about to close*. (B) There is no mention of a bell connected with the elevators mentioned in the announcement. (C) There is no indication that a bell goes off *before* the train arrives. (D) The *red button* should be pressed when in need of assistance, but there is no mention that it sounds a bell.

PART V

101. (C) The infinitive follows *advise* plus object.
(A) *Swimming* is the gerund form. (B) *Swam* is the past tense. (D) *To have swum* is the perfect infinitive.

102. (D) The present perfect is formed by *have* plus the past participle: *has invested*. (A) *Was invested* is the passive voice. (B) The simple present *invest* does not follow *has*. (C) *Investing* is the present participle.

103. (A) *Playing* is used as the gerund. (B) *To go play* is not possible in this context. (C) *Play* is the simple present form. (D) The infinitive, *to play*, does not follow the verb *find*.

104. (B) *Be continued* means *proceed*. (A) *Concurred* means *agreed* and is illogical. (C) *Contoured* means *curved* and is illogical in this context. (D) *Confounded* means *confused* which could not apply to the noun *negotiations*.

105. (A) *Buying and selling* is a thing and therefore, the pronoun *something* should be used. (B) *Somewhere* indicates a place. (C) The pronoun *somehow* indicates *in some manner*. (D) *Somewhat* indicates a degree, or how much.

106. (C) *Generate* is a synonym for *produce*. (A) *Order* is illogical. (B) and (D) The stocks will neither *cause* nor *develop* dividends.

107. (D) The unreal (second) conditional uses *if* plus past tense. (A) *Will be* indicates the future tense. (B) The simple present, *is*, is not used in this conditional sentence. (C) *Has been* is the present perfect.

108. (A) *Than* indicates a comparison; therefore *sooner* is needed. (B) *Soonest* is the superlative form, used when more than two objects are involved. (C) *Soon* is the simple adverb. (D) *Some soon* is not a possible combination.

109. (B) *Affluent* means *rich* and refers to people.
(A) and (D) *Opulent* and *expensive* are used to describe things. (C) *Abundant* refers to quantity.

110. (A) To *look at* is the correct verb plus preposition.
(B) You *look to* someone for advice. (C) You *look on* the table, the floor, etc. (D) If you are trying to find something, you might *look by* the door.

111. (C) *In style* means *in fashion or currently fashionable*.
(A), (B) and (D) *Around*, *through* and *unto* do not combine with *style*.

112. (D) A *license* gives you the authority to do something.
(A) *Presence* is illogical in this context. (B) You may receive a *ticket* if you disobey the laws when driving. (C) A *diploma* is given after completion of some course or program.

113. (A) *Just as* means equally. (B) *Not quite* could be used in this context; *quite* does not fit. (C) *Moreover* is used for emphasis. (D) *Same* is used with the definite article.

114. (B) *Few* is used for countable nouns. The comparative form, *fewer*, is needed to parallel the comparative *slower*.
(A) *Less* is used for non-count nouns such as *sugar*.
(C) The comparative form is needed. (D) *Least* is the superlative form.

115. (A) *Come in* indicates the direction. (B) and (D) *Come over* and *come down* do not indicate the correct direction for the tide. (C) The tide *goes out*.

116. (A) An adjective is needed to precede the noun.
(B) *Hardly* is the adverb and does not precede a noun.
(C) The definite article precedes the superlative form.
(D) *Harden* is the verb form.

117. (C) *Next to* means *almost*. (A) *Because of* starts a clause that explains the previous clause. (B) *By way of* begins a clause indicating *how*. (D) *Close to* would fit; *closest to* implies a comparison.

118. (B) *These* indicates a plural noun. (A) *Plan* is a singular noun. (C) *Planning* can be used as a noun in the form of a gerund, but is considered singular. (D) *Planned* is the past participle.

119. (C) You either *see* or *understand* a point of view.
(A) One person is not able to *think* another person's point of view. (B) *Mind* is illogical in this context. (D) *Reckon* means *to guess* or *to consider*, but is not used with *a point of view*.

120. (A) *Intensive* means *to require a lot of,* as in *labor*.
(B) *Involved* is not used to describe a type of industry.
(C) *Indicative* means *suggestive*. (D) *Incisive* means *sharp*.

121. (D) *Everyone* is considered singular. (A) *Anyone* is used with a negative, usually *not*. (B) *All* requires a plural verb. (C) *One another* is commonly found after a verb.

122. (D) *Hiring* means *to employ*. (A) *Employ* is a transitive verb, i.e. it takes an object. (B) and (C) *Analyzing* and *specifying* are not logical in this context.

123. (D) The simple form of the verb follows *will*.
(A) and (B) The progressive forms *having issued* and *issuing* do not follow the verb *will*. (C) *Will* is never followed by the infinitive.

124. (B) *Anyone* is used with the negative form *not*.
(A) Two negatives, *not* and *no one*, cannot appear in the same clause. (C) *Someone* is not preceded by the negative *not*. (D) *Each one* indicates a specific person.

125. (C) *So* indicates purpose. (A) *Because* is used to explain the previous clause. (B) *But* connects contrasting clauses. (D) *For* in formal English means the same as *because*.

126. (A) *Much* quantifies *more*. (B) *Many more* is followed by a plural noun. (C) *That more* is not a possible combination; *that much more* would be possible. (D) *The more* is used in expressions describing a condition and its result, e.g. *the more attractive the book, the higher the sales*.

127. (A) *Any* is used to refer to all members of a group. (B) *Ones* refers to specific computers. (C) *Many* refers to more than one, and in this sentence we are not sure if one or many computers will be bought. (D) *Other* refers to a specific alternative group.

128. (D) *Cut off* means *stop the supply of something*. (A) *Shut off* has the same meaning but is used to refer to water, electricity, etc. (B) and (C) *Closed off* and *sealed off* mean *to deny access to*.

129. (B) The adjective form *suspicious* describes the buyer. (A) *Suspects* can be used as either a plural noun or a verb. (C) *Suspicion* is a noun. (D) *Suspected* is the past participle form.

130. (C) *Well in advance* describes when. (A) and (B) *Much sooner* or *much faster* could be used to complete the sentence; *well sooner* and *well faster* are not possible. (D) *Well previous* is not possible.

131. (D) *Much* is used for non-count nouns. (A) *Less* is used for comparison. (B) and (C) *Many* and *few* are used for countable nouns.

132. (C) The third conditional expresses an imaginary situation about the past, so the verb is in the simple past. (A) *Would belong* indicates present or future time. (B) *Belong* is the simple present tense. (D) The verb *belong* indicates a state and is not used in the progressive form.

133. (A) *Too* is used to quantify *many*. (B) *Any* indicates *none* and cannot be used with *many*. (C) *Few* is the opposite of *many*. (D) *Hardly* is used with *any*.

134. (A) The modal *must* is followed by the base form of the verb. (B) The infinitive (*to* + verb) never follows *must*. (C) *Functioned* is the past participle. (D) *Functioning* is the present participle; *be functioning* would be possible.

135. (A) An object is needed after the preposition *for*; *the* is followed by the gerund *asking* which is used as a noun. (B) *To ask* is the infinitive and never follows the preposition *for*. (C) *Ask* is a verb and cannot follow *the*. (D) *You asked* is a pronoun plus past tense verb form.

136. (C) The present simple, *connect*, is needed. (A) *Am connected* is the passive voice, and is not followed by an object pronoun. (B) The infinitive form cannot follow the subject pronoun. (D) *Connected* is the past tense; the action is in the present.

137. (A) *Address* means *to talk to*. (B) The preposition *to* is needed with the verb *talk* when who is mentioned. (C) In this context, the preposition *on* would need to accompany the verb *focus*. (D) In this context, the preposition *with* would need to accompany the verb *communicate*.

138. (B) The preposition *at* indicates a specific location. (A) The sentence would need to include the box office and another location. (C) and (D) *Around* and *by* indicate vague locations near the box office; however the box office is a specific location.

139. (D) *By the government* indicates the passive voice (appropriate form of the verb *be* + the past participle). (A) *Will have been* should be followed by the past participle and not the progressive form. (B) *Are being subsidized* would be possible. (C) The government is subsidizing the crops, not vice versa.

140. (A) Somebody can be friendly *with* or *to* someone. (B), (C) and (D) *At, on* and *across* are incorrect prepositions.

PART VI

141. (B) The gerund *surrounding* replaces the relative clause: *which surrounds*. (A) *Wooden* is an adjective used to describe the fence. (C) *Is beginning* is the present progressive. (D) *From rain* is a prepositional phrase.

142. (D) The first verb in the sentence, *resigned*, indicates the past tense; *become* should also be in the past tense. (A) *Head* is an adjective describing *lawyer*. (B) *From* is the correct preposition to follow *resigned*. (C) *When* is a conjunction joining the two clauses.

143. (B) You *search for* something. (A) The noun *tire* forms a compound to describe what kind of industry. (C) *As* is a conjunction meaning *because*. (D) *Are dwindling* is in the present progressive and refers to the *sources*.

144. (D) The past participle *ignored* is needed in the passive voice. (A) The adjective *apparent* follows the verb *to be*. (B) *To expand* is the infinitive. (C) *Into* is the correct preposition to follow the verb, *expand*.

145. (D) *With someone's blessing* means *with their approval*. (A) *Since* is used as a conjunction explaining why. (B) *Herself* is a reflexive pronoun referring to *Mrs. Papin*. (C) *It was assumed* is the passive voice.

146. (C) *And so* refers to a result; *so* should be used here to indicate a reason. (A) The preposition *after* is followed by a noun. (B) *To take* is the infinitive, which follows the verb *decide*. (D) The modal *could* is followed by the base form of the verb *spend* and then an object, *more time*.

147. (A) *Like* can be followed by either the infinitive, *to travel*, or the gerund, *traveling*. (B) The modal *should* is followed by the simple form of the verb. (C) The correct preposition *in* is used. (D) *Travel-related* is an adjective used to describe the noun, *field*.

148. (D) The noun *suitcase* is singular and therefore the singular pronoun *it* should follow. (A) The phrase *almost an hour* describes the length of time. (B) The gerund *realizing* follows the preposition *before*. (C) *Had forgotten* is the past perfect tense, referring to an earlier time period.

149. (D) *That* is required after the noun (*steps*); *what* means *the thing that*, so it replaces the preceding noun. (A) *In order to* introduces a clause explaining what must happen. (B) *According to schedule* is a prepositional phrase. (C) *Have to* is a synonym of *must* and is followed by the bare infinitive.

150. (C) *It's* is a contraction of *it is*; the possessive pronoun is *its*. (A) *Native* describes the noun *population*. (B) The present perfect *has begun* indicates that the documenting started in the past and continues to the present. (D) *Migratory* is the adjective form of the noun *migration*.

151. (A) *Every* is followed by the singular form of the noun. (B) When referring to the range, the prepositions *from* and *to* are used. (C) *Will be inspected* is the passive voice showing future time. (D) The preposition *for* is followed by a noun, *compliance*.

152. (D) The adverb *ahead* cannot precede the noun. (A) The noun *results* is followed by the preposition *of*. (B) The verb *show* refers to *the results*, which is plural. (C) The quantifier *quite* describes the noun *a demand*.

153. (C) The action that happens first should be in the past perfect, followed by the simple past tense *sold*. (A) *From this bill of sale* is a prepositional phrase. (B) The modal *can* is followed by the base form of the verb, *see*. (D) *About six months* is a prepositional phrase.

154. (B) The causative *have* is followed by the past participle, *replaced*. (A) *Is having* is the present progressive. (C) *Second and third* are adjectives describing *floors*. (D) *As well as* means *in addition to*.

155. (C) *Has been* refers to the noun *developments* and should be plural. (A) *Recent* is an adjective that describes *developments*. (B) *In the field of* is a prepositional phrase. (D) *Those who* is a determiner used to specify a group.

156. (B) The application cannot send, therefore the passive voice, *is sent*, is needed. (A) *Initially* is the adverb describing when. (C) *Who must check* is the relative clause giving us more information about *the loan officer*. (D) *Before* is a preposition indicating a time frame.

157. (C) *Authority* is a noun; the adjective *authoritative* is needed to describe the noun *sources*. (A) The subject of the sentence is the plural noun *reports*. (B) *In hotel costs* is a prepositional phrase. (D) *The industry* refers to a specific industry.

158. (B) The reduced relative *used* is required, meaning *which was used*. (A) The subject *tests* is followed by the past tense form of the verb, *revealed*. (C) *Particular* modifies *model*. (D) *Of inferior quality* is a prepositional phrase.

159. (B) This sentence requires the simple past in the passive, *were released*. (A) *When* is a conjunction connecting two phrases with time reference. (C) *Scholars* is the plural subject of the sentence. (D) *Dumbfounded* is the past participle, meaning *surprised* or *shocked*.

160. (D) *Analyses* is the plural form of the noun, therefore, the plural *were* is needed. (A) A gerund follows the preposition *after*. (B) *In profits* is a prepositional phrase. (C) *Were convinced* is the passive voice.

PART VII

161. (B) *To learn* (... *by knowing which tools were best for the job*) and *earn more* (... *my income is rising*). (A), (C) and (D) *To get job offers, to get discounts* and *to understand finances* are not mentioned.

162. (A) One subscriber says that costs have gone down due to *time-saving tips*. (B) *A free CD* is not mentioned. (C) Income is mentioned; however *guaranteed income* is not mentioned. (D) *Free services* are not mentioned.

163. (C) A handyman usually *builds* or repairs things. (A) There is no mention of *cooking*. (B) The *customers* benefit by getting lower costs. (D) An *electrician* might benefit from the guide; but it is primarily for builders.

164. (D) The first sentence in the third paragraph states that the effects may be more deadly or *dangerous* than people think. (A) There is no indication that the author holds a *controversial position*. (B) There is no mention of new *scientific research*. (C) The author would probably be against *selling forests to developers*.

165. (D) The second sentence in the second paragraph indicates that ...*forests are so central to life on Earth* or that the effects *are so widespread*. (A) *Forests are vast* but the effects can be seen. (B) The effects appear at all stages. (C) *The hope of reforestation remains* is illogical.

166. (D) After the forest is cut, it is *cleared by loggers* and exploited by hunters, miners, and farmers. (A) Generally forests are not *reforested*. (B) When forests are not cut, they *stabilize the climate, foster bio-diversity, and stop flooding*. (C) There are several stages between the forest being *cut down and dying*.

167. (A) With the software *you can anticipate your net income*. (B) *Health insurance costs* are mentioned, but not that they will be lower. (C) *Tax shelters* are not mentioned. (D) The buyer should learn about *more deductions*.

168. (C) If you need the software, it is because *taxes are complex*. (A) The ad does not mention *pay raises*. (B) The implication is that more *deductions* could be claimed. (D) There is mention of a *savings potential* but not that *saving money takes time*.

169. (B) The medication should not be taken while driving, therefore, *a chauffeur* should not take it. (A), (C) and (D) *A writer, a waitress* and *a clerk* do not need to drive or operate machinery in their work.

170. (B) *Nausea* means the same as *an upset stomach*. (A) An effect is *dry mouth*, not *dry skin*. (C) *Hunger* is not mentioned. (D) *Headaches* are mentioned, but not *light-headedness*.

171. (D) A *rash* is a *skin irritation* and these people should see a doctor. (A) It does not mention that *people with nausea* should see a doctor. (B) Only those with a rash should see a doctor. (C) Before the person sees a doctor, he or she should *discontinue use*.

172. (C) *Fax* is an abbreviation for *facsimile*. (A) *An express mail transmission* would not indicate the duration. (B) Details such as *pages* and *duration* are not consistent with a *serial number record*. (D) The report refers to *transmission* not *arrival*.

173. (D) The duration was *00:00:38*. (A) *06/18* indicates the date. (B) *06:19* indicates the time that the fax was sent. (C) *01* indicates the number of pages.

174. (A) *01* is indicated after *pages*. (B) The number *6* indicates either the month, June, or the time 6:19. (C) The number *11* is not mentioned. (D) *38* indicates the number of seconds it took to send the fax.

175. (B) Point 2 mentions *items ordered*. (A) The order form is for *electronic equipment*, but the equipment is not described. (C) *Refunds* are not mentioned. (D) The recipient is to *make any corrections* if the address is wrong, but this is not the purpose of the form.

176. (D) It states that a *street address is required for shipment*. (A) *Deliveries cannot be made to P.O. Boxes*. (B) There are several ways to pay; a *credit card* is one option. (C) *Advance payment* is not mentioned.

177. (A) The change is *effective immediately*, or *right away*. (B) Employees should sign up for automatic deposit before *February 23*. (C) Paychecks were handed out on *Fridays*. (D) Paychecks are available on the *first and third Monday of each month*.

178. (A) The memo states that ... *your check will be put directly into your checking account*. (B) The check is deposited into your bank account, not *in the mail*. (C) *Checks will* not *be handed out on Fridays*. (D) *Taxes are withheld regardless of payment method* is unrelated to automatic deposit.

179. (D) The employees must *sign for their check*. (A) *Providing an employee number and photo I.D.* is not mentioned. (B) They need to sign for their check on Monday, not necessarily *work on the Monday*. (C) Employees *must sign up by February 23* if they want their checks to be deposited directly.

180. (D) The last sentence states that the company is not responsible for lost checks and that employees pay any fees. (A) *The employee would pick it up on the next Monday* is illogical. (B) The employee and not *the company would pay for a stop payment*. (C) *A deposit slip would be automatically sent to the employee* is not mentioned.

181. (B) The heading on the memo is: *Attention all hourly employees*. (A) Other employees who are not hourly, but salaried, may also go to *Human Resources*. (C) The notice applies also to people who are not interested in *automatic deposit*. (D) The memo is for hourly employees, not those who are interested in becoming paid by the hour.

182. (D) The heading is *In-flight instructions*, which refers to *planes*. (A) You would read this on a plane, not at *the airport*. (B) *A boat trip* is not referred to as a flight. (C) *A hospital* is not mentioned.

183. (C) The instructions begin with *please go to your seat*. (A) *Going to the pilot* is not mentioned. (B) *Flight attendants* will assist after everyone is in their seats. (D) *Exit ramps* are only mentioned as being clearly marked.

184. (B) ... *an oxygen mask will automatically fall from the overhead compartment*. (A) *Under the seat* is not mentioned. (C) *The exit ramps* are only mentioned as being clearly marked. (D) *In the rear of the cabin* is not mentioned.

185. (A) *If you are with a child, first put on your own mask*. (B) *Calling the attendant* is not mentioned. (C) The parent should put on his or her mask first and then *the child's mask*. (D) *Going to the exit* is not mentioned.

186. (C) The ad is aimed at people who are (buying or) selling houses, i.e. *homeowners*. (A) The service provides photographs, but it is not aimed at *photographers*. (B) The service provides research into the *architects*. (D) *Construction engineers* would not need to find out about the history of a house.

187. (A) The company's offices are on *J Street*. (B), (C) and (D) Some of the houses that were researched were located on *8th Avenue, K Street* and *9th Avenue*.

188. (C) Enclosed with the letter is *information about the convention*. (A) The purpose is not only *to find the location of the convention*, but also to provide more general information. (B) The letter mentions discounts at the *Maxton Hotel*, but this is not its primary purpose. (D) The letter includes information *about accommodations*, it does not ask for information.

189. (B) *Enclosed you will find convention information*. (A) The hotel is offering a discount, however there are no *hotel discount coupons* enclosed. (C) *Reports about last year's convention* is not mentioned. (D) Langh Thien wants to have dinner with *Dr. Jean Delois*.

190. (D) Langh Thien says *"maybe this year your entire staff could join you."* (A) He refers to information that the *special events coordinator* told him. (B) Langh Thien hopes that they can meet at the convention, not at *Levine & Schmidt*. (C) There is no mention of *contacting Dr. Delois*.

191. (C) The title of the article includes the words *why their bites itch*. (A) *Mosquito nesting habits* are not mentioned. (B) *The diet of the mosquito* may consist solely of blood, but this is not the subject of the article. (D) The difficulty of finding blood vessels is mentioned but *how mosquitos find blood vessels* is not stated.

192. (B) *Mosquitos pump in chemicals*. (A) and (C) The chemicals are injected into the *human skin* and *the blood vessels*. (D) *The blood* is thinned by the chemicals.

193. (B) The final paragraph discusses how to find *a good financial advisor.* (A) The advisor may help you decide *which companies to invest in.* (C) *How politics affect company profits* is only mentioned indirectly (*... he watches the local political climate*). (D) The article states that most people do not have time to *research stocks and bonds.*

194. (C) The notice is aimed at *advising investors* (*... trying to find out which investment is best ... the best advice*). (A) The notice gives advice, but is not as strong as *a warning.* (B) The notice is about investing, but it does not directly *encourage investment.* (D) *Supporting independent businesses* is not mentioned.

195. (D) The third paragraph mentions *internal and external factors.* (A) *Access to multiple stocks and bonds* is not mentioned. (B) *A background in politics* is illogical. (C) *A master's degree in economics* may be helpful, but not necessarily.

196. (A) The article says that either you or your advisor has to do the research. (B) *Getting advice from another investor* would be the same as *hearsay,* which the passage does not recommend. (C) *Find a company with a good name* is not mentioned. (D) *Following demand carefully* is only one aspect of managing investments.

197. (C) *... the biggest reason people buy a house is so that they can have a place they can call their own.* (A) and (D) Although 50% said that *they didn't want to pay rent* or *have a landlord* this was not the biggest reason. (B) Only 25% wanted to *have their own yard* or property for their children to play on.

198. (B) *10%* wanted to *buy the house to sell later at a profit,* or in other words, *as an investment.* (A) *5%* wanted room for pets. (C) *25%* wanted property for their children to play on. (D) *50%* did not want to pay rent.

199. (A) *Next to having your own place,* the greatest reason for buying a house is *the urge to build, remodel, and choose design interiors,* i.e. *wanting to renovate and decorate.* (B) *Seeing it as an investment* only counted for 10%. (C) Only 5% were concerned about *having a place for the cats and dogs.* (D) Less than 1% wanted to *impress others.*

200. (D) Less than 1% wanted a home to put them *in a certain social station,* i.e. as a *matter of prestige.* (A) 5% were concerned about *having a yard for animals.* (B) 10% *wanted to build equity* (*motivated by financial reasons*). (C) *Having their own place* was the greatest factor.

Answer Key

Practice Test Four

In the following Answer Key, the first explanation provided for each question is the correct option.

PART I

1. (A) The train *tracks* run *in front of* the people waiting on the platform. (B) The train has windows but no *conductor* is shown in the picture. (C) The sound of *racks* is similar to *tracks* and could be confused. (D) *Rain* sounds similar to *train,* but it is not raining in this picture.

2. (C) The man is looking at food displayed on shelves *behind glass.* (A) There is a menu on the wall, but he does not have one *in his hand.* (B) There are beverages on the shelves behind the glass. We do not know what is *under the counter.* (D) There are drinks machines in the background, but no *coffee* in a *cup.*

3. (D) The lap-top computer is resting on his legs, or *in his lap.* (A) There are *keys* on a keyboard but he does not have any keys in his hand. (B) If he was taking a *nap,* he would be asleep. *Nap* sounds similar to *lap.* (C) The sound of *typing* might be confused with *taping,* but there is no recording device in the picture.

4. (D) The *lights,* or lampposts, are in the middle of the street and there are a few small trees between them. (A) There is an arch design in the building, but no *arch* anywhere else in the picture. (B) Most of the buildings have considerably *more* than one floor, or *story.* (C) There are no visible *stoplights* along this road, only lights, or lampposts.

5. (C) The workers are building a large boat, or *yacht.* (A) The men are *wearing* overalls. They are not *putting them on.* (B) This boat is still being built and is not *ready to sail.* (D) *Lumber* is wood used for building or carpentry. The ship *could* be made of lumber, but there is no other lumber visible in the picture that could also be *for the ship.*

6. (B) The tour *guide* is talking into the *mike,* or microphone. (A) The guide, not a *tourist, leads* the group. (C) *Slides,* or photographs, are associated with *travel,* but there are not any in this picture. (D) This option confuses the sound of *guide* with *guard,* and *mike* with *hike.*

7. (B) She's standing at the *check-out* paying for her shopping. (A) *Tipping* is related to good service in a restaurant or café, but not a shop. (C) The clerk has *cash* in her hand, not a *credit card.* (D) She is looking for something in her handbag, not putting her groceries in bags.

8. (D) The passengers are standing in a line and getting onto the plane one by one. They are *boarding* it. (A) The plane and the passengers are *on the runway* at an airport. However, the plane is stationary, it is not *landing.* (B) The passengers are boarding, or getting onto the plane. They are not *getting off* it. *Get off* sounds similar to *take off,* a phrase associated with planes meaning to leave the ground and begin to fly. (C) The plane is stationary in the picture. It will *take off* when all of the passengers are on board.

9. (C) The *scientist* is looking at, or *peering* at, something under the microscope. (A) The person may be a *chemist,* but he is not *mixing* anything. (B) The person is looking into a *microscope,* not somebody's *mouth.* There is also only one person in the picture whereas this option refers to two. (D) *Focusing* is associated with microscopes, but we do not know what the person is *focusing on* and we cannot see any *shapes* in the picture.

10. (B) The people are walking down the steps. (A) An *escalator* is a type of electrical staircase that moves. These stairs are not moving. (C) A *ladder* has steps, and *climb* is associated with steps, but there is no ladder in this picture. (D) The stairs are made of *brick,* or concrete, not *wood.*

11. (C) The *work space* is open. There are no walls *dividing* one work area from another. (A) A *conference room* is a type of office where people have meetings, usually containing one large table and a number of chairs. This is not a conference room. (B) There are no *doors* in this picture, either open *or* closed. (D) A *warehouse* is used to *store* things. The room *is* full of computers, but they are being used, not stored.

12. (D) Not all of the *seats* have people sitting in them, so some of them are *empty.* (A) The *patrons,* or customers, are *already* in their seats. They are not *being seated,* or shown to their seats. (B) The tables are not neatly arranged *in rows.* They are *randomly* arranged. (C) There are lights, but they are not *on* because it is daytime. Therefore the light cannot be *bright.*

13. (D) He's *using,* or talking on, a *mobile phone.* (A) The man may be *selling* something, and we can clearly see his *socks.* However, there is no indication he is *selling socks.* (B) He may be *waiting* for something or someone, but there is no indication he is waiting for a *part.* (C) He's talking on the phone, but he is not in a *phone booth.*

14. (D) There is a pedestrian *standing by,* or near, *a car* in the picture. (A) There are palm trees lining the street. There is no *park* visible. (B) There is no *stop sign* in the picture. (C) The cars are all on a straight road. None of them are *turning a corner.*

15. (A) The doctors are in the middle of performing an *operation* on a *patient*. (B) *Cutting* is associated with operations, but there is no evidence of cutting happening in this picture. *Meat* is used to refer to dead animals, not human beings. (C) The *tubes* are connected to the body, they are not *being removed*. (D) The body has *muscles*, but the doctors are *operating*, not *massaging*.

16. (B) The restaurant worker is *filling the glass* with a beverage, or a drink. (A) The glass is being *used*, not *cleaned*. (C) The beverage she is pouring is not *coffee*, it is a clear liquid. However, there is a coffee maker behind her. (D) She's *pouring*, not *drinking*, the beverage.

17. (C) The *diners* are sitting at tables eating and drinking *by the water*. (A) The waiter is serving, he is not touching any of the umbrellas. (B) The couples are not *swimming* in the water, they are *sitting* by it. (D) The customers are *being served*, they are not doing the serving.

18. (C) The man *operates an elevator* and he is *pushing a button*. (A) A *bellboy* also works in a hotel, carrying bags to guests' rooms, but there are no *bags* or *guests* in this picture. (B) A *presenter* would be waiting for *attendees* at a conference or seminar. This man may be waiting, but he is not a speaker at a conference. (D) The man is *pushing* a button, not *fastening* the buttons on his jacket.

19. (A) Different types of plants are growing *against the wall* of the building. (B) The bicycle is *in front of* the car, not *on top of* it. (C) A *highway* is much bigger than the road pictured here. A highway would not pass this close to houses. (D) The wall in the picture is *part of* the house, it does not *surround* it.

20. (B) The *cash register* has both bills, or paper money, and *change*, or coins. (A) The *cash* is in the register, not in a *bag*. (C) *Currency* and *safe* are both related to money, but there is no safe shown in the picture. (D) He's *handling* bills, but he is not giving, or handing, anything to a customer.

PART II

21. (B) The ship is arriving as the speakers speak. (A) *Shipments* is related to *ship*, but the questioner is not asking about aspects of *inspection*. (C) If something had arrived, we might expect someone to *get it*, but this option does not answer the question.

22. (A) The person cannot remember the *name* of the song. However, the person does remember that it was an *unusual* name. (B) *Remember* and *name* are repeated in both the question and the answer, but *his* implies a person not a song. (C) *Song* is repeated in *songwriter*, and this option confuses the sounds of *member* with *remember*.

23. (C) The new plane's *top*, or *fastest* speed is *500 miles an hour*. (A) *Plane* is repeated, and *flew* relates to planes. Also, a supersonic plane is very *fast*. However, this option does not answer the question. (B) *Plane* sounds like *plain*, and *travel* is used in both the question and the option.

24. (B) Nobody will be *in charge*, because the office will be *closed*. (A) Since the secretary will be *away all week*, he or she cannot possibly be *in charge*. (C) *Charge* is repeated, but with a different meaning.

25. (C) The respondent says the speaker *can* use the batteries and adds the additional information that four are required. (A) and (B) *Light* is repeated from *flashlight*, but neither of these options is correct.

26. (A) This option confirms that the number of *potential readers* will be established through *marketing surveys*. (B) *Read* is repeated, but the respondent's habits are irrelevant. (C) *Readers* and *book stores* are related, and *twenty-five* answers *how many?* However, book shops are not the topic.

27. (B) The speaker estimates that there are *twenty cars* on the train. (A) *Trains* is repeated, but the questioner is not asking about *speed*. (C) *Cars* is repeated, but this option does not answer the question.

28. (B) When the speaker arrives, she will immediately call. (A) *Call* is repeated in the question and option, but the meanings are different. (C) This option confuses the sound of *hair* with *there*.

29. (A) The speaker hopes that the Seoul office will open by the *end of the month*. While you might normally expect a specific date in answer to this question, the speaker does not *know* an exact date. (B) Next week might be a good answer to *when?* However, this option confuses the words *open* and *openings*. (C) *Proprietor* may relate to *office*, but the sound of *sole* is confused with *Seoul*.

30. (B) The speaker liked the *set* and *costumes*. Rather than saying directly that he liked or did not like the opera, he gives it qualified praise. (A) The words *opera* and *operating* are confused. (C) The words *opera* and *cooperate* are confused.

31. (C) The question assumes that the speaker *has* changed her mind. However, this response shows that the questioner's assumption was wrong – the speaker has *not* changed her mind. (A) *Mind* is repeated, but with a different meaning. (B) *Change* is repeated, but the context is different.

32. (A) The person does not know the answer to the question, but thinks that Mary will. (B) *Report* is used in both the question and option. Also, *should* could indicate a guess about whether the item is the summary report. However, this option does not answer the question. (C) This option confuses the sounds of *summary* and *summer*.

33. (B) The auction is open to the public only *on the weekends.* This type of qualified answer is common on the TOEIC. Rather than a simple *yes* or *no* response, a limitation is given. (A) *Auction* and *function* have the same suffix and may be confused. (C) *Public* is repeated, but this option does not answer the question.

34. (A) The person has not *yet* put an ad in the paper, but plans to do so *in the morning.* (B) This option confuses *ad* with *add.* (C) *Paper* is repeated and this option confuses the sounds of *ad* and *pad.*

35. (B) Selling real estate is more *lucrative,* or profitable. (A) *Sell* and *estate* are repeated, but the context is different. (C) This option confuses the words *choose* and *choosy.*

36. (C) The person does not know the answer to the question, but will *call* to find out. (A) *Express* is repeated, but the meaning is different. (B) This option confuses *press* with *express.*

37. (A) The person cannot *call ahead* because she does not have the telephone number. (B) The sounds of *warmer* and *warn* may be confused. (C) *Ahead* is repeated, but this option does not answer the question.

38. (B) Not only has the person put in a *bid,* but it was the first bid that was *received.* (A) This option confuses the sounds of *bid* and *bib.* (C) *Project* and *plan* may be synonyms, but this option does not answer the question.

39. (C) Of course the speaker *will* come to the celebration. (A) *Came* is the past of *come,* but the question is directed to the speaker, not to other people *(they).* (B) A celebration might start, or finish, at 2:15, but that is not the question.

40. (A) The respondent says the company *used to* sell laboratory equipment and adds the information that they sold it *wholesale.* (B) *Lab* is repeated from *Laboratory,* but the topic is *equipment,* not location. (C) This option confuses the sounds of *laboratory* and *lavatory.*

41. (C) Excessive use of *air conditioning* explains why the electric bill is so high. (A) *High* is repeated in the question and the option, but in different contexts. (B) *Accounts* is repeated in the question and option, but in different contexts.

42. (A) Bill's solution saved the speaker from coming to a complete *standstill,* but a *standstill* was close. A *standstill* is a *stoppage.* (B) This option confuses s*tandstill* and *stand still.* (C) This option confuses *standstill* and *handstand.*

43. (C) The speaker suggests explaining things to the boss *truthfully.* (A) *Explained* and *boss* are repeated, but it is not the boss who will do any explaining. (B) This option confuses the sounds of *explain* and *plain.*

44. (B) Actually, they did not *figure it out,* or solve the problem. Rather, they had the *answer sheet.* (A) *Figure* is repeated, but *skating* is not the topic. (C) Both *figure* and *quickly* are repeated, but this option does not answer the question.

45. (A) The speaker is pleased to accept the invitation for a plant tour. (B) *Plant* is repeated in the option, but the question is not about quantity. (C) This option confuses the sounds of *tour* and *pour.*

46. (A) The speaker agrees to ask the company's lawyer and will do it that afternoon. (B) Not *liking* to do something may be a good reason not to do it, and *lawyer* and *laundry* both start with the same letter. However, the question is not about laundry. (C) *Company* is repeated in both the question and the option, but the meanings are different.

47. (B) The boss has not arrived because his plane has not even landed yet. (A) *Boss* is repeated, and someone who is *driving* can be expected to *arrive.* However, this option does not answer the question. (C) *Five o'clock* may be a time that the boss will *arrive,* but this option refers to somebody in the first-person getting something. It does not refer to the boss' arrival.

48. (A) A tax break, if it were big enough, *would* be incentive. (B) This option confuses the sounds of *incentive* and *insensitive.* (C) *Break* is repeated and the sounds of *tax* and *ax* are confused.

49. (C) A *few hours* is *enough* notice for her. (A) and (B) *Notice* is repeated in both options, but neither answers the question.

50. (B) The speaker plans to *save* the extra income *for a house.* (A) This option confuses the sounds of *suggest* and *guests,* and *come in* with *income.* (C) *Extra* is repeated, but a reply to somebody asking for a suggestion is unlikely to be in the past tense.

PART III

51. (B) The speakers are discussing a bill for a meal, so they are in a *restaurant*. (A) and (C) *Bills* and *paying* are often associated with *stores* and *theaters*, but neither of these answers is correct. (D) There is no indication that they are in a *train station*.

52. (A) The new accountant wants to *see*, or *inspect*, the records from *last year*. (B) *Taste* might be confused with *sample*, but food is not the topic. (C) *Storage* is repeated in the option, but there is no mention of the accountant *buying* anything in the dialog. (D) *Box up* and *pack up* can be synonyms, and *records* and *files* can be related. However, this option is not the correct answer.

53. (D) Stefan has been taking time off by pretending to be sick. He has therefore not been doing his job. (A) *Sick* is repeated, and *boss* and *manager* often refer to the same person. However, there is no mention of any of the managers being sick. (B) A person who is looking for a new job, as Stefan may soon be doing, may be *unemployed*, but *rising unemployment* is not the topic of this dialog. (C) It is *Stefan* who was reprimanded.

54. (A) Because the woman wants the rooms *recarpeted*, she must be talking to a *carpet installer*. (B) *Office* is repeated, and *manage* might be confused with *manager*. However, he is not an *office manager*. (C) A *janitor* might clear out the rooms, but is unlikely to do the carpeting. (D) *Manager* is repeated, and *restaurant* and *cafeteria* have similar meanings, but the woman is not talking to a *restaurant manager*.

55. (C) *Vapors* and *gas* have the same meaning. (A), (B) and (D) These options are all materials that could require safety equipment, but it is unlikely that any would *give off poisonous vapors*. Also, there is no mention of any of these materials.

56. (D) Because the speakers are discussing *requirements for a position*, we know that the woman is *applying for a job*. (A) One job requirement is *bilingualism*, but the woman is not currently *learning a language*. (B) In the dialog, French refers to the language. (C) The woman can *speak* Spanish. She is not currently *studying* it.

57. (B) The man is planning a *vacation* and asking about special *package tours*, so we know that he is talking to a *travel agent*. (A) *Swimming* is associated with *lifeguards*, but the man is not *talking to* a lifeguard. (C) *Package* and *wrapper* have similar meanings, but there is no mention of a gift in the dialog. (D) *Being active* can include going to a gymnasium, but the man is not talking to a *gymnasium manager*.

58. (B) The woman's car has been stolen, so she is asking the man to call the police. (A) The man asks politely about her evening (*last night*), but the woman doesn't want him to ask any *more* questions. (C) The woman's car is the subject of the dialog, but information about cars is not the woman's concern. (D) *Stolen* and *taken* can be synonyms, but the woman *knows* what was taken.

59. (D) The woman points out they do not have a final decision yet on which computers to buy, so a *purchasing decision* must have been the goal of their meeting. (A) *Demonstration* and *protest* can be related, but here they have different meanings. (B) *Time* and *schedule* can be related, but this is not the correct answer. (C) *Computers* is the topic, but the demonstration was not for training purposes.

60. (A) *Funds*, *savings account*, *passbook*, and *investment brochure* are all things that we would expect to find at a bank, so we can conclude that the man is talking to a *banker*. (B) *Account* and *accountant* have the same root, but the man is not talking to an *accountant*. (C) A *travel agent* might also give you a *brochure*, but the brochure in this dialog is about *investments*, not *travel*. (D) There is no reference to a *library* or *librarian* in this dialog, although you might confuse *passbook* with *book*, and books are associated with libraries.

61. (C) Because the man is asking about advice on *foreign computer markets,* we know that he is thinking of selling computers abroad. (A) *Indonesia* is the market of his interest, but he's not *just* planning a visit there. (B) *Taxes* is repeated in the dialog and the option, but the man is not talking about *paying them*. (D) Many computer specialists start *consulting businesses*, but the man does not mention this plan.

62. (D) *Taxi* and *cab* are synonyms. (A) The woman asks about the *time* of the show, but they do not discuss going to an *earlier* show. (B) There is no mention of a *boxing match*. (C) *George* is one of the speakers, so they cannot be planning to call him.

63. (C) *Crooked* and *askew* are synonyms. The tray of a printer is often called the *paper tray*, or the *supply tray*. (A) The red *light* is mentioned in the dialog, but there is not a problem with the *print*. (B) Jammed paper is often a source of problems with fax machines, but in this case, *the paper is fine*. (D) The printer is not broken.

64. (D) The man cannot check the inventory records until the computer is back on line. In order to *check* something, you need to be able to *access* it. (A) *Other office* and *branches* can be synonymous, but the man *agrees* to call the other office, and there is no mention of his *transfering* there. (B) There is no reason to believe the inventory is not *up-to-date*. (C) *Inventory* and *stock* have similar meanings, and a chair is what the woman wants. However, we do not know if there are none in stock.

65. (B) *Ladies rooms* means *bathrooms* (for ladies). (A) There is no mention of *offices*. (C) and (D) A modern *dining room* or *bedroom* might have some of the features mentioned here; *glass, mirrors, recessed lighting*, but neither of these options is correct.

66. (A) Deciding which projector is best is Sonya's task. *Decide* and *select* are synonyms here. (B) A presentation is upcoming, but it is not Sonya's responsibility. (C) Sonya has been calling the *sales people*, not those *attending the meeting*. (D) Sonya is trying to reach salespeople, but *training* them is not her job.

67. (B) The man asks Maria to buy him a *dictaphone* while she's in Hong Kong, and a dictaphone is a piece of *office equipment*. (A) *Dictaphones* save the man time, which could mean that he *works faster*, but he's not asking *Maria* to do this. (C) Maria is traveling to Hong Kong, but *getting brochures* is not the man's request. (D) Maria asks the man to give her the model number. *He* does not ask *her* to write it down.

68. (C) Because the woman is leaving on *Thursday afternoon,* the man suggests meeting *Thursday morning.* (A) and (B) *Monday* and *Tuesday* are not referred to in the dialog. (D) The man initially suggests a *Friday* meeting, but the woman cannot make it.

69. (B) The man is shopping for suits, so we can guess that he is in a *clothing store*. (A) People often wear suits to church, and churches have *aisles*, but the speakers are not *in a church*. (C) The man is looking to buy something to *wear* at the office. (D) People often wear suits when they're out to dinner, but a *dinner* is not mentioned here.

70. (A) Because Ms.Carreras checks *toner* and *collators* on machines, we can figure that she is a *copy machine mechanic*. (B) The *course booklet* needs to be copied, but Ms.Carreras is not a *lecturer*. (C) Copy machines serve the *function* of printing, but Ms.Carreras is not *printing* anything. (D) *Marketing* and *advertising* are related, but this is not the correct answer.

71. (D) The woman wants to buy, or *purchase*, a Japanese newspaper and a copy of the *Korean Sun*. (A) *Korea* is mentioned, but we are not told she would like to visit there. (B) *Baggage* and *luggage* have the same meaning, and the *baggage claim area* is referred to. However, the woman's *personal* luggage is not referred to in the dialog. (C) *International* is mentioned, and *international flights* are associated with airports. The woman is obviously in an airport, but there is no suggestion she is intending to book a flight.

72. (C) The man suggests that Rita join the new bowling league, even though she's not a good bowler. (A) This option confuses *bowl* with *bowling* and *bowler*. (B) It might be reasonable to suggest to a poor bowler that she or he *practices more,* but this is not what the man suggests. (D) *Award* and *trophy* are similar in meaning, but the man says they are *not trying* to win a trophy.

73. (C) The man was impressed that the woman could *fix the program*. *Fix* means *solve*. (A) The woman *does* use the same software, but this is not what impressed the man. (B) *Program* is repeated, but the woman did not *write* any programs. (D) This option may confuse the sounds of *expensive* with *impressive*.

74. (A) The donation goes to the *Environmental Clean-Up Fund,* which involves *cleaning up pollution*. (B) *System* is repeated in the dialog and the option. *Security* and *safeguarding* have similar meanings, but this is not the correct answer. (C) *Art* is repeated in the dialog and the option, but with different meanings. (D) *Lubricants* is repeated in the dialog and the option, but there is no mention of *researching* anything.

75. (B) *Seats* and *flight* indicate that the speakers are in an airport. (A) A bus has *seats*, and a bus schedule may include a *five o'clock shuttle*, but buses do not have *flights*, so this is not a *bus station*. (C) A *meeting* is associated with *an office*, but the woman has not arrived at it yet. (D) *Seat* may be connected with *theater*, but this is not where the woman is.

76. (C) Only a taxi driver can reasonably be asked to take a different route. (A) *Route* and *airport* are both associated with travel, but the man is on his way somewhere. He is not in a *travel agency*. (B) *Rush hour* refers to traffic, and buses are part of traffic, but one passenger would not ask a bus driver to *change* his or her route. (D) *Route* may be associated with *tour*, but the man is referring only to himself, not a group.

77. (B) Downsizing includes *laying people off*, or making them redundant. (A) *Marketing* is repeated in both the dialog and the option, but there is no mention of *strategies*. (C) This option confuses the words *copy* and *copier*. (D) In the dialog, *finance* refers to the *department*, not personal expenditure.

78. (C) The man is concerned about getting a sofa in time for his *family reunion*. (A) Car size is mentioned in both the dialog and the option, but the man is not planning to *buy* a larger car. (B) The man will be *meeting his family* at a reunion, but he does not express concern about this. (D) The man needs to get the *sofa* home quickly, not *himself*.

79. (D) The man needs a *new ink cartridge*. (A) The man does not want a *printer*. (B) This option confuses the sound of *socks* with *stock*. (C) *Printers* may be associated with *paint*, but this is not the correct answer.

80. (B) Orders are being *canceled* because of a strike. (A) *Strike* and *hit* can mean the same thing, but not in this case. (C) *Meeting* and *canceled* are repeated in both the dialog and the option, but in different contexts. (D) The man is *meeting* with the *representatives*, but there is no reference to anybody having *called* them.

PART IV

81. (A) Because the speaker gives her radio identification numbers and channel, we know that she is a *radio announcer*. (B) The residents of Blair County are mentioned, but they are being spoken about.
(C) and (D) A *newspaper reporter* and the *police* might both give news similar to this, but there is no indication that this report is coming from either.

82. (C) The residents are advised to *keep traveling to a minimum*. This includes *avoiding driving*. (A) The hail is described as *baseball-size*, but a baseball *game* is not mentioned. (B) The streets are flooding and will probably eventually need to be *cleaned up*, but this report is not giving that advice at this time. (D) *Report* and *changes* are repeated, but this option is not correct.

83. (D) John is not at work today because his wife went to the hospital *over the weekend*, so we can determine that today is *Monday*. (A) There is no mention of *Friday*.
(B) and (C) *Saturday* and *Sunday* are weekend days, and the weekend is mentioned in the message, but it is mentioned in the past tense.

84. (A) We can assume that John was with his wife, who went to the delivery room of a *hospital* (to have a baby).
(B) *Mr. Stokes* is going to the airport, not John.
(C) Mr. Stokes *will be* with the *company president*, but we have no reason to believe that John was with him over the weekend. (D) *Delivery* is repeated in both the message and the option, but in different contexts.

85. (C) The theater is called *Crown Movies*. (A) The theater is next to *Bernstein and Company*. (B) The theater is in the *North Star Shopping Center*. (D) *Gemstones for Sale* is the name of a movie at the theater.

86. (B) The recording gives *movie names* and *show times*.
(A) and (C) Theater recordings often give information such as *directions* or *coming attractions*, but this one does not.
(D) We know that this recording was *not* used to advertise in the shopping center, because at the end it thanks the listener for *calling*. It must be a telephone recording.

87. (C) The speech is about *safeguarding* a national treasure – the country's *waterways*, or *river system*.
(A) Protecting rivers will undoubtedly affect the budget, but that's not the topic of this speech. (B) *Heritage* suggest history and *treasury* may be confused with *treasures*. However, this option is incorrect. (D) *Laws* is repeated in the option and mentioned several times in the speech, but the speech is not concerned with how laws are made.

88. (A) Some *western lawmakers* are *against* the idea because they believe it will give the government *greater say* on the use of private land. (B) There is no indication that water use will be restricted. (C) *Financial assistance* is mentioned, but there is no suggestion that land prices will increase. (D) A proposal is being *reviewed*, and there is no mention that there has not been enough *research*.

89. (D) Lawmakers in the west are resisting the plan.
(A) Local people should *like* the plan because it will help them apply for protection of their rivers. (B) *Shipping* is not mentioned, although it may be associated with rivers.
(C) Environmentalists can be expected to *support* a plan that protects waterways.

90. (A) The study talks about female *longevity* and *childbearing*. (B) *Female hormones* may relate to longevity and childbearing, but they are not discussed here.
(C) Children are under discussion but not in terms of their *behaviour*. (D) The *turn of the century* (1896) is mentioned in both the study and the option, but *styles* is not the topic.

91. (B) *Two* groups of women were studied. (A) The groups are compared, so each is mentioned *individually*.
(C) The age of *seventy-three* is mentioned in the study.
(D) *The fifth decade* is mentioned in the study.

92. (C) Women who live longer were four times as likely to have had children in their *forties*. (A) *All* of the women in the study were born in the late nineteenth century.
(B) Family size is not mentioned in the study.
(D) The age of the women's parents is not discussed.

93. (C) The report says that people feel *confident* about the economy. (A) Europeans are described as being *extremely worried*, but it's not the *economy* that they are worrying about. (B) While the report takes a look at *pessimism*, or *guarded optimism*, among Europeans, the pessimism is not over the economy. (D) *Stress, unhappiness*, and *concerns* may be associated with feeling *upset*, but this is not over the economy.

94. (B) Europeans are worried because their wages have not been keeping up with *inflation*. (A) *Taxes* are mentioned, but not in terms of being *heavy*. (C) *Corporate* is mentioned in the report in terms of *downsizing*, but not in terms of *wages*. (D) The economy is described as *healthy* in the report.

95. (D) The report says that Europeans are worried that taxes are not being *put to good use*. In other words, they are being used *wastefully*. (A) Companies are *downsizing*, not *relocating*. (B) The *speed of economic growth* is not one of the problems. (C) The report is about *workers*, but not about productivity.

96. (B) The announcement affects people who *drink alcohol*. (A) *Law enforcement officials* may mean the same as *local authorities*, but this is not who the announcement is directed at. (C) People who do *not* drink alcohol would not be affected by this announcement. (D) *Park officials* are more likely to be *making* this announcement.

97. (A) The announcement makes it clear that alcohol is prohibited *everywhere* in the fairgrounds, so we can conclude that only *outside* the fairgrounds is alcohol allowed. (B) Only *non-alcoholic* beverages will be served in the restaurants. (C) *No area is designated for alcohol* this year. (D) *Refreshment* means *beverage*, and they are only serving *non-alcoholic drinks* at the *beverage stands*.

98. (C) The speaker wants to go over *scheduling*.
(A) People *know* which department to go to, so there is no need to *assign work areas*. (B) Individual work times are *not* fixed. Rather, they have *flextime*, which means *flexible hours*. (D) *Let go* may relate to the time you finish your work, or it can mean *being dismissed.* This is not the correct option.

99. (C) Everyone must be at work during the *ten to three o'clock* period, so they must be there by *ten o'clock*.
(A) and (B) *Eight o'clock* and *nine o'clock* are standard times to start work, but not at this company. (D) By *eleven o'clock,* everybody should have arrived.

100. (D) Monthly overtime cannot be more than *ten hours.*
(A) *Thirty-seven* and *three* may be confused. (B) *Forty-one* and *four* may be confused. (C) *Thirty-seven* and *seven* may be confused.

PART V

101. (B) *Accumulate* means *to gather or build up.*
(A) Snow cannot *heighten.* (C) Snow does not *develop.*
(D) *Raise* is a synonym for *heighten.*

102. (C) *Take up residence* means *to start living somewhere.* (A) *Take in* means *to include* or *to make an article of clothing smaller.* (B) *Take out* means *to escort* or *to carry away.* (D) *Take with* means *to carry something from one place to another.*

103. (C) The reduced relative is formed using the gerund *listing.* (A) The clause cannot be started with the third person singular, present tense form of the verb, *lists.* (B) *Listed* is the past tense, and could be used if *which* preceded it. (D) *To list* is the infinitive form.

104. (C) The base form *satisfy* follows the verb *be able to.* (A) *Satisfactorily* is the adverb. (B) *Satisfaction* is the noun form. (D) *Satisfies* is the third person singular, present tense form.

105. (C) There is an understood clause, *than we arrived,* which therefore calls for a comparative form, *sooner.* (A) *Earliest* is the superlative form. (B) and (D) The adjective *previous* and the preposition *past* cannot stand alone at the end of the sentence.

106. (B) The preposition used in the idiom is *right on the mark,* meaning *accurate.* (A), (C) and (D) *Over, against* and *into* are incorrect prepositions.

107. (D) The conjunction *and* joins two clauses.
(A) The conjunction *but* indicates some contradiction.
(B) and (C) *Above* and *beyond* are prepositions and do not join the clauses.

108. (D) The pronoun *it* refers to the singular noun, *account.* (A) *Them* is the plural pronoun. (B) *That* is a relative pronoun. (C) *Those* is the plural form of the pronoun *that.*

109. (D) The reflexive pronoun is used with the verb *resigned.* (A) The verb *given up* is not followed by *to.* (B) The verb *admitted* is not followed by the reflexive pronoun in this sense. (C) *Relinquished* means *to let go of.*

110. (D) *That* refers to one specific *tractor.* (A) *It* is a subject pronoun and cannot be followed by another noun, *one.* (B) and (C) *Those* and *these* are plural pronouns.

111. (D) This is a general truth and requires the simple present tense. (A) *Determined* is the past tense. (B) *Had been determined* is the passive voice in the past perfect tense. (C) *Determining* is the gerund.

112. (C) *Sensible* means *reasonable* and is close in meaning to *down-to-earth.* (A) *Scented* means *to have a smell* and does not modify *arguments.* (B) *Sensational* is the opposite of *down-to-earth.* (D) *Sensuous* is related to the senses and does not logically modify *arguments.*

113. (B) A project is either *ahead of, behind* or *on schedule.* (A), (C) and (D) *Forward, onward* and *atop* are incorrect prepositions to use with *schedule.*

114. (A) *Records* is a plural noun and therefore the plural form *were* is needed. (B) The sentence cannot be in the present tense, because it does not refer to a general truth or a repeated action. (C) *Was* is the singular form of the verb. (D) *Has been* is a singular form.

115. (C) You book a flight *for* somebody. (A) You book a flight *to* somewhere. (B) You book a flight *with* an airline or a travel agent. (D) *By* does not combine with the expression *to book a flight.*

116. (A) The correct idiom, meaning *waiting,* is *biding his time.* (B), (C) and (D) *Activity, wherewithal,* and *wait* are not used in combination with the verb *biding.*

117. (A) *In regard to* means *concerning.* (B) *As* is used with the plural form *regards.* (C) and (D) The prepositions *for* and *from* do not combine with *regard.*

118. (C) The use of past tense in the first clause indicates the need for the past tense in the *if*-clause of this mixed conditional sentence. (A) The first clause of the sentence needs to be in the present tense, if the verb *want* is to be used. (B) *Had wanted* indicates that two actions at different times are involved. (D) *Wanting* is the gerund form and cannot follow the subject pronoun.

119. (D) *In* is the preposition that combines with the verb *participate.* (A), (B) and (C) In this sentence, the passive voice would need to be used with *involve, associate* and *concern.*

120. (B) The correct idiomatic phrase is *out of the question,* meaning *impossible.* (A) *Above* is an incorrect preposition. (C) and (D) *Overhead* and *outside* are adverbs which do not combine with *the question.*

121. (A) *Need* is the correct noun to use, in this sentence meaning *reason.* (B) *Dire* is an adjective. (C) *Must* is a verb. (D) *Responsibility* is a noun, but it is illogical in this context.

122. (B) *Than* indicates that the comparative form is needed. (A) The superlative form, *most,* is used when more than two objects are being compared. (C) and (D) *Many* and *much* indicate quantity and are illogical in this context.

123. (B) *Facility* is a noun meaning *ease.* (A) *Fertility* means *the ability to produce.* (C) *Compatibility* means *to get along with* and is illogical in this context. (D) Potentiality means *the ability to develop* and does not fit in this context.

124. (B) *Both,* meaning *the two,* is followed by a plural noun. (A) and (D) *Neither* and *each* modify singular nouns. (C) *None of* is followed by the article *the.*

125. (C) The preposition *from* combines correctly with the verb *divert.* (A), (B) and (D) The prepositions *over, into* and *throughout* are not used with the verb *divert.*

126. (D) *If*, meaning *on condition that*, introduces the second clause of this conditional sentence. (A) *While* is used when something is happening at the same time as something else. (B) The conjunction *or* involves a choice between two ideas. (C) *Because* is used to explain a previous statement.

127. (B) The gerund is used as a reduced relative here; it means *who are vacationing.* (A) The understood *who are* is not followed by the past participle *vacationed.* (C) Vacation is the noun form. (D) *Vacations* is the plural noun form.

128. (B) *Then* is the conjunction connecting two clauses, with the meaning *in that case.* (A) The conjunction *because* is not used after an *if*-clause. (C) *For* is a formal equivalent of *because*, or a preposition. (D) *Since* is followed by a reason.

129. (D) *All* means *the whole amount* and is frequently combined with *of.* (A) *Everything* means *all things* and cannot combine with *of.* (B) *About* cannot be combined directly with the verb *give.* (C) To *give forth* means *to give out or send out* and cannot combine with *attention.*

130. (D) *Whenever possible* means *when something is able to be done.* (A) *Available* is illogical in this context. (B) *Present* would refer to a person. (C) *Aboard* refers to a specific, physical location.

131. (D) *Cut off* means *to be discontinued.* (A) *Taken off* means *removed.* (B) and (C) *Closed off* and *sealed off* are usually used to refer to buildings or roads.

132. (A) *By* indicates that the passive voice should be used, *starting January first* indicates the future. (B) *Absorbed* is the past participle. (C) *Will absorb* is the active voice in the future. (D) *Absorbing* is the progressive form.

133. (B) The conjunction *as* is used to connect actions that are occurring at the same time. (A) *When* is illogical in this context. (C) *Besides* is a preposition and is not used to connect ideas. (D) *However* connects two contradictory statements.

134. (C) A noun follows the article *the.* (A) *Constructive* is an adjective which needs to modify a noun. (B) *Constructs* is the third person singular, present tense verb form. (D) *Constructed* is the past participle form.

135. (A) The preposition *before* introduces a clause that indicates *when.* (B) *Since* introduces a clause explaining something. (C) and (D) *In front of* and *near to* are prepositions indicating location or place.

136. (C) *Concern* means *worry.* (A) *Compliance* indicates that something is being done as it should be and is illogical in this context. (B) *Consent* means *agreement* and is illogical in this context. (D) Mrs. Davis' problem is that she has *no control* over Paul Roger's expenses.

137. (D) The modal *should* followed by the simple form of the verb *arise* is used in this sentence instead of an *if*-clause. (A) and (B) The modals *could* and *would* are not interchangeable with *if.* (C) In this sentence, if *if* begins the clause, the past simple is used.

138. (D) A product is *recalled* when there is a problem with it and it is returned to the manufacturer. (A) A worker can be *rehired*, but not a thing. (B) When a product is new, it is *released.* (C) *Resent* in this case is illogical.

139. (A) You understand or *see* a point of view. (B) One person cannot *think* another person's point of view. (C) *Reckon* is illogical in this situation. (D) The preposition *out* could be used with the verb *figure*, which means to understand.

140. (A) *Than* indicates that the comparative should be used. (B) *Lesser* is used for non-count nouns. (C) *Less* is used with non-count nouns. (D) *Lower* is the comparative form, but is not used to refer to a number of things.

PART VI

141. (C) If the quantity is 100, then the article *a* must accompany *hundred.* The expression *hundreds of consumers* could also be used to indicate an indeterminate amount. (A) *When* is correctly used as a conjunction. (B) *Hit* is the past tense form of the verb. (D) *Flocked to* means *to come to.*

142. (B) *Has* like *book* follows *will*, so it should be in the base form: *have.* (A) The base form *book* follows the future tense indicator *will.* (C) *Picked up* is the correct past participle form following the causative *have.* (D) The phrase *when you arrive* indicates the time.

143. (A) *Altogether* means *completely.* In this context, the adverb *together* is needed. (B) *So that* means *in order that.* (C) The base form of a verb follows *would.* (D) *To carry* is the infinitive which follows the adjective.

144. (A) The base form of the verb follows *would.* (B) The second conditional requires a past tense in the *if*-clause. (C) *Refresher* describes the noun *course.* (D) *According to* is a preposition meaning *as stated by.*

145. (D) The passive is formed by the form of *be* plus the past participle, *handled.* (A) *Even today* describes the time frame. (B) *Transmission* is the noun form. (C) *Both of which* refers to *the transmission* and *the billing.*

146. (B) There are two subjects in the clause: *economy* and *it.* *It is* should be replaced by *as.* (A) *Reported* is the past tense. (C) *In a steady* describes *direction.* (D) *Direction* is the noun form.

147. (A) The plural verb form *are provided* indicates a plural subject: *basics.* (B) *You'll need* is the contraction for *you will need.* (C) *Own* is a reflexive adjective. (D) *Are provided* is the passive form.

148. (C) *Will* changes to *would* in reported speech.
(A) *When* is used as a conjunction. (B) *He was told* is the passive voice in the past tense. (D) *Canceled* is the past participle used in the passive voice.

149. (C) When *year* is used as an adjective preceding the noun, it does not carry an *-s*. (A) *Did you know that* is an introductory clause formed with the past tense.
(B) *Top* describes the noun *floor*. (D) *Adjacent,* meaning *next to,* describes the *storage area*.

150. (B) The subject of the sentence is *Mr. Rossini* and must be followed by the singular form of the verb: *has.*
(A) The clause *who already heads* describes *Mr. Rossini*.
(C) *Yet another* describes *position*. (D) The preposition *in* denotes location.

151. (D) The adjective form used to describe *trip* is *intriguing; intrigued* would be used to describe a person.
(A) The subject and past tense form of the verb begin the sentence. (B) *To the Far East* is a prepositional phrase describing where. (C) *Adventurous* is an adjective describing *trip*.

152. (B) The adjective form to describe *application* is *completed*. (A) *Initially* is an adverb. (C) *Who must check* is a relative clause describing the *loan officer*.
(D) The gerund form follows the preposition *before*.

153. (D) The adverbial phrase *all over* is needed in this context. (A) *First, global* and *pollution* are all adjectives describing *convention*. (B) Someone held the convention, therefore if *convention* is used as the subject, the passive voice is used. (C) *Was attended* is a parallel structure to *was held*.

154. (A) The past participle of the verb *fly* is *flown*.
(B) The gerund form *negotiating* follows the preposition *after*. (C) *Long-awaited* is an adjective describing *agreement*. (D) You have an *agreement with* someone.

155. (B) The subject of the verb is the singular *piano;* therefore the verb should also be singular. (A) *Newly arrived* is an adjective describing *guests*. (C) *With live jazz* is a prepositional phrase. (D) The gerund *starting* replaces the pronoun + verb *which starts at*.

156. (C) *Children* is a plural noun that does not take the *-s* ending. (A) *We spent* is the subject followed by the past tense of the verb. (B) *Playing* is the gerund used as a noun. (D) *At the beach* is a prepositional phrase describing where.

157. (B) The correct preposition used with *situation* is *in*.
(A) The preposition *with* follows *familiar*. (C) The base form of the verb, *condone,* follows the modal *can't*.
(D) *Negligent* is an adjective describing the noun *behavior*.

158. (C) *Knowledgeable* is followed by the preposition *about*. (A) The relative clause *who is employed by* gives the reader more information about *the consultant*. (B) The third person singular, present tense form of the verb *to be* is used to correspond with the singular subject, *the consultant*. (D) *Junk* tells us what kind of *bonds*.

159. (D) The article *a* is needed. (A) The plural form *dozens* indicates that there were at least 24 candidates.
(B) *Showed up* is a two-word verb meaning *to appear*.
(C) *When it came time* is another way to say *When the time came*.

160. (C) Two objects, introduced by *both* are joined by the conjunction *and*. (A) *On our tour* is a prepositional phrase.
(B) The subject of the sentence is *we* and the verb is the past tense *saw*. (D) *Of crude oil* describes the object *by-products*.

PART VII

161. (B) The first line states that the exhibition *will be held in Madrid*. (A) *London* is not mentioned. (C) and (D) *Paris* and *Lisbon* are mentioned because the embassies in those cities will make contributions.

162. (C) An orphanage is *a home for children without parents*. (A) and (B) *Private investors* and *the contributing embassies* are contributing to the exhibit, but they will not directly benefit from it. (D) *The Filipino Art Gallery* is not mentioned.

163. (A) He is seeking a *similar managerial position* after 15 years *with a main bank*. (B) The man has knowledge of *marketing;* however that is not his main field of expertise.
(C) *Linguistics* is not mentioned, although the man speaks several languages. (D) The man is educated; however the field of *education* is not mentioned.

164. (B) The man is a *Turkish native speaker*. (A) The man speaks *English* well. (C) and (D) The man is proficient, but not fluent, in *Russian* and *French*.

165. (D) Subscriptions are for *magazines* or newspapers.
(A) The magazine is about *homes*. (B) Information about *alarm systems* or *security systems* is included in the magazine. (C) *Financial securities* are not mentioned.

166. (B) Half is 50% and therefore the person would pay *$17.00*. (A) *$10.00* is the postage charge for foreign orders.
(C) The person would save 65% if he paid *$23.95*.
(D) *$34.20* is the newsstand price.

167. (A) The form asks for the *address* or *where one lives*.
(B), (C) and (D) *Country of origin, age,* and *how long one has been a homeowner* are not mentioned.

168. (C) The first sentence *thanks* Mr. Malloy.
(A) Mr. Malloy has given Mr. Barr *investment advice* in the past. (B) Mr. Barr is a client of MFM, but is not asking for *a position*. (D) Mr. Barr is a member of MFM, but there is no mention of *renewing a membership*.

169. (B) ... *the greatest value is having time to myself again*. (A), (C) and (D) *Mr. Malloy's assessment ability, the investment in a growth fund* and *reading about investment possibilities* are mentioned; however, they are not the most valuable aspect.

170. (D) The letter indicates that Mr. Malloy knows a lot, or is *well-informed* about investments. (A) *Considerate* or kind is not mentioned. (B) Mr. Barr and not Mr. Malloy is very *appreciative*. (C)*Persistent* is not mentioned.

171. (C) *They will be doing their ... park clean-up.*
(A) People should bring *cleaning equipment.* (B) *Planning the future of the park* will be done after the park clean-up. (D) *To offer assistance to local residents* is not mentioned.

172. (A) The Jeffrey Logan Park is in *Lenour Heights.*
(B) *The beach* is not mentioned. (C) The park is north of *the historic district.* (D) The meeting after the clean-up will be *in the downtown area.*

173. (D) *The Friends of Jeffrey Logan* are known as the Local Guardians. (A) The *subscribers to the newspaper* are the readers, but not the Local Guardians. (B) *Residents of the Historic District* are not mentioned. (C) The *young people in Lenour Heights* will work with the Local Guardians to clean up the park.

174. (B) The meeting in the library is to *discuss a two-year plan for the recreational development of the park.*
(A) Food will be provided, but eating is not the main purpose of the meeting. (C) *Daniella Bard* is the organizer, but there is no mention of a lecture. (D) They will *meet other area residents,* but it is not the purpose.

175. (A) The first sentence states that *at a stockholders meeting ...Corporation announced.* (B) The *advertising* campaign helped improve sales. (C) There is no mention of *a news conference.* (D) The *management* was praised.

176. (B) The *advertising campaign was credited for the upswing* or the *rise in profits.* (A) The *stockholders* were *loyal,* but not necessarily *tenacious.* (C) *The company leadership* or the management was praised, but did not get the most credit. (D) The efforts of the *marketing team,* not the *sales team,* deserved the most credit.

177. (B) *The marketing group deserved most of the credit.*
(A), (C), and (D) were mentioned, but not as the ones deserving the credit.

178. (C) There was another sales exemption at the beginning of the year. (A) The exemption is from *North Carolina's taxes.* (B) Both exemptions are *sales exemptions.* (D) *A longer exemption* is not mentioned.

179. (B) There have been two two-week exemptions.
(A) The current exemption is *two weeks.* (C) and (D) *Six-* and *eight-*week exemptions are not mentioned.

180. (C) The first exemption was $500 and the second exemption is $100, so the difference is *$400.* (A) The current exemption is *$100.* (B) In the previous exemption, *$200* could be broken down into two $100 items.
(D) The first exemption was for *$500.*

181. (D) Footwear includes *shoes.*
(A), (B) and (C) *Jewelry, watches* and *hats* remain taxable as under the previous rules.

182. (C) *A head scarf,* like *hats,* would remain taxable.
(A), (B) and (D) *Yarn to repair a shawl, buttons for a winter coat* and *dress-making fabric* would be included because they would count as part of the actual clothing.

183. (D) *$27,124* is the figure for *total assets,* or *property, plant and equipment.* (A) *$2,232* is the operating cash flow. (B) *$7,890* is the total revenue. (C) $14,913 is the total debt.

184. (B) *$1,862* was the operating cash flow and the available money. (A) *$134* was the net earnings, which was a loss. (C) *$2,845* was the combined equity, but may not have been immediately available. (D) *$5,256* was the revenue, but does not reflect costs.

185. (C) *$14,913* is the *total debt,* or *total liabilities.*
(A) *$1,863* is the stockholder equity. (B) *$7,890* is the total revenue. (D) $27,124 is the total assets.

186. (D) Profits are the net earnings and fell *440%.*
(A) *15%* reflects the change in debt. (B) *18%* reflects the change in assets, which include more than profits.
(C) *35%* includes both debt and assets.

187. (B) *A civil engineer* works with roads or highways.
(A) *A mechanical engineer* works with machines.
(C) *A chemical engineer* works with chemicals.
(D) *An electrical engineer* works with electrical energy.

188. (A) *A mechanical engineer* works with equipment or machines. (B) *A military engineer* works with areas related specifically to the military. (C) *A chemical engineer* works with chemicals. (D) *A civil engineer* works with roads.

189. (C) Electricity runs through *power lines.*
(A) and (B) A civil or mechanical engineer would work with *rock drilling equipment* or *various building materials.*
(D) A civil engineer would work with *surveying techniques* to build roads, etc.

190. (B) The banks are worried that the credit standards have been *lowered* or that they are *too lax.* (A) and (C)The article does not mention that *the IMF is running out of money* or that *the IMF is exercising too much influence.*
(D) How fast *the Third World economies are changing* is not mentioned.

191. (D) The developing countries used to carry *51%* of the debt. (A) *9%* is the amount of debt carried by the industrial nations. (B) *45%* is the percentage of loans to countries with a GNP of less than $700 per person.
(C) *49%* is the amount of debt that used to be carried by the industrial nations.

192. (A) Industrial nations carry *9%* of the debt.
(B) *49%* is the amount of debt that used to be carried by the industrial nations. (C) The developing countries used to carry *51%* of the debt. (D) *91%* is the percentage currently carried by the developing countries.

193. (A) *El Niño creates weather patterns that affect the world.* (B) *El Niño* produces drought and rainstorms which are not *benign.* (C) The article does not say for how long *El Niño* lasts. (D) The weather pattern is becoming more constant, not *decreasing.*

194. (C) *The warming of the Pacific Ocean* creates the weather pattern. (A) Australia may experience a drought, not *rainstorms.* (B) Chile may experience severe rainstorms, not *drought.* (D) The southwestern part of the U.S. may experience unusually heavy rains, not *dryness.*

195. (C) *El Niño will bring unusually heavy rains to the southwestern part of the United States.*
(A), (B) and (D) *Pakistan, Australia* and *central U.S.* will be drier.

196. (D) *Global warming* is not mentioned.
(A), (B) and (C) *Droughts, heavy rainfalls,* and *weak monsoons* are all mentioned as effects of *El Niño.*

197. (B) The advertisement is aimed at business people *who communicate a lot by phone.* (A) People who are out of touch may be *lonely,* but the ad is not aimed at lonely people. (C) and (D) These options are not mentioned.

198. (A) It is important to *maintain communication ... with your clients.* (B) The phone advertised has *a fast modem.* (C) If you are not in touch with your clients, your competitors will *learn about your clients.* (D) The company selling the phone claims that they *have the solution.*

199. (B) According to the advertisement, because it is digital, *communication is protected* or *secure.* (A) The price of the phone is not mentioned. (C) The advertisement does not say whether *the modem is faster* or not. (D) The advertisement does not mention if only digital phones *store e-mail messages.*

200. (D) You can plug it into *a phone jack* to pick up messages. (A), (B) and (C) *An executive order, a battery pack* and *a password* are not mentioned.

Answer Sheets

Answer Sheet Practice Test 1

Listening Comprehension

Part I

1	A	B	C	D
2	A	B	C	D
3	A	B	C	D
4	A	B	C	D
5	A	B	C	D
6	A	B	C	D
7	A	B	C	D
8	A	B	C	D
9	A	B	C	D
10	A	B	C	D
11	A	B	C	D
12	A	B	C	D
13	A	B	C	D
14	A	B	C	D
15	A	B	C	D
16	A	B	C	D
17	A	B	C	D
18	A	B	C	D
19	A	B	C	D
20	A	B	C	D

Part II

21	A	B	C
22	A	B	C
23	A	B	C
24	A	B	C
25	A	B	C
26	A	B	C
27	A	B	C
28	A	B	C
29	A	B	C
30	A	B	C
31	A	B	C
32	A	B	C
33	A	B	C
34	A	B	C
35	A	B	C
36	A	B	C
37	A	B	C
38	A	B	C
39	A	B	C
40	A	B	C
41	A	B	C
42	A	B	C
43	A	B	C
44	A	B	C
45	A	B	C
46	A	B	C
47	A	B	C
48	A	B	C
49	A	B	C
50	A	B	C

Part III

51	A	B	C	D
52	A	B	C	D
53	A	B	C	D
54	A	B	C	D
55	A	B	C	D
56	A	B	C	D
57	A	B	C	D
58	A	B	C	D
59	A	B	C	D
60	A	B	C	D
61	A	B	C	D
62	A	B	C	D
63	A	B	C	D
64	A	B	C	D
65	A	B	C	D
66	A	B	C	D
67	A	B	C	D
68	A	B	C	D
69	A	B	C	D
70	A	B	C	D
71	A	B	C	D
72	A	B	C	D
73	A	B	C	D
74	A	B	C	D
75	A	B	C	D
76	A	B	C	D
77	A	B	C	D
78	A	B	C	D
79	A	B	C	D
80	A	B	C	D

Part IV

81	A	B	C	D
82	A	B	C	D
83	A	B	C	D
84	A	B	C	D
85	A	B	C	D
86	A	B	C	D
87	A	B	C	D
88	A	B	C	D
89	A	B	C	D
90	A	B	C	D
91	A	B	C	D
92	A	B	C	D
93	A	B	C	D
94	A	B	C	D
95	A	B	C	D
96	A	B	C	D
97	A	B	C	D
98	A	B	C	D
99	A	B	C	D
100	A	B	C	D

Reading

Part V

101	A	B	C	D	121	A	B	C	D
102	A	B	C	D	122	A	B	C	D
103	A	B	C	D	123	A	B	C	D
104	A	B	C	D	124	A	B	C	D
105	A	B	C	D	125	A	B	C	D
106	A	B	C	D	126	A	B	C	D
107	A	B	C	D	127	A	B	C	D
108	A	B	C	D	128	A	B	C	D
109	A	B	C	D	129	A	B	C	D
110	A	B	C	D	130	A	B	C	D
111	A	B	C	D	131	A	B	C	D
112	A	B	C	D	132	A	B	C	D
113	A	B	C	D	133	A	B	C	D
114	A	B	C	D	134	A	B	C	D
115	A	B	C	D	135	A	B	C	D
116	A	B	C	D	136	A	B	C	D
117	A	B	C	D	137	A	B	C	D
118	A	B	C	D	138	A	B	C	D
119	A	B	C	D	139	A	B	C	D
120	A	B	C	D	140	A	B	C	D

Part VI

141	A	B	C	D
142	A	B	C	D
143	A	B	C	D
144	A	B	C	D
145	A	B	C	D
146	A	B	C	D
147	A	B	C	D
148	A	B	C	D
149	A	B	C	D
150	A	B	C	D
151	A	B	C	D
152	A	B	C	D
153	A	B	C	D
154	A	B	C	D
155	A	B	C	D
156	A	B	C	D
157	A	B	C	D
158	A	B	C	D
159	A	B	C	D
160	A	B	C	D

Part VII

161	A	B	C	D	181	A	B	C	D
162	A	B	C	D	182	A	B	C	D
163	A	B	C	D	183	A	B	C	D
164	A	B	C	D	184	A	B	C	D
165	A	B	C	D	185	A	B	C	D
166	A	B	C	D	186	A	B	C	D
167	A	B	C	D	187	A	B	C	D
168	A	B	C	D	188	A	B	C	D
169	A	B	C	D	189	A	B	C	D
170	A	B	C	D	190	A	B	C	D
171	A	B	C	D	191	A	B	C	D
172	A	B	C	D	192	A	B	C	D
173	A	B	C	D	193	A	B	C	D
174	A	B	C	D	194	A	B	C	D
175	A	B	C	D	195	A	B	C	D
176	A	B	C	D	196	A	B	C	D
177	A	B	C	D	197	A	B	C	D
178	A	B	C	D	198	A	B	C	D
179	A	B	C	D	199	A	B	C	D
180	A	B	C	D	200	A	B	C	D

Answer Sheet Practice Test 2

Listening Comprehension

Part I				
1	A	B	C	D
2	A	B	C	D
3	A	B	C	D
4	A	B	C	D
5	A	B	C	D
6	A	B	C	D
7	A	B	C	D
8	A	B	C	D
9	A	B	C	D
10	A	B	C	D
11	A	B	C	D
12	A	B	C	D
13	A	B	C	D
14	A	B	C	D
15	A	B	C	D
16	A	B	C	D
17	A	B	C	D
18	A	B	C	D
19	A	B	C	D
20	A	B	C	D

Part II			
21	A	B	C
22	A	B	C
23	A	B	C
24	A	B	C
25	A	B	C
26	A	B	C
27	A	B	C
28	A	B	C
29	A	B	C
30	A	B	C
31	A	B	C
32	A	B	C
33	A	B	C
34	A	B	C
35	A	B	C
36	A	B	C
37	A	B	C
38	A	B	C
39	A	B	C
40	A	B	C
41	A	B	C
42	A	B	C
43	A	B	C
44	A	B	C
45	A	B	C
46	A	B	C
47	A	B	C
48	A	B	C
49	A	B	C
50	A	B	C

Part III				
51	A	B	C	D
52	A	B	C	D
53	A	B	C	D
54	A	B	C	D
55	A	B	C	D
56	A	B	C	D
57	A	B	C	D
58	A	B	C	D
59	A	B	C	D
60	A	B	C	D
61	A	B	C	D
62	A	B	C	D
63	A	B	C	D
64	A	B	C	D
65	A	B	C	D
66	A	B	C	D
67	A	B	C	D
68	A	B	C	D
69	A	B	C	D
70	A	B	C	D
71	A	B	C	D
72	A	B	C	D
73	A	B	C	D
74	A	B	C	D
75	A	B	C	D
76	A	B	C	D
77	A	B	C	D
78	A	B	C	D
79	A	B	C	D
80	A	B	C	D

Part IV				
81	A	B	C	D
82	A	B	C	D
83	A	B	C	D
84	A	B	C	D
85	A	B	C	D
86	A	B	C	D
87	A	B	C	D
88	A	B	C	D
89	A	B	C	D
90	A	B	C	D
91	A	B	C	D
92	A	B	C	D
93	A	B	C	D
94	A	B	C	D
95	A	B	C	D
96	A	B	C	D
97	A	B	C	D
98	A	B	C	D
99	A	B	C	D
100	A	B	C	D

Reading

Part V									
101	A	B	C	D	121	A	B	C	D
102	A	B	C	D	122	A	B	C	D
103	A	B	C	D	123	A	B	C	D
104	A	B	C	D	124	A	B	C	D
105	A	B	C	D	125	A	B	C	D
106	A	B	C	D	126	A	B	C	D
107	A	B	C	D	127	A	B	C	D
108	A	B	C	D	128	A	B	C	D
109	A	B	C	D	129	A	B	C	D
110	A	B	C	D	130	A	B	C	D
111	A	B	C	D	131	A	B	C	D
112	A	B	C	D	132	A	B	C	D
113	A	B	C	D	133	A	B	C	D
114	A	B	C	D	134	A	B	C	D
115	A	B	C	D	135	A	B	C	D
116	A	B	C	D	136	A	B	C	D
117	A	B	C	D	137	A	B	C	D
118	A	B	C	D	138	A	B	C	D
119	A	B	C	D	139	A	B	C	D
120	A	B	C	D	140	A	B	C	D

Part VI				
141	A	B	C	D
142	A	B	C	D
143	A	B	C	D
144	A	B	C	D
145	A	B	C	D
146	A	B	C	D
147	A	B	C	D
148	A	B	C	D
149	A	B	C	D
150	A	B	C	D
151	A	B	C	D
152	A	B	C	D
153	A	B	C	D
154	A	B	C	D
155	A	B	C	D
156	A	B	C	D
157	A	B	C	D
158	A	B	C	D
159	A	B	C	D
160	A	B	C	D

Part VII									
161	A	B	C	D	181	A	B	C	D
162	A	B	C	D	182	A	B	C	D
163	A	B	C	D	183	A	B	C	D
164	A	B	C	D	184	A	B	C	D
165	A	B	C	D	185	A	B	C	D
166	A	B	C	D	186	A	B	C	D
167	A	B	C	D	187	A	B	C	D
168	A	B	C	D	188	A	B	C	D
169	A	B	C	D	189	A	B	C	D
170	A	B	C	D	190	A	B	C	D
171	A	B	C	D	191	A	B	C	D
172	A	B	C	D	192	A	B	C	D
173	A	B	C	D	193	A	B	C	D
174	A	B	C	D	194	A	B	C	D
175	A	B	C	D	195	A	B	C	D
176	A	B	C	D	196	A	B	C	D
177	A	B	C	D	197	A	B	C	D
178	A	B	C	D	198	A	B	C	D
179	A	B	C	D	199	A	B	C	D
180	A	B	C	D	200	A	B	C	D

Answer Sheet Practice Test 3

Listening Comprehension

Part I

	A	B	C	D
1	A	B	C	D
2	A	B	C	D
3	A	B	C	D
4	A	B	C	D
5	A	B	C	D
6	A	B	C	D
7	A	B	C	D
8	A	B	C	D
9	A	B	C	D
10	A	B	C	D
11	A	B	C	D
12	A	B	C	D
13	A	B	C	D
14	A	B	C	D
15	A	B	C	D
16	A	B	C	D
17	A	B	C	D
18	A	B	C	D
19	A	B	C	D
20	A	B	C	D

Part II

	A	B	C
21	A	B	C
22	A	B	C
23	A	B	C
24	A	B	C
25	A	B	C
26	A	B	C
27	A	B	C
28	A	B	C
29	A	B	C
30	A	B	C
31	A	B	C
32	A	B	C
33	A	B	C
34	A	B	C
35	A	B	C
36	A	B	C
37	A	B	C
38	A	B	C
39	A	B	C
40	A	B	C
41	A	B	C
42	A	B	C
43	A	B	C
44	A	B	C
45	A	B	C
46	A	B	C
47	A	B	C
48	A	B	C
49	A	B	C
50	A	B	C

Part III

	A	B	C	D
51	A	B	C	D
52	A	B	C	D
53	A	B	C	D
54	A	B	C	D
55	A	B	C	D
56	A	B	C	D
57	A	B	C	D
58	A	B	C	D
59	A	B	C	D
60	A	B	C	D
61	A	B	C	D
62	A	B	C	D
63	A	B	C	D
64	A	B	C	D
65	A	B	C	D
66	A	B	C	D
67	A	B	C	D
68	A	B	C	D
69	A	B	C	D
70	A	B	C	D
71	A	B	C	D
72	A	B	C	D
73	A	B	C	D
74	A	B	C	D
75	A	B	C	D
76	A	B	C	D
77	A	B	C	D
78	A	B	C	D
79	A	B	C	D
80	A	B	C	D

Part IV

	A	B	C	D
81	A	B	C	D
82	A	B	C	D
83	A	B	C	D
84	A	B	C	D
85	A	B	C	D
86	A	B	C	D
87	A	B	C	D
88	A	B	C	D
89	A	B	C	D
90	A	B	C	D
91	A	B	C	D
92	A	B	C	D
93	A	B	C	D
94	A	B	C	D
95	A	B	C	D
96	A	B	C	D
97	A	B	C	D
98	A	B	C	D
99	A	B	C	D
100	A	B	C	D

Reading

Part V

	A	B	C	D		A	B	C	D
101	A	B	C	D	121	A	B	C	D
102	A	B	C	D	122	A	B	C	D
103	A	B	C	D	123	A	B	C	D
104	A	B	C	D	124	A	B	C	D
105	A	B	C	D	125	A	B	C	D
106	A	B	C	D	126	A	B	C	D
107	A	B	C	D	127	A	B	C	D
108	A	B	C	D	128	A	B	C	D
109	A	B	C	D	129	A	B	C	D
110	A	B	C	D	130	A	B	C	D
111	A	B	C	D	131	A	B	C	D
112	A	B	C	D	132	A	B	C	D
113	A	B	C	D	133	A	B	C	D
114	A	B	C	D	134	A	B	C	D
115	A	B	C	D	135	A	B	C	D
116	A	B	C	D	136	A	B	C	D
117	A	B	C	D	137	A	B	C	D
118	A	B	C	D	138	A	B	C	D
119	A	B	C	D	139	A	B	C	D
120	A	B	C	D	140	A	B	C	D

Part VI

	A	B	C	D
141	A	B	C	D
142	A	B	C	D
143	A	B	C	D
144	A	B	C	D
145	A	B	C	D
146	A	B	C	D
147	A	B	C	D
148	A	B	C	D
149	A	B	C	D
150	A	B	C	D
151	A	B	C	D
152	A	B	C	D
153	A	B	C	D
154	A	B	C	D
155	A	B	C	D
156	A	B	C	D
157	A	B	C	D
158	A	B	C	D
159	A	B	C	D
160	A	B	C	D

Part VII

	A	B	C	D		A	B	C	D
161	A	B	C	D	181	A	B	C	D
162	A	B	C	D	182	A	B	C	D
163	A	B	C	D	183	A	B	C	D
164	A	B	C	D	184	A	B	C	D
165	A	B	C	D	185	A	B	C	D
166	A	B	C	D	186	A	B	C	D
167	A	B	C	D	187	A	B	C	D
168	A	B	C	D	188	A	B	C	D
169	A	B	C	D	189	A	B	C	D
170	A	B	C	D	190	A	B	C	D
171	A	B	C	D	191	A	B	C	D
172	A	B	C	D	192	A	B	C	D
173	A	B	C	D	193	A	B	C	D
174	A	B	C	D	194	A	B	C	D
175	A	B	C	D	195	A	B	C	D
176	A	B	C	D	196	A	B	C	D
177	A	B	C	D	197	A	B	C	D
178	A	B	C	D	198	A	B	C	D
179	A	B	C	D	199	A	B	C	D
180	A	B	C	D	200	A	B	C	D

Answer Sheet Practice Test 4

Listening Comprehension

Part I

#				
1	A	B	C	D
2	A	B	C	D
3	A	B	C	D
4	A	B	C	D
5	A	B	C	D
6	A	B	C	D
7	A	B	C	D
8	A	B	C	D
9	A	B	C	D
10	A	B	C	D
11	A	B	C	D
12	A	B	C	D
13	A	B	C	D
14	A	B	C	D
15	A	B	C	D
16	A	B	C	D
17	A	B	C	D
18	A	B	C	D
19	A	B	C	D
20	A	B	C	D

Part II

#			
21	A	B	C
22	A	B	C
23	A	B	C
24	A	B	C
25	A	B	C
26	A	B	C
27	A	B	C
28	A	B	C
29	A	B	C
30	A	B	C
31	A	B	C
32	A	B	C
33	A	B	C
34	A	B	C
35	A	B	C
36	A	B	C
37	A	B	C
38	A	B	C
39	A	B	C
40	A	B	C
41	A	B	C
42	A	B	C
43	A	B	C
44	A	B	C
45	A	B	C
46	A	B	C
47	A	B	C
48	A	B	C
49	A	B	C
50	A	B	C

Part III

#				
51	A	B	C	D
52	A	B	C	D
53	A	B	C	D
54	A	B	C	D
55	A	B	C	D
56	A	B	C	D
57	A	B	C	D
58	A	B	C	D
59	A	B	C	D
60	A	B	C	D
61	A	B	C	D
62	A	B	C	D
63	A	B	C	D
64	A	B	C	D
65	A	B	C	D
66	A	B	C	D
67	A	B	C	D
68	A	B	C	D
69	A	B	C	D
70	A	B	C	D
71	A	B	C	D
72	A	B	C	D
73	A	B	C	D
74	A	B	C	D
75	A	B	C	D
76	A	B	C	D
77	A	B	C	D
78	A	B	C	D
79	A	B	C	D
80	A	B	C	D

Part IV

#				
81	A	B	C	D
82	A	B	C	D
83	A	B	C	D
84	A	B	C	D
85	A	B	C	D
86	A	B	C	D
87	A	B	C	D
88	A	B	C	D
89	A	B	C	D
90	A	B	C	D
91	A	B	C	D
92	A	B	C	D
93	A	B	C	D
94	A	B	C	D
95	A	B	C	D
96	A	B	C	D
97	A	B	C	D
98	A	B	C	D
99	A	B	C	D
100	A	B	C	D

Reading

Part V

#					#				
101	A	B	C	D	121	A	B	C	D
102	A	B	C	D	122	A	B	C	D
103	A	B	C	D	123	A	B	C	D
104	A	B	C	D	124	A	B	C	D
105	A	B	C	D	125	A	B	C	D
106	A	B	C	D	126	A	B	C	D
107	A	B	C	D	127	A	B	C	D
108	A	B	C	D	128	A	B	C	D
109	A	B	C	D	129	A	B	C	D
110	A	B	C	D	130	A	B	C	D
111	A	B	C	D	131	A	B	C	D
112	A	B	C	D	132	A	B	C	D
113	A	B	C	D	133	A	B	C	D
114	A	B	C	D	134	A	B	C	D
115	A	B	C	D	135	A	B	C	D
116	A	B	C	D	136	A	B	C	D
117	A	B	C	D	137	A	B	C	D
118	A	B	C	D	138	A	B	C	D
119	A	B	C	D	139	A	B	C	D
120	A	B	C	D	140	A	B	C	D

Part VI

#				
141	A	B	C	D
142	A	B	C	D
143	A	B	C	D
144	A	B	C	D
145	A	B	C	D
146	A	B	C	D
147	A	B	C	D
148	A	B	C	D
149	A	B	C	D
150	A	B	C	D
151	A	B	C	D
152	A	B	C	D
153	A	B	C	D
154	A	B	C	D
155	A	B	C	D
156	A	B	C	D
157	A	B	C	D
158	A	B	C	D
159	A	B	C	D
160	A	B	C	D

Part VII

#					#				
161	A	B	C	D	181	A	B	C	D
162	A	B	C	D	182	A	B	C	D
163	A	B	C	D	183	A	B	C	D
164	A	B	C	D	184	A	B	C	D
165	A	B	C	D	185	A	B	C	D
166	A	B	C	D	186	A	B	C	D
167	A	B	C	D	187	A	B	C	D
168	A	B	C	D	188	A	B	C	D
169	A	B	C	D	189	A	B	C	D
170	A	B	C	D	190	A	B	C	D
171	A	B	C	D	191	A	B	C	D
172	A	B	C	D	192	A	B	C	D
173	A	B	C	D	193	A	B	C	D
174	A	B	C	D	194	A	B	C	D
175	A	B	C	D	195	A	B	C	D
176	A	B	C	D	196	A	B	C	D
177	A	B	C	D	197	A	B	C	D
178	A	B	C	D	198	A	B	C	D
179	A	B	C	D	199	A	B	C	D
180	A	B	C	D	200	A	B	C	D